NORTH CAROLINA
Craft Beer
& BREWERIES

JOHN F. BLAIR, PUBLISHER
Winston-Salem, North Carolina

NORTH CAROLINA

Craft Beer

& BREWERIES

ERIK LARS MYERS AND SARAH H. FICKE

JOHN F. BLAIR,
Publisher
1406 Plaza Drive
Winston-Salem, North Carolina 27103
blairpub.com

Library of Congress Cataloging-in-Publication Data

Names: Myers, Erik Lars, author. | Ficke, Sarah H., author.
Title: North Carolina craft beer & breweries / by Erik Lars Myers and Sarah H. Ficke.
Other titles: North Carolina craft beer and breweries
Description: Second edition. | Winston-Salem, North Carolina : John F. Blair, [2016] | Includes index.
Identifiers: LCCN 2016003569| ISBN 9780895876621 (alk. paper) | ISBN 9780895876638 (eISBN)
Subjects: LCSH: Beer—North Carolina. | Breweries—North Carolina—Guidebooks North Carolina—Guidebooks.
Classification: LCC TP577 .M94 2016 | DDC 338.7/6634209756—dc23 LC record available at http://lccn.loc.gov/2016003569

10 9 8 7 6 5 4 3 2 1

Design by Debra Long Hampton
page i: Brewery 99, New Bern/Brewery 99; pages ii-iii: Check Six Brewing Company, Southport/Erik Lars Myers
Cover Images
    Bottle cap: ©Illpos/Shutterstock
    Red grunge: ©Kjpargeter/Shutterstock
    Taps: ©blizzard_77/iStock
    Bottom image: A colorful flight at Innovation Brewing, Sylva/Erik Lars Myers

CONTENTS

CHARLOTTE AREA

THE TRIAD

THE TRIANGLE
209

THE SANDHILLS AND THE COAST

PREFACE

WE LIKE TO TELL PEOPLE THERE'S NO BETTER PLACE TO DRINK A BEER THAN IN NORTH CAROLINA.

The four years since the first edition of this book have brought an amazing transformation in our state. The number of breweries has exploded, growing roughly 300 percent in those four years. It's staggering.

That growth meant that the second edition was a daunting task. Rather than tracking down a few breweries here and there to add to the chapters, we had to make a series of marathon trips to reach breweries. On the way, however, we ran into some beautiful stories that you'll read in the following pages.

Since the first edition, some of the breweries we profiled have exploded. They've doubled or tripled in size, started new facilities, and done amazing, innovative things. Of course, new breweries have also opened, some in popular beer towns such as Asheville and others in small towns without a brewery since before Prohibition. We saw towns whose new economic focus is now a local brewery that is the engine of economic development. One brewer told us that since he opened in 2013, he has had to open a second location and now employs over 50 people—in a town of only 1,300.

While we ran into some closures along the way, at least one of those breweries has since been bought by a new owner, who has also completed a new production facility expansion, all since the last edition.

Certainly, read about the breweries in the following pages, but do yourself a favor and hit the road to visit them. Some readers told us they have taken dog-eared copies of *North Carolina Craft Beer & Breweries* on road trips around the state and had brewers sign their pages. We invite you to follow in these explorers' footsteps—to find a North Carolina brewery, raise a glass, and marvel at the wonderful industry that has grown across our beautiful state.

We hope you enjoy exploring the breweries as much as we enjoy telling you about them.

ACKNOWLEDGMENTS

THIS BOOK WOULD NOT HAVE BEEN POSSIBLE without the help of Margo Knight Metzger and Lisa Parker of the North Carolina Craft Brewers Guild, Dave Tollefsen and Glenn Cutler of NC Beer Guys, and the incredible and thorough reporting of Daniel Hartis of the *Charlotte Observer* and *All About Beer* magazine (and author of *Charlotte Beer* and *Beer Lover's: The Carolinas*).

We also owe our publisher, our editor, and the whole team at John F. Blair our thanks for their patience and hard work in assembling what turned out to be a much larger project than anticipated. They handled our complicated updates with grace and professionalism and ultimately created what you have in your hands.

A huge thanks to the North Carolina craft beer community for its incredible enthusiasm and passion. Not only did it drive us to write this second edition, but the never-ending stream of smiles, support, kind words, and, of course, great beer sustained us through our work.

Finally, an enormous helping of thanks to the staff and partners at Mystery Brewing, who dealt with a harried and hectic boss, coworker, and partner—or maybe we should say *even more* harried and hectic. Without their hard work, support, and friendship, this book would simply not exist.

A HISTORY OF NORTH CAROLINA BEER AND BREWING

TRADITIONAL HISTORIES OF NORTH CAROLINA SAY LITTLE OR NO BREWING was done in the state's past. They cite the warm, humid climate and ignore the generations of British, Scottish, German, and Czech immigrants who settled North Carolina. Having arrived from beer-drinking cultures, those immigrants were unlikely to forgo their favorite beverage simply because of a little weather.

However, North Carolina's beer history is significantly more complicated than that of beer-producing states in the North such as Pennsylvania and New York. Early on, barley was difficult to grow in North Carolina, and many traditional brewing ingredients had to be imported or improvised. The Revolutionary War and the Civil War both had significant impacts on ingredient availability and imports. Then came our country-wide "noble experiment": Prohibition.

Through it all, in just 200 years, North Carolina has gone from being one of the lowest beer-producing states to being the heart of the southeastern beer market and one of the most exciting emerging beer scenes in the country.

Brewing in the Colonial Period

Brewing has been practiced in North Carolina since the early days of the colony. Christoph von Graffenried included in his *Account of the Founding of New Bern* (the town was founded in 1710) a letter from a colonist to a kinsman in Germany requesting that he send brewing equipment "because my wife understands brewing so well and has done it for years, and the drink is very scarce here."[1]

John Brickell, an Irishman who traveled in North Carolina between 1729 and 1731, published a book called *Natural History of North Carolina* in 1737. In it, he reported on the popularity of beer, imported rum, brandy, and "Mault Drink." According to Brickell, "The following are made in Country, viz. Cyder, Persimon-Beer, made of the Fruit of that Tree, Ceder-Beer, made of Ceder-Berries; they also make Beer of the green stalks of Indian-Corn, which they bruise and boyle. They likewise make Beer of Mollosses, or common Treacle, in the following manner, they take a Gallon of Mollosses, a Peck of Wheaten Bran, a Pound of Hops, and a Barrel of Fountain Water, all which they boile together, and work up with Yest, as we do our Malt Liquors; this is their common Small-Beer, and seems to me to be the pleasantest Drink, I ever tasted, either in the Indies or Europe, and I am satisfied more wholsom. This is made stronger in proportion, as People fancy."[2]

Brickell noted that traditional brewing was not widespread: "It is necessary to observe that though there is plenty of Barly and Oats in this Province, yet there is no Malt Drink made, notwithstanding all kind of Malt Liquors bear a good Price, nor have any of the Planters ever yet attempted it."[3]

Some evidence suggests that larger-scale brewing existed in the colony as well. When the town of Cross Creek (now part of Fayetteville) in Cumberland County was mapped in 1770, a brewery was one of the buildings marked.[4] A brewery was also a key part of the town of Salem, founded by the Moravians, early immigrants to North Carolina with a Czech background. The Single Brothers—as the unmarried Moravian men were called—ran several industries in town, including a brewery, which existed from 1774 to 1813.[5]

However, histories also report almost unanimously that the climate in the Southern colonies was not ideal for growing barley. The heat was cited as causing storage problems. In *Brewed in America: A History of Beer and Ale in the United States*, author Stanley Baron noted that farmers experimented with growing barley and hops in the Carolinas and that "the usual home brewing" took place, but that "rum is supposed to have taken over here particularly early and thus reduced the beer requirements."[6]

What were Carolinians really drinking during the colonial period? Rum was certainly popular, but pricing lists for taverns in that period show that they also carried a variety of beers, including "strong malt beer of America," "strong malt beer of Britain," and "British ale or beer bottled and wired in Great Britain," as well as both "Northern" and "Carolina" ciders. Carolina cider was the least expensive of those drinks per quart, and a beer "bottled and wired in Great Britain" was the most expensive by far.[7] The histories report that most beer in the Southern colonies was imported either from the North or from Britain. In fact, Baron's book explained that refusing to import beer from Britain was one step the Americans took during the Revolutionary War to break from the mother country.

From the Revolutionary War to the Civil War

Brewing continued in North Carolina after the Revolutionary War, both at home and on a larger scale. William Lenoir's plantation distilling book, kept from 1806 to 1808, included instructions on malting barley and a recipe for making three kinds of beer (strong beer, middle beer, and small beer), to be brewed in one session using the same grain for all three beers.[8] In 1807, Henry Gunnisson used the *Wilmington Gazette* to announce that he had started a brewery "in Wilkinson's Alley, on the West side of Front Street"—just a few blocks from where Wilmington's Front Street Brewery stands today.[9]

The North Carolina brewer most active in the newspapers during this period was Thomas Holmes of Salisbury, who ran a series of advertisements in the *Western Carolinian*. Holmes announced that he was opening a public house in October 1821. By December 1822, he was advertising for barley for his brewery. In April 1823, he opened a "new establishment . . . where he intends to keep a constant supply of Beer and Porter."[10] Holmes encouraged local production of brewing ingredients. In June 1823, he advertised for hops "for which he will pay 30 cents pr. Pound, if picked in a good season, when not too dry."[11] He also encouraged people to drink local beer over liquor. Holmes continued to run periodic advertisements until the spring of 1827, when he announced he was returning to a former location in town to run a "house of entertainment."[12] At that point, he and his brewery dropped out of the newspaper records. However, the August 19, 1828, edition of the *Western Carolinian* reported that "a highly respectable and enterprising gentleman of Salisbury, fitted up a Brewery here about a year since; and was in the 'full tide of successful experiment,' when lately his principal workman, an experienced brewer, died, and the operations of the brewery had consequently to be suspended for a time." In a burst of local pride, the paper added that "the Beer and Porter produced at this establishment, was superior to any liquor of the kind ever manufactured in this part of the country; it was getting to be generally used by our citizens, and promised to have a salutary tendency to check the excessive use of ardent spirits."[13] The article did not name names, though, so the connection between this brewery and the one run by Thomas Holmes is unknown.

Although small-scale brewing was practiced in North Carolina during the first half of the 19th century, it was not enough to register in the national histories of the industry. *One Hundred Years of Brewing*, a history and collection of 19th-century brewing statistics published in 1903 and sponsored by the trade journal *Western Brewer*, didn't mention any breweries south of Maryland and Washington, D.C., in its pre–Civil War section.

The comparatively small amount of North Carolina–brewed beer during this period didn't mean people weren't drinking beer. While rum and whiskey were definitely popular, so was beer, but it was often imported from other states or Europe. North Carolina newspaper articles from the post–Revolutionary War period contained advertisements from stores selling bottled and casked porter from England, barrels of porter from Philadelphia, ale from Albany, and "Scotch ale."

When North Carolinians made beer, it often stretched the boundaries of what might be considered beer today. While they did make traditional English ales out of barley malt, hops, yeast, and water, a wide variety of recipes from the early 19th century involved many more ingredients—everything from other types of grain or corn to herbs, fruits, spruce, extra sugars, and even raw eggs. Based on recipes published in newspapers and other publications at the time, most homebrewed beer in North Carolina was table beer, meant to be a refreshing, low-alcohol beverage served regularly at meals.

In August 1828, the *Western Carolinian* offered this recipe: "The following ingredients make a palatable and healthy table beer; take 3 lbs. sugar or molasses, 1 gallon wheat bran, and 3 ozs. hops; put them into 4 gals. water, boil it three quarters of an hour, strain the liquor through a sieve, put it in a cool place a short time, then into a cask, and add six gals. of cold water, and put in half a pint of yeast. After it works, it will be an excellent beverage, better than whiskey, brandy, rum, gin, wine, cider, or ale."[14]

In July 1847, the *Carolina Watchman* concluded its article on what farmers should drink out in the fields with a recipe for "Chinese Beer." The beer contained "spices," lemon, cream of tartar, sugar, and one bottle of "old porter."[15]

Molasses seems to have been a popular ingredient in early beer recipes, sometimes providing most of the fermentable sugar. This fits with the idea that barley malt was hard to come by in the Carolinas. Though it certainly existed, it may not have been available in the quantity needed to make a lot of beer—an issue that lingers today.

Brewing and the Civil War

The Civil War had a significant impact on North Carolina's beer brewing and consumption habits, since the state imported so much of its beer, malt, and other ingredients from the North. Tensions between North and South may have affected Southern beer as early as 1850, when the *Carolina Watchman* reprinted an article from the *Mobile Herald and Tribune* responding to some anti-Southern resolutions passed by the Massachusetts Senate. The article proposed several responses, one of which was "that we encourage Southern agriculture by giving preference to all produce cultivated in the Southern States, viz. . . . that we drink no ale, porter, or cider made in the north, but encourage the growth of Southern hops and apples, and the establishment of Southern breweries."[16]

After the war started, the Southern states did at least try to restrict beer imports. The 1861 publication *Tariff of the Confederate States of America* listed "fifteen per centum ad valorem" taxes on goods including "beer, ale, and porter, in casks or bottles,"[17] while the 1864 *Statutes at Large of the Confederate States of*

America prohibited importing "beer, ale and porter."[18] Southern recipe books proposed home-brewed alternatives to imported beer. *The Confederate Receipt Book: A Compilation of Over One Hundred Receipts, Adapted to the Times* contained recipes for table beer, spruce beer, and ginger beer that all used molasses as the fermentable sugar and only sometimes used hops. The book *Resources of the Southern Fields and Forests* focused on ingredients available in the Southern states. The author included a section on how to make Russian kvass out of rye and a section on growing hops for medicinal and brewing purposes. He addressed the climate problem this way: "Ale and beer can be made in the Confederate States, though not with the same advantage as in colder climates. Though without practical experience, I am forced to the conviction that the desideratum is cool cellars. In the rural districts what are called dry cellars are constructed in the clay, just above the water-bearing stratum, the top enclosed or covered with a closed house. The temperature of these cellars is quite low, and they are used in keeping milk, butter, melons, cider, etc. I think their temperature would allow the manufacture and preservation of either wine, ale or beer."[19]

During the war, the North Carolina General Assembly gradually prohibited the making of liquor and then beer from grain, in order to protect the state's food supply.[20]

Brewing after the Civil War and the Onset of Prohibition

Beer imports rose again after the Civil War. On June 14, 1866, the *Old North State* paper advertised the sale of Cockade City Brewery beer (from Petersburg, Virginia) in Salisbury, and on November 8, 1877, the *Carolina Watchman* mentioned importing beer from the Bergner & Engle's brewery of Philadelphia. In 1890, the *Branson's North Carolina Business* directory listed beer bottlers in Tarboro, Elizabeth City, Wilson, and Fayetteville. Robert Portner Brewing Company, based in Alexandria, Virginia, opened a bottling and storage operation in Wilmington after the war that lasted the rest of the century.

However, there is little evidence of brewing in North Carolina during this period. *One Hundred Years of Brewing* listed a few breweries for Virginia, South Carolina, Tennessee, and Georgia between 1876 and 1902, but none in North Carolina whatsoever. The book's tables listing "Production, in barrels, of malt liquors in the United States," "Summary of sales of malt liquors by states," and "Production in barrels of malt liquors in the United States" showed North Carolina as having significantly lower numbers than surrounding states. In some cases, surrounding states reported hundreds of thousands of barrels, while North Carolina had none. Virginia, Georgia, and Tennessee reported over

100,000 barrels of malt liquor (the legal term for beer at the time) for 1897 (roughly 50 times more than those states reported 100 years later). North Carolina reported zero barrels in 1897.

The enormous gap suggests a reporting issue, not just a lack of breweries. The numbers were most likely reported from tax sources. The federal government started taxing alcohol in the years immediately following the war. North Carolina, as a strong center of Confederate feeling, may have resisted reporting barrels (or anything else) for taxation.

F. W. Salem's book *Beer: Its History and Its Economic Value as a National Beverage* contained more specific data about North Carolina, saying that the state had one brewery—J. W. Lancashire Brewery in Fayetteville—that sold four barrels of beer in 1878–79, a ludicrously small number. The same information can be found in William L. Downward's *Dictionary of the History of the American Brewing and Distilling Industries*. However, that book also stated that North Carolina had 273 grain distilleries with a capacity of 1,073 bushels/2,773 gallons. The sheer number of distilleries suggests that either North Carolinians really did love whiskey more than any other drink (which is possible) or that beer production occurred under the umbrella of whiskey distilling and therefore didn't show up separately in government reporting. After all, *beer* was a word frequently used to refer to the product before it was distilled. Alternately, it is possible that neighboring states produced much more grain alcohol than beer and merely reported beer production, instead of distillation. The fact that malting grain and making yeast for beer and whiskey were often spoken of together, as in the Lenoir plantation records, suggests the processes weren't considered wholly different from each other in the 19th century.

Another important issue in postwar North Carolina was Prohibition. Following small restriction movements in the state throughout the 19th century, efforts grew after the Civil War. In 1874, North Carolina passed the "local option" law, which allowed townships, and eventually counties, to vote to prohibit the sale of liquor. Statewide prohibition was attempted in 1881 but was defeated by popular vote. However, laws mandating more gradual implementation were passed, such as the Watts Bill (1903), which prohibited both the sale and manufacture of liquor outside incorporated towns, and the Ward Law (1905), which prohibited the manufacture of liquor in towns of fewer than 1,000 people.

The interesting thing about these early laws is their struggle to categorize beer. In a proposed 1881 law, homebrewed wines and beers would have been exempted. In the final version of that law, wines and cider were exempted, and beer wasn't mentioned at all. Of the laws that actually passed, the Watts Bill exempted wines, cider, and fruit brandies sold in large quantities but said nothing about beer.

In 1908 came another statewide vote on prohibition. The debate was hot and heavy. National organizations got involved. "It is well known that the Brewers' Association . . . determined to spend millions in trying to stem the temperance wave in the South," noted Daniel Jay Whitener in *Prohibition in North Carolina: 1715–1945.*[21] This time, the prohibition vote passed. According to Whitener, this meant that "to sell or manufacture any spirituous, vinous, fermented or malt liquors, or intoxicating bitters was made unlawful. Druggists were allowed to sell upon written prescription of a licensed physician for sickness only. Wine and cider made from grapes, berries, or fruits could be manufactured and sold, provided the sale was made at the place of manufacture and in sealed packages of not less than two and one-half gallons. Cider could be sold in any quantity by the manufacturer from fruit grown on his lands."[22]

That law went into effect in January 1909, well before nationwide Prohibition. But it had numerous loopholes. For instance, retail sales were permitted to male "social clubs." In 1923, when Congress passed the Volstead Act, North Carolina passed the Turlington Act to bring its dry laws in line with the national law.

Prohibition lasted until 1933. When it became obvious that national repeal was on the horizon, the North Carolina General Assembly considered several bills to pave the way for the legal sale of alcohol. The one that passed, after much debate, was a beer and wine bill. "By it the sale of beer, lager beer, ale, porter, fruit juices, and light wines containing not more than three and two-tenths per cent of alcohol by weight was legalized," according to Whitener. "To raise revenue, taxes of two dollars per barrel and two cents per bottle were authorized."[23] This went into effect as soon as national Prohibition was lifted.

Post-Prohibition and the Birth of Craft Beer

Although making low-alcohol beer was legal in North Carolina after repeal, brewing did not take off. According to Reino Ojala's *20 Years of American Beers: The '30s & '40s*, no breweries were qualified to operate in North Carolina as of July 1, 1935. However, beer was widely distributed in the state. In 1936, Atlantic Brewing Company (headquartered in Atlanta) began operating a brewery and bottling plant in Charlotte, and beer was once again being made in North Carolina. However, like regional breweries in most of the rest of the country, Atlantic couldn't keep up with national competition from Anheuser-Busch, Pabst, and other brewing giants. It closed its doors in 1956.

Stroh Brewery Company opened a plant in Winston-Salem in 1970 (it closed in 1999), and Miller Brewing Company opened one in Eden in 1978. But aside from those two industry giants, nothing popped up in North Carolina until the 1980s. That shouldn't come as a surprise. At the end of the 1970s, only 44 breweries existed in the entire United States, down from a peak of 3,200 prior to Prohibition.

In 1980, Uli Bennewitz emigrated from Germany to the United States, eventually ending up in Manteo. He missed the rich German lagers he had grown up with and decided to open a German-style combination brewery and restaurant. He faced only one obstacle: it was illegal. Undaunted, Bennewitz lobbied the North Carolina General Assembly. In 1985, a law passed that allowed brewpubs to operate in the state. With that act, Bennewitz changed the future of North Carolina brewing. He opened his brewpub, Weeping Radish, in 1986 in Manteo, where it remained until moving to Jarvisburg in 2006. Bennewitz also opened a brewpub in Durham in 1988; it has since closed.

From 1990 on, North Carolina has seen a rush of brewery development, closely following the national trend. The state's industry grew from four breweries in 1990 to 28 by 2000, even through the rash of brewery closings the industry saw nationwide.

The brewing industry in North Carolina received an additional boost after passage of the Pop the Cap law (HB 392) in 2006, which raised the legal alcohol limit for beer to 14.9 percent ABV. From 28 breweries in 2000, the state was up to 48 by the end of 2010, despite seeing 20 closings in as many years, and now has over 145 just a few short years later.

Today, the state's brewing industry is thriving. Despite its checkered past, North Carolina has become one of the most notable brewing centers in the southeastern United States.

Notes

[1] Christoph von Graffenried, *Christoph von Graffenried's Account of the Founding of New Bern*, ed. and trans. by Vincent H. Todd and Julius Goebel (1920; online edition, Documenting the American South, University Library, UNC–Chapel Hill, 2003), docsouth.unc.edu/nc/graffenried/graffenried.html (accessed Nov. 7, 2011), 319.

[2] John Brickell, *The Natural History of North Carolina* (Dublin: James Carson, 1737), archive.org/details/naturalhistoryof00bric (accessed Nov. 8, 2011), 38.

[3] Ibid. 39.

[4] Claude Joseph Sauthier, *Plan of the Town of Crosscreek in Cumberland County, North Carolina* (map, 1770, North Carolina State Archives, Raleigh).

[5] James D. Kornwolf and Georgiana Wallis Kornwolf, *Architecture and Town*

Planning in Colonial North America (Baltimore: Johns Hopkins University Press, 2002), 462.

[6] Stanley Baron, *Brewed in America: A History of Beer and Ale in the United States* (Boston: Little, Brown, 1962), 50.

[7] Chowan County, Ordinary Bonds and Records, 1739–1867, North Carolina State Archives, Raleigh.

[8] William Lenoir's distilling book, Folder 289, Lenoir Family Papers #00426, Southern Historical Collection, Louis Round Wilson Special Collections Library, UNC–Chapel Hill.

[9] Henry Gunnisson, "Brewery," *Wilmington Gazette* (Wilmington, NC), May 12, 1807, digital.ncdcr.gov/cdm/ref/collection/p15016coll1/id/23205 (accessed Jan. 25, 2016).

[10] Thomas Holmes, "Beer and Porter House," *Western Carolinian* (Salisbury, NC), Apr. 1, 1823, digital.ncdcr.gov/cdm/ref/collection/p15016coll1/id/18029 (accessed Jan. 25, 2016).

[11] Thomas Holmes, "Hops," *Western Carolinian* (Salisbury, NC), June 10, 1823, digital.ncdcr.gov/cdm/ref/collection/p15016coll1/id/18057 (accessed Jan. 25, 2016).

[12] Thomas Holmes, "House of Entertainment," *Western Carolinian* (Salisbury, NC), May 8, 1827, digital.ncdcr.gov/cdm/ref/collection/p15016coll1/id/18998 (accessed Jan. 25, 2016).

[13] "Domestic Beer, Porter, &c.," *Western Carolinian* (Salisbury, NC), Aug. 19, 1828, digital.ncdcr.gov/cdm/ref/collection/p15016coll1/id/19327 (accessed Jan. 25, 2016).

[14] Ibid.

[15] "Recipe for making Chinese Beer," *Carolina Watchman* (Salisbury, NC), July 22, 1847, digital.ncdcr.gov/cdm/ref/collection/p15016coll1/id/1068 (accessed Jan. 25, 2016).

[16] "A Remedy Proposed," *Carolina Watchman* (Salisbury, NC), June 20, 1850, digital.ncdcr.gov/cdm/ref/collection/p15016coll1/id/1784 (accessed Jan. 25, 2016).

[17] Confederate States of America, *Tariff of the Confederate States of America* (1861; online edition, Documenting the American South, University Library, UNC–Chapel Hill, 1999), docsouth.unc.edu/imls/tariff/tariff.html (accessed Nov. 8, 2011), 5.

[18] James M. Matthews, ed., *The Statutes at Large of the Confederate States of America, Passed at the Fourth Session of the First Congress, 1863–64* (1864; online edition, Documenting the American South. University Library, UNC–Chapel Hill, 2001), docsouth.unc.edu/imls/23conf/23conf.html (accessed Nov. 8, 2011), 179.

[19] Francis Peyre Porcher, *Resources of the Southern Fields and Forests* (1863; online edition, Documenting the American South. University Library, UNC–Chapel Hill, 2001), docsouth.unc.edu/imls/porcher/porcher.html (accessed Nov. 8, 2011), 279–80.

[20] Daniel Jay Whitener, *Prohibition in North Carolina, 1715–1945* (Chapel Hill: University of North Carolina Press, 1946), 50.

[21] Ibid., 166.

[22] Ibid., 162.

[23] Ibid., 199.

HOW BEER IS MADE

Ingredients

ALL BEER IS MADE FROM FIVE ESSENTIAL INGREDIENTS.

Water is the most important ingredient in beer. Beer is mostly water, so it is essential to have clean water that tastes good in order to make good beer. Many of the world's classic beer styles have evolved because of good local water profiles—the balance of minerals and salts naturally dissolved into the water that give it a hard or soft character, as well as a distinctive flavor.

Most of North Carolina has good, neutral, relatively soft water that makes excellent beer.

Malted barley is the source of most of the sugar in beer. Barley is a grain commonly grown throughout the world but especially in northern Europe, the American Midwest, Canada, and Australia. Unlike other cereal grains, it is high in starch and low in protein and has a fibrous husk. All of these characteristics make it ideal for use in making beer.

When barley is harvested, it is not immediately ready for beer production. It must first be malted. Malting is a process in which the grain is soaked in water, which causes germination of the seed to start. Natural enzymes in the barley then begin to change the starch already present in the kernel into sugar. Other enzymes break down cell walls in the barley, making the hard, pebble-like barley kernel soft and sugary. The maltster then applies heat, arresting the germination process and caramelizing the sugar in the kernel.

Maltsters use many different types of heating and roasting techniques to make different colors and flavors of malt, ranging from extremely light pilsner malt, used as a base malt in the lightest beers, to deep black roasted malt, which can impart an espresso-like character and color to a beer. A vast array of caramel and toasted malts lies in between. Brewers can choose from over 200 different types of malts from different maltsters and suppliers. All impart different flavors, colors, and even textures to beer.

Hops are the flowers and fruiting bodies of the plant *Humulus lupulus*. They have bright green flowers resembling pine cones growing in bunches from perennial bines 20 to 30 feet tall. Brewers use hops to add bitterness to beer to counteract the sweetness of the malt. The hundreds of different types of cultivated hops provide their own flavors to beer. The flavors can range from citrusy and pine-like to grassy, earthy, or leathery, and even to apple, pear, blueberry, or other fruit flavors.

Hops haven't always been used in beer. Throughout history, many other herbs have been put into beer to counteract sweetness, among them sweet gale, yarrow, spruce, pine, heather, bee balm, and even some fairly dangerous ingredients such as wormwood and witch hazel. Over time, hops were adopted not only for their pleasant flavor but because they are a natural antibacterial agent. Their presence in brewing has significantly increased the shelf life of beer.

Yeast is unique as an ingredient in brewing because it is actually a living organism. For thousands of years, brewers merely made liquids they knew would eventually turn into beer, then left them out for the apparently spontaneous reaction that would sooner or later occur. They knew that if they added some of the beer from previous batches, or even bread made from a previous batch of beer, that the reaction would happen more quickly. It wasn't until Louis Pasteur's groundbreaking work in the mid-19th century that people understood that live organisms in the liquid were eating the sugar-rich solution and excreting carbon dioxide and ethanol—two of the components that make beer most pleasant to drinkers—as well as up to 900 other chemicals that add flavor.

Brewers use two major families of yeast: ale yeast and lager yeast. These are often incorrectly referred to as "top fermenting" yeast (ale yeast) and "bottom fermenting" yeast (lager yeast) because of how brewers used to harvest the yeast before the advent of modern technology. In reality, fermentation takes place throughout the solution. The primary difference between ale yeast and lager yeast is the temperature at which they best ferment. Ale yeast ferments around room temperature, from 60 degrees to 75 degrees Fahrenheit, whereas lager yeast ferments best between 45 degrees and 60 degrees. Ale yeast also tends to have a much more robust ester profile, evoking a wide range of fruit flavors, while lager yeast creates much more neutral, crisp, clean beers.

Thousands of yeasts from these two families are used around the world to make beer.

Adjuncts often get a bad rap. Adjuncts are sources of sugar used for brewing that are not malted barley. When people speak of adjuncts in brewing, they are typically referring to a macrobrewery's use of corn and rice in light American lagers, primarily to add more fermentable sugar to the beer without adding flavor or character.

However, adjuncts can also be used to add an enormous amount of flavor to beer. Any non-barley grain is considered an adjunct. Rye, wheat, oats, buckwheat, spelt, and sorghum are all used as additions, and all impart their own flavors. Adjuncts can also refer to sugar additions such as turbinado, demerara, brown sugar, molasses, agave syrup, candi sugar, honey, and maple syrup. Finally, many clever brewers use a wide range of fruits and vegetables as sources of starch and sugar as well. These include sweet potatoes, pumpkins, and squash. Anything with natural starch or sugar can be used as an adjunct in beer.

The Brewing Process

Milling

When a brewer starts a batch of beer, the first thing he does is mill the barley. Barley usually comes to a brewery in whole-kernel form. Those kernels must be crushed to expose the insides to water more efficiently in the later steps. Brewers only crush grain. They do not mill it to flour. They want to leave the husks of the barley intact to use as a natural filter later in the process.

Mashing

Once the grain is milled, the brewer adds heated water. The heat and water reactivate the enzymes that were at work in the barley during germination, which restarts the conversion of starches into sugars. Since water is an excellent solvent, it also acts as a base for the sugars to dissolve into, meaning that the sugars can easily be extracted from the grain.

Lautering

Lautering is the process of removing the liquid—now considered *wort*—from the grain. The wort is drained through the grain itself, the husks from the barley acting as a natural filter bed. While this is happening, clean, hot water is sprayed over the top of the grain bed in a process called *sparging*. Sparging rinses the remaining sugar from the grain bed, allowing the brewer to use as much as possible of the sugar that was originally present in the barley.

Boiling

The wort is then transferred to a kettle and boiled. Boiling serves several important functions in brewing. It sterilizes the wort, ensuring that no bacteria or wild yeasts are present. It drives off volatile sulfuric compounds naturally found in barley that can lend beer an unpleasant egg or cabbage flavor and aroma. Boiling allows for the formation of certain calcium compounds that help protein precipitate from the solution to create clearer beer. Finally, boiling is when brewers add the majority of the hops—and sometimes other ingredients—to the beer.

Brewers are careful about when hops are added to the boil. The longer hops are in contact with the boiling wort, the more bitterness is derived from the hops, and the less aroma and flavor. Because of this, brewers normally use a hop schedule that specifies the amount of hops to be added at the beginning or middle of the boil for bitterness, and the amount to be added near the end of the boil for flavor and aroma. Since aroma compounds are delicate and can easily be boiled off, any ingredients whose aromas the brewer wishes to retain are normally added right at the end of the boil.

Fermentation and Conditioning

Boiling normally takes an hour at minimum. Afterward, the wort is chilled to fermentation temperature and yeast is added. It is at this point that the liquid actually becomes beer. Yeast can finish fermenting in as little as three days to as many as 30 days, depending on the strain of yeast, the amount of sugar in the solution, and the temperature of fermentation. Brewers often allow the beer to sit through a period of cold conditioning after fermentation is complete.

Packaging and Distribution

After the fermenting and conditioning are completed, the beer is carbonated and packaged. In North Carolina, every available type of packaging is employed: bottles, cans, growlers (32-ounce and 64-ounce glass jugs), and kegs of all sizes. Once the beer has been packaged, it is on its way to consumers for their enjoyment.

A PRIMER ON BEER STYLES

BEER STYLES ARE IN A CONSTANT STATE OF FLUX. Most of the familiar styles have grown out of European brewing traditions over the past few hundred years. As with art, more new styles—often new takes on traditional styles—are invented every day.

Style guidelines are used for judging beers in competitions, both at amateur and professional levels. Perhaps most importantly, style definitions allow consumers to know what to expect when they pick a beer from the shelf or order a drink in a bar.

Most beer falls into two basic categories: ales and lagers. This refers to the type of yeast used in brewing. All ales are brewed with *Saccharomyces cerevisiae*. Hundreds, if not thousands, of strains of *S. cerevisiae* are used around the world in brewing and baking—even in the bread yeast consumers buy at the store. All lagers are brewed with *Saccharomyces pastorianus*. Two major strains of *S. pastorianus* are used in brewing worldwide. Some brewers use wild yeasts or other controlled yeasts such as *Brettanomyces bruxellensis, lambicus,* or *clausenii* and even bacteria such as *lactobacillus, pediococcus,* or *acetobacter* for different flavors in fermentation.

Ale yeast and lager yeast were once misidentified as, respectively, "top fermenting" and "bottom fermenting" because of the observations that brewers made before modern science. It is now known that fermentation takes place throughout the liquid. However, the terms are still in frequent use.

The following is not a complete list of beer styles, but one that attempts to highlight most of the styles available in North Carolina. Many of the beers brewed in the state defy conventional style guides and are well worth seeking out. For more information, check out the Beer Judge Certification Program (bjcp.org/stylecenter.php) and the Brewers Association Beer Style Guidelines (brewersassociation.org/resources/brewers-association-beer-style-guidelines).

Lagers

Lager literally means "to store." This is in reference to the origin of many lager beers, which were stored in caves during the warm summer months to complete fermentation. In the 1800s, brewing scientists discovered that the yeast in lagers was actually a different type than was used in ales. It ferments at a lower temperature for a longer period of time. Lager yeast has few esters (the fruity flavors normally present in ales) and often has a lingering light sulfuric flavor, giving lagers their characteristic dryness and crispness.

In 2011, scientists discovered a yeast identified as *Saccharomyces eubayanas* in Patagonia that is thought to be the parent organism of lager yeast.

International-Style Lager. The most common beer in the world. Very pale. Highly carbonated. Not malty or hoppy. High use of adjuncts such as corn and rice lighten the body of the beer without adding flavor. Commercial examples: Budweiser, Miller Genuine Draft. No craft examples in North Carolina.

Lite American Lager. A "light" version of premium American lager with less residual sugar, less alcohol, and less flavor. Commercial examples: Bud Light, Coors Light. No craft examples in North Carolina.

Munich Helles. Sweet, malty, crisp golden lager brewed using traditional German noble hops, which lend a light, spicy, floral aroma. North Carolina examples: Olde Mecklenburg Mecklenburger, Red Oak Hummin' Bird.

Bohemian Pilsner. Light, grainy, malty, and complex. Traditionally brewed using Saaz hops, which lend a light bitterness and a spicy and floral character. North Carolina examples: Aviator Crazy Pils, Foothills Torch Pilsner.

German Pilsner. Traditionally, a German copy of Bohemian pilsner. Generally drier and crisper than Bohemian pilsner, brewed using other traditional German hops and having slightly higher carbonation. North Carolina examples: Olde Mecklenburg Captain James Jack Pilsner, Weeping Radish Corolla Gold.

Vienna Lager. A rich, malty amber lager. No hop aroma or flavor. Even though this beer has a sweet flavor, it finishes crisp and dry. North Carolina examples: Red Oak Amber Lager, Draft Line Vienna Lager, Nickelpoint Vienna Lager.

Märzen/Oktoberfest. Traditionally a version of Vienna lager brewed in Munich, this beer is now associated primarily with the annual Oktoberfest there. North Carolina examples: Foothills Oktoberfest, Highland Clawhammer Oktoberfest.

Munich Dunkel. *Dunkel* means "dark" in German. A dark, rich, malty lager that often has notes of chocolate, caramel, coffee, or toast. Based on traditional Märzen but darker, more complex, and higher in alcohol. North Carolina examples: Mother Earth Dark Cloud Munich Dunkel, Olde Mecklenburg Dunkel Lager.

Schwarzbier. Literally "black beer." Similar to a Munich dunkel but not normally as sweet and rich. Flavors tend toward roasted or coffee bitterness and moderate hop bitterness. Sometimes referred to as "black pilsner." North Carolina examples: Duck-Rabbit Schwarzbier, Weeping Radish Black Radish.

Bock. A dark, strong, toasty, malty lager that originated in the northern German city of Einbeck. Bock is a corruption of *Einbeck* in the Bavarian dialect. Since *bock* means "goat" in German, goats are often used in advertising. Bocks sometimes have flavors reminiscent of dark or dried fruits. North Carolina examples: Olde Mecklenburg Frueh Bock, Bull City "Goat" Bullock Bock.

Maibock/Helles Bock. A paler version of traditional bock. Sometimes drier or more hoppy, often with rich, malty complexity but none of the dark fruit flavors. *Helles* means "pale" and *Mai* means "May," referring to the fact that Maibock is traditionally served in the springtime. North Carolina examples: Foothills Gruffmeister Maibock, Carolina Brewing Company Carolina Spring Bock.

Doppelbock. A richer, more alcoholic version of a bock, sometimes with notes of caramel or chocolate in addition to rich fruitiness. *Doppel* means "double." Doppelbocks are normally much sweeter and stronger than traditional bocks. Most are dark, but occasional versions are pale. North Carolina examples: Duck-Rabbit Doppelbock, Olde Hickory Doppelbock.

Baltic Porter. A version of traditional English porter originating from countries around the Baltic Sea. Similar to English porters in its coffee, chocolate, and caramel notes, but sweeter and more alcoholic, with notes of molasses and dark fruit. North Carolina examples: Duck-Rabbit Baltic Porter, Front Street Baltic Porter.

Ales

The one trait all ales have in common is that they are made with some strain of ale yeast. Ale yeasts ferment quickly at close to room temperature. Their notable flavor characteristics come from esters, which can contribute a wide range of fruit flavors, and fusel alcohols, which contribute flavors reminiscent of port or sherry. Ale yeast is one of the most common organisms in the world and was the first organism to have its genome mapped.

Bitter, Best Bitter, Extra Special Bitter. These are British pale ales. They generally have a rich, malty body, often with caramel or toffee notes, and a notable hop presence. Bitter (or standard/ordinary bitter) is the mildest version. A slightly stronger, hoppier version would be called special bitter, best bitter, or premium bitter. Stronger and hoppier yet is extra special bitter or strong bitter. North Carolina examples: Gibb's Hundred The Guilty Party, Pig Pounder Extra Special Pig, Fortnight ESB.

Mild English Brown Ale. The word *mild* was originally applied to a beer that was young or fresh. Now, it refers to a light brown ale with moderate hop bitterness. There are two varieties of English brown ale. Southern English brown is sweet, malty, and nutty and has notes of chocolate and dark fruit. Northern English brown is drier and hoppier. North Carolina examples: Mystery Brewing Pickwick, Natty Greene's Old Town Brown, Hi-Wire Bed of Nails.

American Brown Ale. Similar to English brown ale—sweet, malty, nutty, and chocolaty—but with a much larger hop profile. American brown normally uses citrusy American hops. North Carolina examples: Lonerider Sweet Josie Brown, Carolina Brewing Company Carolina Nut Brown Ale, Birdsong Lazy Bird Brown.

Brown Porter. Porters are essentially dark brown ales. Brewers tend to use "black" or "black patent" malt to flavor porters, giving them a distinctive coffee/espresso note, along with chocolate, malt, and nutty notes. Brown porters are the lighter and sweeter of the two porters and in some cases may not be easily distinguished from brown ales but for the inclusion of black malt. North Carolina examples: Mash House Brown Porter, Boylan Bridge Pullman Porter, Mystery Brewing Jack Thorne.

Robust Porter. Robust porters are darker, roastier, more alcoholic versions of brown porters. They have a definite coffee/espresso note from the inclusion of black malt and can also have notes of dark chocolate or burnt caramel. North Carolina examples: Foothills People's Porter, Duck-Rabbit Porter, Lonerider Deadeye Jack Porter.

Scottish Ale. A wide range of Scottish ales exists, but few make their way into the American market. Malty ales with almost no hop character, they can range from very light and fairly dry to rich, dark, and sweet. They sometimes exhibit a light smoky character but rarely contain peated or peat-smoked malt (the type made for use in Scotch whiskey). Scottish ales are traditionally named in shilling amounts, the lightest being a 60 Shilling (alternately written as "60/-"). Also available are 70 Shilling (70/-), 80 Shilling (80/-), and versions that are gradually darker, sweeter, roastier, smokier, and more alcoholic. North Carolina examples: Highland Tasgall Ale, Bull City Bonnie Brae 60 Shilling Scottish Ale, Mystery Brewing Ballantrae.

Wee Heavy. The darkest and heaviest of Scottish ales. The Scottish version of barleywine, Wee Heavies are sweet, rich, malty, and nutty, with notes of caramel and smoky roastiness. North Carolina examples: Duck-Rabbit Wee Heavy, Huske Hardware Filthy Kilt Wee Heavy, French Broad Wee Heavy-er Scotch Ale, Front Street Dram Tree.

Irish Red Ale. Similar to Scottish ale, but often drier with more caramel or toffee character. It is named for the reddish hue it gains from the addition of roasted (but not malted) barley. North Carolina examples: Highland Gaelic Ale, Aviator Hotrod Red.

American Pale Ale. The American version of British pale ale. Malty with a light sweetness. But American pale ale (like anything with *American* in the name) is really about hops. The least bitter showcase for American hops, it normally exhibits notes of citrus, grass, or pine, depending on the type of hops used. It can have a slight lingering bitter finish. North Carolina examples: Natty Greene's Southern Pale Ale, Lonerider Peacemaker Pale Ale, Carolina Brewing Company Carolina Pale Ale, Pisgah Pale Ale.

Dry Stout. Dry and bitter, with notes of coffee, espresso, and cocoa. Creamy and jet-black with a tan- or brown-colored head. North Carolina examples: Bull City Jack Tar, Fonta Flora Irish Table, Heinzelmännchen Black Forest Stout.

Sweet Stout/Milk Stout. Sweet stouts (or milk stouts) are made using lactose. Lactose is not fermentable by yeast, so the beers are left with much more residual sweetness. They often exhibit chocolate, coffee, or espresso flavors; the end product can taste like sweetened coffee or, because lactose often has a milky tang, a chocolate bar. North Carolina example: Duck-Rabbit Milk Stout.

Foreign Extra Stout. Foreign extra stouts are traditionally brewed for tropical markets. They are higher in alcohol than dry or sweet stouts and often exhibit rather fruity characteristics, as well as the traditional coffee, chocolate, burnt, or roasty notes typical of stouts. North Carolina example: Mystery Brewing Papa Bois.

American Stout. Like other American versions, this is high in hops. Because this stout is bitter, the tannic character of the malt tends to stand out, giving the beer notes of bittersweet chocolate or baking chocolate, or even a bitter coffee note. American hops lend a grassy, citrusy, or piney flavor. North Carolina examples: Foothills Total Eclipse Stout, Highland Black Mocha Stout.

Russian Imperial Stout. Big, complex Russian imperial stouts are often favorites in the craft beer market. They are high in alcohol and tend to have big, rich palates full of chocolate, coffee, molasses, caramel, and toffee, as well as dark fruit flavors such as plum, raisin, prune, or date. They are intense beers. North Carolina examples: Duck-Rabbit Rabid Duck Russian Imperial Stout, Natty Greene's Black Powder Imperial Stout.

English IPA. India pale ales are highly hopped pale ales. By the 1760s, English brewers were advised to add extra hops to beer for export to warm climes. By the early 1800s, "pale ale prepared for the Indian market"—soon to be referred to as "India pale ale"—was on sale in England. English IPAs aren't as bitter as their American cousins. While they exhibit the same light, sweet, caramel palate, they are traditionally made with British hops, which provide an earthy, floral, and sometimes even leathery flavor. North Carolina examples: Mystery Brewing Hornigold, Carolina Brewery Flagship IPA.

American IPA. American IPAs are filled with American hops. While a sweet, malty body exists, it is mainly there to support the hops. American hops are more bitter than many other hops and have flavors reminiscent of citrus, pine, or hemp. These beers tend to have a lingering, bitter finish. North Carolina examples: Big Boss High Roller, Foothills Hoppyum IPA, NoDa Hop Drop and Roll, Wicked Weed Pernicious IPA, Fonta Flora Hop Beard.

Imperial/Double IPA. A big, bold, alcoholic IPA with tons of hops. This beer often resembles a barleywine in strength and character, with rich caramel flavors dominating, but it is really a showcase for hops. It can exhibit citrus, pine, grassy, earthy, floral, herbal, or hemp tones. Some examples even have a note of sulfur to them, which dries out the ultra-sweet body and adds another layer of flavor complexity. North Carolina examples: Lynnwood Brewing Concern Hubris, Trophy Double Death Spiral, Wicked Weed Freak of Nature.

Black IPA. An IPA made with a slight addition of roasted malt for an extra layer of complexity. The added malt is generally either malted wheat or dehusked barley, to avoid a harsh tannic bitterness. The majority of the bitterness in a black IPA is derived from the hops. The added bitterness can lend a bitter cocoa flavor. Versions made with American hops are reminiscent of a chocolate orange. North Carolina examples: Lonerider Grave Robber Black IPA, Olde Hickory Black Raven IPA, Lynnwood Brewing Concern Once You Go.

English Barleywine. Barleywine gets its name from its strength, which is often nearly as high as that of wine. It's a strong, rich, malty beer with notes of caramel, toffee, or molasses. It can exhibit bread, nut, and fruit characteristics. English versions are made with mild English hops, which often lend a leathery or woody character to a barleywine. Many barleywines are now vintage-dated and can be aged. Their flavor can change significantly in the bottle over the course of a couple of years. North Carolina examples: Duck-Rabbit Barleywine, Olde Hickory Irish Walker, Pisgah Hellbender.

American Barleywine. American barleywines, like their English cousins, are sweet, malty, and strong. However, like every other style labeled "American," they have a much higher hop content and a much more bitter character. Because of the sweet backbone of these beers, American barleywines often become a showcase for American hops. They can be very citrusy or piney without being overpoweringly bitter. North Carolina example: Carolina Brewing Company Old 392 Barleywine.

Weizen/Weissbier. The words *weizen* ("wheat"), *weissbier* ("white beer"), and *hefeweizen* ("yeast wheat") refer to light German beers that are made with high proportions of wheat and very few hops. Wheat lends a full, creamy feel to the beers. Since these beers are often served young, with yeast still in suspension, they often have a light, bready quality. The yeast used in most weissbiers also provides a blend of flavors reminiscent of bananas and cloves—a unique flavor profile. North Carolina examples: Lonerider Shotgun Betty Hefeweizen, Mother Earth Sunny Haze Hefeweizen, Four Saints German Hefeweizen.

Dunkelweizen. *Dunkelweizen* means "dark wheat." This is exactly what it sounds like: a wheat beer made with dark malts to create a dark beer with a complex palate. The wheat still provides a full, rich feel, but the result is often much more reminiscent of rich malts, caramels, and at times even chocolate. These beers can have a wide range of flavors, from bananas like their "white" brethren to cloves, bubblegum, or vanilla. North Carolina example: Big Boss D-icer.

Witbier. A witbier is a light, wheat-based ale like a weissbier, traditionally made with additions of coriander and bitter (Curaçao) orange peel. Light and zesty, it has a citrus character from the spice additions and the same milky cloudiness and hazy character of other wheat beers. North Carolina examples: Big Boss Blanco Diablo, Mother Earth Weeping Willow Wit, Natty Greene's Wildflower Witbier.

Saison/Biere de Garde. A saison is traditionally a farmhouse ale brewed for workers in the fields. The original versions were low in alcohol and used left-over farm grains—rye, oats, spelt, buckwheat, or whatever else was around. Today's versions are much higher in alcohol and typically use mostly barley. They have a distinctive yeast that produces dry, spicy beer. Some versions have added spices ranging from star anise, cloves, and black pepper to rosemary, thyme, sage, and basil. The color can range from bright yellow to orange. Most versions are highly carbonated. North Carolina examples: Mystery Brewing Evangeline, Haw River Mille Fleur, Fonta Flora Southern Saison, Burial Haysaw Saison.

Abbey Ale. Abbey ales refer to a range of complex, dry Belgian beers that have traditionally been produced in Trappist monasteries. But only beers produced in eight specific abbeys in Belgium and the Netherlands are allowed to be called "Trappist ales." Although two main styles are recognized—dubbel and tripel—many Belgian- and abbey-style ales defy categorization. Dubbels are dark, dry, malty beers with vinous notes of dark fruit and chocolate. Tripels are high-alcohol golden beers with rich, malty palates and fruity notes. Belgian and abbey ales tend to be quite dry, "digestible," and highly carbonated. North Carolina examples: Highland Seven Sisters Abbey-Style Dubbel, Four Saints Genesis Belgian-Style Dubbel, Mother Earth Tripel Overhead, Aviator Devils Tramping Ground Tripel.

Hybrid Styles

Hybrid in this case refers to beers that cross the border between ales and lagers in terms of process. They do not actually use hybrid yeasts, but rather ale yeasts fermented at colder temperatures (as lagers would) or lager yeasts fermented at higher temperatures (as ales would).

Kölsch-Style Beer. A Kölsch is light, clean, and crisp. It is similar to a pilsner, but Kölsch is fermented with clean ale yeasts at low temperatures. Kölsch beers tend to have a light, malty sweetness and a clean, grainy quality. Unlike pilsners, they tend to have a light fruitiness and only a light hop bitterness. Technically, only beer brewed in and around Köln, Germany, is allowed to be called Kölsch. North Carolina examples: Mother Earth Endless River Kölsch, White Street Kölsch, French Broad Kölsch, Weeping Radish OBX Kölsch.

California Common/Steam Beer. "California common" beers or "Steam" beers are a certain type of amber lager made with a lager yeast fermented at higher temperatures like an ale. The style originated in San Francisco prior to refrigeration, when brewers attempted to make traditional lagers in the naturally cool climate of the Bay Area. The beer is fruity and malty, with notes of grain, caramel, and—because of the lager yeast—a bit of sulfur, which dries it out and allows the hops to shine through. The name *Steam Beer* is trademarked by Anchor Brewery in San Francisco, so the style is generally referred to as California common. North Carolina examples: Fullsteam Southern Lager, Aviator Steamhead.

Other Styles

The following are variations, rather than strict styles. Fruits or spices can be added to any beer, and anything can be put into a barrel (though brewers might not want to do so).

Fruit Beer. Simply put, this is beer made with fruit. Berries—raspberries, blueberries, strawberries, blackberries, etc.—tend to be the most popular additions. Wheat beers are one of the most popular bases for fruit beers. In North Carolina, beer/fruit combinations run the gamut from the lightest of pilsners to the darkest of stouts, employing everything from common fruits to really strange ones. For a long time, fruit beers were seen as "starter" beers or "easy" beers. But in the right brewer's hands, these are delicious concoctions full of rich complexity that all beer drinkers should be eager to try. North Carolina examples: Fullsteam First Frost (abbey-style dubbel made with persimmons), Liberty Blackberry Wheat (blackberry hefeweizen), Big Boss Big Operator (black ale made with raspberries).

Spice Beer. Beer made with spices—it seems simple but is actually quite complex. Hundreds of different spices can be used in beer. Anything in the kitchen—including rosemary, basil, black pepper, sage, saffron, allspice, vanilla, and ginger, to name only a few—can fall into a brewer's kettle, with amazing results. Spice beer also refers to beers made with coffee or chocolate. North Carolina examples: Mystery Brewing Six Impossible Things Chocolate Breakfast Stout, Big Boss Harvest Time (made with pumpkin pie spice), Outer Banks LemonGrass Wheat Ale, Fullsteam Summer Basil, Birdsong Jalapeño Pale Ale.

Smoked Beer. In these beers, a portion of the grain is smoked, much as traditional North Carolina barbecue is smoked. They can range from the slightly smoky to the intensely smoky, which can taste a little like drinking a smoked sausage. Some brewers smoke their own grain, but most buy grain presmoked. North Carolina examples: Fullsteam Hogwash Hickory-Smoked Porter, Natty Greene's Smoky Mountain Porter.

Barrel-Aged Beer. Barrel-aged beers are stored in barrels after fermentation to pick up flavor from the barrels—or, most often, to pick up flavor from what used to be in them. North Carolina has a rich history of bourbon distilleries and is home to a wide range of bourbon-barrel-aged beers. Often, brewers will barrel-age a portion of a batch of beer. Other breweries make beer specifically to be aged in barrels. North Carolina examples: Olde Hickory The Event Horizon (barrel-aged imperial stout), Mother Earth Tripel Overhead (bourbon barrel aged).

Sour Beer/Wild Ale. The two basic types of sour beers are those that are soured prior to fermentation (via sour mash or flavor additions) and those that are soured after fermentation (via spontaneous fermentation or controlled fermentation using yeast/bacteria blends). Sour mash beers are typically high in lactic acid, which can provide a refreshing, lemony tang. In high concentrations, these beers can have notes that resemble yogurt or sour milk but—amazingly—are quite delicious. Spontaneously fermented beers and those fermented using souring blends are complex, dry beers. Their wide range of flavors runs from vinegar (acetic acid), lemon, apple cider, and tropical fruits to more funky flavors sometimes described as "hay," "horse blanket," and "barnyard." Some brewers add fruit to sour beers, which complement them well. North Carolina examples: Wicked Weed Genesis, D9 Viking Fraoch, Mystery Brewing Mythos, Haw River Major Arcana, Fonta Flora Vestige Bloom.

SYMBOL KEY

 Has a taproom

 Serves food

 Sells beer to-go in growlers

 Sells beer to-go in bottles/cans

 On-site parking

 Dog-Friendly

 Kid-Friendly

 Offers tours

MOUNTAIN BREWERIES

Andrews
Andrews Brewing Company

Bryson City
Nantahala Brewing Company

Franklin
Lazy Hiker Brewing Company

Highlands
Satulah Mountain Brewing Company

Sylva
The Sneak E Squirrel
Heinzelmännchen Brewery
Innovation Brewing

Waynesville
BearWaters Brewing Company
Frog Level Brewing Company
Boojum Brewing Company
Tipping Point Brewing

Brevard
Brevard Brewing Company

Hendersonville
Southern Appalachian Brewery

Asheville
Altamont Brewing Company
Oyster House Brewing Company
Asheville Pizza and Brewing Company
Hi-Wire Brewing
Thirsty Monk Pub & Brewery
Twin Leaf Brewery
Burial Beer Company
Green Man Brewery
Wicked Weed Brewing
One World Brewing
Lexington Avenue Brewery
French Broad Brewing Company
Wedge Brewing Company
Highland Brewing Company

Weaverville
Blue Mountain Pizza and Brew Pub

Morganton
Fonta Flora Brewery

Morganton/Asheville
Catawba Brewing Company

Lenoir
Lee's Brewing Company
Howard Brewing

Black Mountain
Pisgah Brewing Company
Lookout Brewing

Spruce Pine
Dry County Brewing Company

Plumtree
Blind Squirrel Brewery

Beech Mountain
Beech Mountain Brewing Company

Banner Elk
Flat Top Brewing Company

Granite Falls
Granite Falls Brewing Company

Hickory
Olde Hickory Brewery

Boone
Lost Province Brewing Company
Appalachian Mountain Brewery
Booneshine Brewing Company

Blowing Rock/Hickory
Blowing Rock Brewing Company

West Jefferson
Boondocks Brewing

ANDREWS BREWING COMPANY

565 Aquone Road
Andrews, NC 28901
828-321-2006
Email: drink@AndrewsBrewing.com
Website: andrewsbrewing.com
Hours: Monday–Tuesday and Thursday–Saturday,
    noon–8 P.M.
Founders: Eric and Judy Carlson
Head Brewer: Eric Carlson
Brewer: Dusty Davis
Opened: 2013

NESTLED IN THE GREAT SMOKY MOUNTAINS is North Carolina's westernmost brewery, Andrews Brewing Company. This small craft brewery features a rotating lineup of six beers and beautiful scenery to enjoy while sipping. The recipes at Andrews tend to be straightforward. "We do not push the limits of craft beer as most small breweries do," cofounder and brewer Eric Carlson says, though he adds, "That will probably change as we bring our local following along through some fun styles."

Eric and his wife, Judy, are relative newcomers to the craft beer business, but not to the business of alcohol production. They opened their winery, Calaboose Cellars, in 2007 after starting to grow grapes on their property in Andrews. The winery is named in honor of its old stone building, the town's first jail. The Carlsons added the brewery after seeing North Carolina's growing interest in locally produced craft beer. It seemed like a natural step, but Eric is the first to admit there are "stark differences between making wine and beer." He explains, "With wine, we harvest the grapes and start the wine. Then it sits there for months. Then we filter it. Then it sits there for months. Then we bottle it. Beer making? Different! Constant! We can experiment with our recipes monthly."

Since opening the brewery, the Carlsons have continued to experiment with beer making and to expand. In 2014, their Double Arrowhead beer won third place in the highly competitive IPA category at the NC Brewers Cup.

They recently purchased a 9,000-square-foot building in downtown Andrews and have plans to expand their brewing facility and open a brewpub, which will take pressure off their smaller original location.

The patio in front of Andrews Brewing Company
Andrews Brewing Company

NANTAHALA BREWING COMPANY

61 Depot Street
Bryson City, NC 28713
828-488-BEER (2337)
Email: ken@nantahalabrewing.com
Website: nantahalabrewing.com
Hours: Monday–Thursday, noon–10 p.m.;
   Friday–Saturday, noon–midnight;
   Sunday, noon–10 P.M. (These are summer hours;
   verify seasonally.)
Owners: Ken Smith, Joe Rowland
Brewmaster: Greg Geiger
Opened: 2009

Nantahala Brewing Company is tucked far into the Great Smoky Mountains in downtown Bryson City, now a major outdoor tourism destination. Bryson City is just a few miles from both the start of the Blue Ridge Parkway and Kituwah, the oldest Cherokee Indian village on record, dating back thousands of years. The brewery is named after the Nantahala River, a whitewater-rafting destination known for its rapids. The river even serves as a training ground for Olympic athletes.

The brewery is housed in an old Quonset hut left by the government after the Army Corps of Engineers built nearby Fontana Dam. The large arched space has developed organically as the brewery has grown. The floors, walls, and stairways are made of rustic-looking wood. The place has, co-owner Joe Rowland says, the feel of a treehouse. The brewery is across the street from the Great Smoky Mountains Railroad depot, where tourists can ride the old railway into the mountains on day trips. From the front deck of the brewery, patrons can watch as the old steam engines roll into the station.

The building stands next to what was Mike Marsden's Across the Trax bar. Marsden always thought it would be a great place for a brewery. Soon after he met Chris and Christina Collier, a homebrewing couple who dreamed of opening their own brewery, the three began sketching plans. A short year later,

Nantahala Brewing Company opened its doors, brewing on used equipment from South Carolina's RJ Rockers brewpub.

The brewery has an enormous tasting room that opened in 2011. Its interior façade—complete with a two-story balcony, siding, a shingled roof, and an awning over the long bar that runs in front of the entire brewery—makes patrons feel as if they're outside. Tall tables and multiple games dot the brewery. Sports events can be projected on the big wall, complementing the two flat-screen televisions over the bar. The corner of the tasting room is dominated by a raised stage where live bands play on the weekends.

Nantahala's beers are now distributed around the state, though most of its sales are concentrated in the mountains it calls home.

Looking down on Nantahala's taproom just before opening
Erik Lars Myers

LAZY HIKER
BREWING COMPANY

188 West Main Street
Franklin, NC 28734
828-349-BEER
Email: getlazy@lazyhikerbrewing.com
Website: lazyhikerbrewing.com
Hours: Monday–Thursday, noon–9 P.M.;
    Friday–Saturday, noon–11 P.M.; Sunday, noon–6 P.M.
Founders: Tommy Jenkins, Lenny Jordan, Ken Murphy
Founding Brewer: Noah McIntee
Opened: 2015

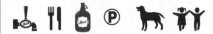

AS THE NAME SUGGESTS, LAZY HIKER BREWING COMPANY is located near the heart of mountain-hiking territory in western North Carolina. Its hometown, Franklin, is officially an Appalachian Trail community; the Appalachian Trail is 14 miles from the brewery, while the Bartram Trail is just three miles away. However, Lazy Hiker welcomes everyone, not just hardcore hikers. As head brewer Noah McIntee says, "The name Lazy Hiker is an invitation for all hikers, including thru-hikers bound for faraway states as well as year-round residents of the area that tread the local trails, to slow down and relax with a beer."

At Lazy Hiker's taproom, visitors will find up to 12 beers on tap, a food truck in the parking lot, and occasional live music. The brewery and taproom are at the old Franklin Town Hall, which seems like a lucky location. As McIntee explains, "Our private event room is the same room where the town board voted to allow a referendum on alcohol sales within the town limits."

The brewery's 15-barrel system sits in what was a large maintenance garage out back, and the main taproom is the former garage for the town's fire department. Now, it is filled with wooden tables and chairs where thirsty people enjoy Lazy Hiker's beers. As might be expected, Lazy Hiker's recipes lean toward the classic and/or refreshing. Its styles range from light (IPA and golden ale) to dark (porter and stout), offering drinkers plenty of range.

Lazy Hiker has been in operation only a short time, but it started off with a bang. "Our brewery and our beers have been met with such success in our local market that we are happily expanding our capacity and our distribution,"

Lazy Hiker is a beacon of beery light for those hiking the nearby Appalachian Trail.
Lazy Hiker Brewing Company

McIntee says. "We still hand-deliver every keg in the six westernmost counties of North Carolina, but we are gearing up to answer the growing calls from Asheville, Charlotte, and North Georgia."

Although opening the brewery has been a whirlwind so far, it has proven highly rewarding. As McIntee says, "The town and all of our supporters were cheering the whole time."

SATULAH MOUNTAIN BREWING COMPANY

454 Carolina Way
Highlands, NC 28741
828-482-9794
Website: satulahmountainbrewing.com
Hours: Thursday–Saturday, 2 P.M.–midnight
Founder: Dale Henry Heinlein
Head Brewer: Dale Henry Heinlein
Opened: 2014

SATULAH MOUNTAIN BREWING COMPANY, Macon County's first post-Prohibition brewery, is located in a small strip mall on Carolina Way in the tourist-friendly town of Highlands. The brewery is named for one of the local mountains surrounding this town in the southwestern part of the state. Dale Heinlein, the owner and brewer, explains that he chose the name "because of my family, because of history, and because of what this mountain represents to the people who share and love its beauty."

There are many reasons for visitors to stop in and enjoy this small-town brewery. The bar has a friendly, modern look. Light-colored wood lines the walls and ceiling. Seating is provided by a mixture of tall ladder-back barstools and soft leather chairs. Behind the shining bar, 12 taps pour a mixture of Satulah Mountain's beers and craft guest taps from around the country. The taproom doesn't have a full menu but does serve pretzels with beer mustard to complement the brews.

Heinlein uses his small system to crank out a wide variety of styles—"everything from smoked Belgians to stouts to IPAs," he says, as well as "kombucha and root beer" for visitors who want something on the nonalcoholic side. Because Satulah Mountain's lineup constantly changes, there's no predicting what beers will be on tap at any given time. But there's certain to be something

Patrons at the bar at Satulah Mountain Brewing Company
Satulah Mountain Brewing Company

tasty for visitors looking to meet up with friends, enjoy the occasional live music, or just relax in this mountaintop town.

THE SNEAK E SQUIRREL

1315 West Main Street
Sylva, NC 28779
828-586-6440
Email: sneakesquirrel@yahoo.com
Website: facebook.com/THESneakESquirrel
Hours: Monday–Saturday, 2 P.M.–midnight
Founder: John Duncan
Brewer: Joe Rehak
Opened: 2015

IN AUGUST 2015, SYLVA GOT ITS THIRD CRAFT BREWERY: The Sneak E Squirrel. To find the Squirrel, curious drinkers just need to travel west out of town on Main Street until they see it on the left. The building, an old Pontiac dealership, is low and wide with a sloping roof and, as might be imagined, plenty of parking spaces. Inside, the bar/restaurant is filled with small wooden tables that offer flexible seating for groups of friends and family. The white walls are the backdrop for work by local artists, which rotates frequently so there is often something new and intriguing to see. The bar serves up 10 taps of The Sneak E Squirrel's beer, all crafted by John Duncan and Joe Rehak on their copper-sheathed seven-barrel brewing system.

The Sneak E Squirrel is the brainchild of Duncan, a native of the North Carolina Piedmont who fell in love with the mountains. Duncan's background contains a wide variety of experiences, from stints in the United States Army and the Coast Guard to teaching martial arts. It took years for Duncan to get hooked on craft beer. But once it happened, it didn't take long for him to grow deeply involved as a homebrewer and entrepreneur. He opened a homebrew store, Dingleberry's Brewing Supplies, in Sylva in 2001 and ran it for 14 years before starting his own full-scale brewery. Duncan still runs Dingleberry's, which is now located inside The Sneak E Squirrel.

As a new brewery, The Sneak E Squirrel is still building a name for itself in western North Carolina, but there are many reasons for visitors to check it

The tasting bar at The Sneak E Squirrel
The Sneak E Squirrel

out: the food, the pool table, the trivia nights, the retro video-game events, and, of course, the constantly evolving beer list.

HEINZELMÄNNCHEN BREWERY

545 Mill Street
Sylva, NC 28779
828-631-4466
Email: gnome@yourgnometownbrewery.com
Website: yourgnometownbrewery.com
Hours: Monday–Thursday, 11 A.M.–7 P.M.;
    Friday–Saturday, 11 A.M.–9 P.M.
Owners: Dieter Kuhn, Sheryl Rudd
Brewmaster: Dieter Kuhn
Opened: 2004

DIETER KUHN, HEINZELMÄNNCHEN'S *BRAUMEISTER*, WAS BORN AND RAISED in Heidelsheim, Germany, a village near the Black Forest. As the legend goes, the Heinzelmännchen—little gnomes that garden gnomes (yes, with the red pointy hats) are modeled after—used to come out of the forest at night and do work so the townspeople could relax all day. One night, a curious villager who wanted to see what the Heinzelmännchen looked like scattered peas on the floor of a workshop so they would slip and fall. Insulted and angry, the Heinzelmännchen never returned, leaving the people to do all the work themselves.

Kuhn sees the legend differently. In fact, he takes inspiration from the gnomes. "The Heinzelmännchen were helpers. They teach us that if we all help each other, life is much better. It's a sort of pay-it-forward kind of thing."

Kuhn came to the country via Chicago and entered the United States Marine Corps out of high school. It was when traveling between Chicago and his marine base on the East Coast that he discovered the mountains of western North Carolina. "It was sort of a halfway point," he says. "I used to camp here while I was traveling. It really reminded me of home, in Germany. I knew it was a place that I wanted to be with my family."

He finally moved to Sylva in 1991. But as beautiful as the mountains were, the small, isolated communities lacked one thing: good beer. "In Germany, beer was part of life," Kuhn says. "There was always beer at the table."

Remembering that his father made beer at home, he set out to do the same. He found a store that sold malt syrup, a health-food store that sold hops as a

**Heinzelmännchen
Brewery in Sylva**
Erik Lars Myers

sleep aid, and a local bakery from which he could get yeast. The results, he says with a laugh, were horrible. "It didn't taste anything like beer!"

Knowing he could do better, he pursued higher-quality ingredients via mail order. Friends loved the beer and urged him to start his own brewery. Over time, a group of them agreed to invest in Kuhn and help him start a business. He attended the Siebel Institute in Chicago and was ready to hit the ground running.

When he returned to North Carolina, though, he found that the process was considerably more expensive than he had thought, so he started looking at ways to cut costs. That's when he discovered Specialty Products International, a company that produces malt extract for the Beadle Brewing System, brewpub equipment that requires no mashing and no lautering. Kuhn wasn't entirely convinced, but after trying some of the beers and ensuring that he was receiving only the freshest extract, he moved forward, using his knowledge of brewing to supplement the extracts with specialty grains. Heinzelmännchen was off the ground.

Now, Kuhn has a seven-barrel mash tun/lautertun in place and a plan for further growth. "I need to move out of here to expand production," he says, gesturing to the small storefront his brewery currently occupies. "I'm full."

The brewery is compact, yet comfortable. As guests walk in through the beveled-glass doors, they see a small seating area to the right where regulars and new drinkers can enjoy beer and conversation. The small brewing space is on the left. A shelf displays brewery merchandise (featuring gnomes, of course) and related local goods for sale. The back of the room is dominated by a friendly wooden bar and the brewery's cold room, with taps sticking out of it through the end of a barrel. And in the middle of it all stands Kuhn, warmly welcoming guests into his brewery and offering samples of his beer and house-made sodas.

Literature posted around the brewery proclaims Heinzelmännchen as "Beer for food." Kuhn's beers are mostly traditional German beers or variations on other styles made to more closely resemble those German traditional beers. He talks about how he's made an IPA using malts from near his hometown in Germany, and how he uses pilsner malt and German and English hops to get more of the crisp dryness he prefers in his beer, a theme that is constant throughout each of his offerings, whether it be his seasonal Dunkel Weise or his Black Forest Stout.

A table covered with binders containing pictures of Sylva and of Heinzelmännchen at local events shows that Kuhn's goal of bringing good beer to the North Carolina mountains has also led to fruitful relationships among the brewery, the community, and the tourists who travel here for the beer. The Heinzelmännchen would no doubt approve.

INN⚙VATION BREWING
Sylva, NC

414 West Main Street
Sylva, NC 28779
828-586-9678
Website: innovation-brewing.com
Hours: Monday–Thursday, 2 P.M.–midnight;
   Friday–Saturday, noon–midnight;
   Sunday, noon–11 P.M.
Founders: Nicole Dexter, Charles Owen
Head Brewers: Chance Clendenin, Charles Owen
Brewing Staff: Nicole Dexter
Opened: 2013

INNOVATION BREWING, THE SECOND BREWERY TO OPEN IN SYLVA, is perched on the edge of Scott Creek. Its shaded patio, which overlooks the water, captures the laid-back feeling of this small-town brewery. Inside, the wood-paneled tap-room gives off a feeling of rustic comfort. The small, inventive touches here and there include metal gears and patterns made of different types of grain laid under the bar's transparent surface, as well as flight trays cut from irregular wooden logs.

Inventive also describes the beer list at Innovation. Its flagship list features classic styles such as brown ale, IPA, and Irish stout, while its special and seasonal offerings range far afield, with ingredients including juniper, beets, ginger, jalapeños, and peaches. It also has a small barrel program that produces wine-aged and sour beers. As owner Nicole Dexter explains, Innovation walks a fine line with its brews: "We like to push the envelope with our beer ideas and recipes while consistently putting out a quality and clean product."

Dexter and her co-owner, Charles "Chip" Owen, have devoted considerable time and effort to making Innovation what it is. According to Dexter, limited resources mean that much of the brewery is handcrafted: "We built everything ourselves, from the brew system to the keg washer to the tables and chairs for the pub."

The name Innovation came to Dexter during one of their building sessions. The team was assembling a preowned walk-in cooler and struggling to get the panels locked in place. In desperation, Dexter climbed on top of the cooler to

A rustic flight at Innovation Brewing
Erik Lars Myers

force a reluctant panel. "While I was on top of the cooler trying to use my body weight to get the ceiling panel close enough to the wall panel to allow Chip to snap it together, all while trying to balance on this very unstable unattached ceiling panel, I suggested the name Innovation, and it stuck!"

While *Innovation* accurately describes the brewery's ethos, the name hasn't been without its own challenges. In 2015, Bell's Brewery of Michigan started trademark proceedings against Innovation because it believed the name too closely overlapped with two of its slogans: "Bottling Innovation since 1985" and "Inspired Brewing." At the time of this writing, the dispute had not been resolved. But Dexter and Owen remain hopeful they will be able to reach a positive solution that will allow them to use the brand name in which they have invested so much.

In the meantime, they remain focused on growing their business by expanding their brewing capacity and their barrel program and by cultivating the craft beer community in Sylva.

BEARWATERS BREWING COMPANY

130 Frazier Street #7
Waynesville, NC 28786
828-246-0602
Email: hello@bwbrewing.com
Website: bwbrewing.com
Hours: Monday–Saturday, 1 P.M.–9 P.M.
Founders: Kevin Sandefur, Heidi Dunkelberg
Head Brewer: Kevin Sandefur
Opened: 2012

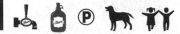

BEARWATERS BREWING COMPANY, WAYNESVILLE'S SECOND CRAFT BREWERY, experienced a rocky beginning.

In 2010, the Haywood County Chamber of Commerce granted cofounder Kevin Sandefur startup funding to help turn his passion for homebrewing into a professional concern. In the two years following that grant, Sandefur and his business partner, Heidi Dunkelberg, converted a warehouse in Waynesville into a small brewing operation. The brewery opened in May 2012 with great support from the local community.

However, less than a year later, the brewery, then called Headwaters Brewing, received a legal notice from Victory Brewing in Pennsylvania. In the time since Headwaters started planning, Victory had trademarked the name of its Headwaters Pale Ale. The Waynesville brewery would have to change its name or forever limit its distribution to the state of North Carolina.

Sandefur and Dunkelberg weighed their options and decided to invest in a name change. In 2013, Headwaters Brewing Company became BearWaters Brewing Company—a small change but a costly one for a new business.

Despite that setback, BearWaters Brewing has seen great success. Sandefur's recipes, ranging from dark and malty to light and hoppy, have won medals at the Carolinas Championship of Beer competition, and the BearWaters taproom has

Locals crowd the bar on a busy Saturday night at BearWaters Brewing Company.
Erik Lars Myers

become a popular destination. Although the brewery and taproom are in a warehouse in an industrial part of Waynesville, a rustic-looking porch added to the front of the building softens the entrance and hints at the friendly space inside. The taproom is long and narrow, with a wooden bar running down one side and a small stage at the back for live music on weekends. Comfortable seating options and a family-friendly atmosphere add to its appeal.

Although the brewery hit a road block early on, that clearly did not damage the long-term potential of this Waynesville business.

FROG LEVEL
BREWING COMPANY

56 Commerce Street
Waynesville, NC 28786
828-454-5664
Email: froglevelbrewing@gmail.com
Website: froglevelbrewing.com
Hours: Monday–Saturday, noon–9 P.M.
Owner: Clark Williams
Brewmaster: Clark Williams
Opened: 2011

FROG LEVEL, SAYS BREWMASTER AND OWNER CLARK WILLIAMS, is a reference to the frost line on the mountains that rise around Waynesville. Above the frost line, frogs can't live. But below the line, they thrive. In the bottom of the valley along the banks of Richard Creek, where Frog Level Brewing Company makes its home, it must be very froggy indeed.

Another story says that the Frog Level section of Waynesville is so nick-named because of historical flooding. It's a part of this small mountain town that's been going through a resurgence, and Williams is in the middle of it with his brewery.

Williams is a retired marine who has his priorities in line. "Beyond my wife and family," he says, "I have two loves—this town and this state. I'll do whatever I can to help the things I love. If having a brewery here means that five guys who have never been to Waynesville before come into town to try a beer, go next door and get a cup of coffee, and head down the street for a sandwich, well, that's five guys that weren't here before, helping the community."

Frog Level Brewing Company started as a nanobrewery, one of the state's smallest. Williams brewed on a system built out of half-barrel kegs, making 10 gallons of beer at a time. He came up with the idea while traveling with his wife on a vacation to New Mexico. "I kept coming across all of these small breweries," he says. "Just really small places—though not this small—with guys working their butts off, but they were happy. When we came home, I realized, *I've got to do this.*"

Frog Level's funky skid-mounted, direct-fire brewhouse keeps churning out great beers at river level in Waynesville.
Erik Lars Myers

The beautiful space he occupies in Waynesville—in the Frog Level section—once served as a carriage house and stable for the famous Vanderbilts from nearby Asheville. It's a long, century-old building with rough, exposed bricks along one side and deep red walls and brightly polished timbers along another. A high bar runs around the brewery toward the back of the building and empties onto a large back deck that overlooks Richard Creek. The large pieces of art that span the walls and flow up into the space came from a local gallery that had to close. Williams couldn't bear to see the community lose the business, so he offered his wall space. The art adds to the comfortable atmosphere of the tasting room and shows the close connection between the brewery and the Frog Level community.

Over the years, Williams has expanded the brewery, changing what was once the bar area into a full production space with a direct-fired three-barrel system, which makes considerably more beer than his old keggle system did. It hasn't changed the homey atmosphere and beautiful outdoor patio, though. Visitors will always have a good time below the frost line.

BOOJUM BREWING COMPANY

Production facility:
357 Dayton Drive
Waynesville, NC 28786
828-944-0888
Hours: By appointment only

Taproom:
50 North Main Street
Waynesville, NC 28786
828-246-0350
Hours: Monday, Wednesday, Thursday, noon–10 P.M.;
      Friday–Saturday, noon–midnight; Sunday, noon–9 P.M.

Email: Info@BoojumBrewing.com
Website: boojumbrewing.com
Founders: Kelsie Baker and Ben Baker
Head Brewer: Ben Baker
Assistant Brewer: Keller Fitzpatrick
Opened: 2015

THE LEGENDARY BOOJUM OF HAYWOOD COUNTY is a seven- or eight-foot-tall creature covered in shaggy hair and with the face of a man. According to the stories, he roams the Balsam Mountains in search of precious gems.

The legend of the Boojum grabbed the imaginations of siblings Kelsie and Ben Baker when they started visiting the Waynesville area as children, so it seemed a fitting name when they returned as adults to start their own craft brewery.

Boojum Brewing is a 15-barrel brewery that makes seven year-round beers and a variety of seasonal and special one-off recipes. Some of its beers are classic styles—brown ale, pale ale, and double IPA—but others push the envelope by incorporating nontraditional ingredients such as blueberries, jalapeños, and peanut butter.

Ben Baker brews the beer at Boojum's production facility, a warehouse north of downtown Waynesville. The place to taste the beer and pick up growlers to go, though, is the taproom, located on Main Street just minutes from the other

Pristine brewing equipment at Boojum Brewing Company
Dave Tollefsen, NC Beer Guys

local breweries. Boojum's taproom is a square, blue-walled space with a rustic-looking wooden bar backed by shelves of glassware and two large televisions. The beer menu is projected on the wall opposite the door, creating a clean-looking and easy-to-update list. A colorful artist's rendering of the legendary Boojum is painted on another wall to remind patrons of the brewery's inspiration.

Although just a year old at the time of this writing, Boojum is growing. It recently signed a distribution deal for the western part of the state and is starting to can some of its regular beers, including its King of the Mountain Double IPA.

Boojum Brewing seems poised to take advantage of the craft beer excitement in the mountains of North Carolina, with or without help from its mythical namesake.

TIPPING POINT
BREWING

190 North Main Street
Waynesville, NC 28786
828-246-9230
Email: info@tippingpointtavern.com
Website: tippingpointtavern.com
Hours: Monday–Thursday, 11:30 A.M.–midnight;
    Friday–Saturday, 11:30 A.M.–1 A.M.
Founders: Jon Bowman, Dan Elliott, Doug Weaver
Head Brewer: Jon Bowman
Assistant Brewer: Chris Perella
Opened: 2012

SITTING RIGHT ON MAIN STREET IN THE HEART OF DOWNTOWN is Tipping Point Brewing. It isn't Waynesville's oldest brewery—that honor goes to Frog Level—but Tipping Point's planning began before Waynesville had any craft breweries. Jon Bowman, cofounder and head brewer, explains that at the time he and his partners started thinking about it, "Waynesville did not have much to choose from in the way of pubs and had no breweries. We thought we could bring about a positive change for the downtown area, a 'Tipping Point.' " Bowman doesn't credit Malcolm Gladwell's well-known book for the name. "I did not even know about the *Tipping Point* book until I Googled the name after thinking of it." But Gladwell's ideas capture the concept Bowman had for the brewery. He now has a quote from the book on his website and admits, "We keep a copy at the bar."

The tavern opened as a bar and restaurant in 2010, serving up beer from other craft breweries and a tasty pub menu. The brewery was part of the plan from the beginning, but equipment is expensive, and finding the funding delayed that part of the business for two years. In that span, Frog Level Brewing and Headwaters Brewing (now BearWaters) had opened, establishing Waynesville as a craft beer–friendly town. Tipping Point added to the town's attractions. Its combination restaurant and taproom is a popular place to hang out and enjoy food and beer.

The long, narrow tavern is lined with booths on one side and a bar filled with stools on the other. The wall behind the bar is packed with bottles, glassware, televisions, and a chalkboard sign, making the most of the compact space. The beer list can be found on a large chalkboard at the end of the room, enticing visitors to walk in and discover what's on tap. Tipping Point serves nine of its own beers, in addition to bottles and cans of other beers. Bowman describes his brews as "ales, typically in the English style, and also the American IPA and pales." Tipping Point's seasonal lineup features both classic styles such as an ESB and more unusual takes such as a smoked imperial stout.

At the moment, the Waynesville tavern is the best place to find Tipping Point's beer. Bowman explains that the partners have considered packaging and selling their brews, but that will most likely happen through something like a mobile canning unit. "We are out of space," he admits, "so anything else would require opening an off-site brewery." According to Bowman, an expansion brewery isn't currently in the cards for Tipping Point. For now, its focus remains on "small production with big quality" and on enhancing Waynesville's reputation as a great beer town.

The cozy taproom at Tipping Point Brewing
Erik Lars Myers

BREVARD BREWING COMPANY

63 East Main Street
Brevard, NC 28712
Email: brevardbrewing@gmail.com
Website: brevard-brewing.com
Hours: Monday–Thursday, 2 P.M.–11 P.M.;
    Friday–Saturday, noon–midnight;
    Sunday, 2 P.M.–10 P.M.
Founder: Kyle Williams
Head Brewer: Kyle Williams
Opened: 2012

DRIVING OR WALKING DOWN EAST MAIN STREET IN BREVARD, it is hard to miss Brevard Brewing Company. The business's stone façade stands out from the brick surrounding it, and its double doors sport the yellow and green Brevard Brewing logo. Inside, a square bar thrusts into the roomy space, backed by a red-painted wall, a chalkboard listing the beers on tap, and T-shirts and other Brevard Brewing merchandise. To the left of the bar, doors give a glimpse of Brevard's sizable brewing system in the next room. Wooden tables are scattered around the room, and the atmosphere is laid back and friendly.

Kyle Williams, the founder and head brewer, has been working in the industry since 2006. He was a brewer at Black Mountain's Pisgah Brewing Company when he decided to start his own place. Kyle's wife, Elizabeth, had family connections in Brevard going back generations, which made it a logical place for them to open their brewery.

Kyle is a fan of lagers, and it shows in Brevard's beer lineup. Lagers are unusual in small craft breweries because their long fermentation time ties up tank space and slows down production. Well-made lagers are always exciting finds for craft beer drinkers, and Brevard provides plenty of them. Its flagship beer is a Bohemian-style pilsner, and its list also includes a Munich dunkel and an American premium lager, which, as Brevard Brewing cheerfully states on its website,

The spacious taproom at Brevard Brewing Company
Erik Lars Myers

"proves it's OK for beer geeks to drink 'lawnmower beer.'" Visitors who aren't into lagers may find an IPA or pale ale on tap, as well as guest beers in other styles.

Brevard is a production brewery that focuses on selling pints and growlers in its taproom and kegs to select local accounts. A larger brewing system acquired in 2014 has allowed Kyle to start distributing kegs to some bars in Asheville, but Brevard's reach is still very local.

SOUTHERN APPALACHIAN BREWERY

822 Locust Street
Hendersonville, NC 28792
Email: mail@sabrewery.com
Website: sabrewery.com
Hours: Wednesday, 4 P.M.–9 P.M.; Thursday 4 P.M.–10 P.M.;
　　Friday, 4 P.M.–11 P.M.; Saturday, 2 P.M.–11 P.M.;
　　Sunday, 2 P.M.–9 P.M.
Owners: Andy and Kelly Cubbin
Brewmaster: Andy Cubbin
Opened: 2003

WHEN ANDY AND KELLY CUBBIN FIRST CONSIDERED GETTING INTO BREWING, they didn't even live in North Carolina. The couple was in Chicago, working as photographers and looking for a change. Andy had been homebrewing for years. When they found a brewery for sale in Rosman, North Carolina, they decided to jump at the chance to get out of the city.

The property they bought was Appalachian Brewery. "It was really small," says Andy, "somewhere between a nano and a micro. It was a five- or six-barrel Frankensteined kind of system, basically like a small homebrewing operation." But it gave him something to cut his teeth on. The couple renamed the place Appalachian Craft Brewery, to distinguish it from Appalachian Brewing Company in Harrisburg, Pennsylvania. Andy and Kelly moved the brewery to Fletcher and started making beer.

It was not at that point a full-time undertaking. Unsure that the small brewery was going to support them, they kept pursuing photography. But over the next four years of brewing and perfecting recipes, they resolved to make a run at it. "We decided that we just couldn't do it halfway," says Andy. "We said to ourselves, *We're good at it. We can do it. Let's go for it.*"

They immediately began looking for a larger system and a new space for the brewery. They had planned to move to Asheville, but during the four years the Cubbins were looking at the city, four new breweries opened. So they decided to make their stand elsewhere and eventually settled on Hendersonville. It was a town they liked and could see themselves living in. It was also close enough

Locals crowd in to see a band play in front of brewing equipment at Southern Appalachian Brewery
Erik Lars Myers

to Asheville to be part of the "Beer City" phenomenon. And they found what they describe as "the perfect space." They bought a new, better, larger system and started the move.

Since the brewery wasn't their primary source of income, they closed it to move. "We basically said to people, 'We're going to be gone for a while. I hope you put us back on tap,' " recalls Andy. They also renamed the brewery, to further distance it from Appalachian Brewing Company. "People recognized us as Appalachian Craft Brewery, so we needed it to be similar. But it was still an issue, so we renamed it Southern Appalachian Brewery, really, to get to the other end of the alphabet."

What followed were six months of bureaucratic delays. By April 2011, they were back in business, with a whole new set of challenges. "Now, we're running a bar," says Andy. "We've never done that before, so every day is a new learning experience."

Their taproom is a space carved out of one end of their brewery building. On nice days, events spill into the parking area outside. Rectangular wooden tables provide rustic, casual seating for the brewery's patrons, who can enjoy one—or more—of the 12 beers on tap. On the frequent live-music nights, the musicians set up in front of the brewing tanks, which form a striking backdrop.

Andy is a self-taught brewer, and he's proud of that fact. "I think that there are two types of brewers," he says, "some who follow the science of brewing, and some that live in the art and the craft of it. If you can make good beer, you can always learn more of the science. But I think the hardest thing about brewing, just like it is with cooking, is being able to taste something and then improve upon it."

Asheville, NC

ALTAMONT BREWING COMPANY

1042 Haywood Road
Asheville, NC 28806
828-575-2400
Website: altamontbrewing.com
Hours: Daily, 2 P.M.–2 A.M.
Founders: Gordon Kear, Ben Wiggins
Head Brewer: Gordon Kear
Opened: 2012

ALTAMONT BREWING COMPANY IS THE PERFECT FIT for its West Asheville neighborhood. To appeal to a variety of drinkers, this casual bar features its own house-brewed beers, guest taps, and a small liquor selection. Inside, the space is dominated by a raised stage that plays host to live music every weekend and an open-mic night the first Tuesday of each month. On days without music, a ping-pong table, foosball, and televisions provide entertainment for the groups of drinkers who congregate at this popular spot.

Gordon Kear, the brewer at Altamont, became familiar with western North Carolina during his time as a student at Warren Wilson College. Although he moved to Arizona to join Flagstaff Brewing Company, he kept his eye on North Carolina. After six years as a brewer at Flagstaff, he returned to North Carolina to cofound Altamont with longtime friend Ben Wiggins. The business is named after the town in Thomas Wolfe's novel *Look Homeward, Angel*, a fictionalized retelling of the author's early life in Asheville.

Since breweries are expensive, Wiggins and Kear took an incremental approach to their business. They opened Altamont as a bar in 2011, serving craft beer from other breweries. In 2012, they started brewing and selling their own beer. With three years of successful brewing under their belts, the Altamont team expanded in the fall of 2015 by opening a restaurant in an adjoining space. The restaurant's small menu ranges from sandwiches and wings to a noodle bowl and a hummus plate. The flavors are designed to complement the brewery's beers, which lean heavily toward American IPAs and other mainline styles.

Fermenters stand quietly at the back of Altamont's taproom.
Erik Lars Myers

OYSTER HOUSE BREWING COMPANY

625 Haywood Road
Asheville, NC 28806
828-575-9370
Email: billy@oysterhousebeers.com
Website: oysterhousebeers.com
Hours: Monday–Thursday, 3 P.M.–11 P.M.;
    Friday, 3 P.M.–midnight; Saturday, noon–midnight;
    Sunday, noon–11 P.M.
Owner: Billy Klingel
Brewmaster: Billy Klingel
Opened: 2009

OYSTER HOUSE BREWING COMPANY STARTED AS ONE OF THE MOST NON-TRADITIONAL breweries in North Carolina—or anywhere else, for that matter. It wasn't really a brewpub so much as a seafood restaurant that happened to make its own beer.

Billy Klingel, the owner and brewer, started the business while working at The Lobster Trap, a popular restaurant in downtown Asheville. He was a long-time employee of the restaurant and also happened to be "a geeked-out home-brewer," in his own words. Tres Hundertmark, the original general manager and executive chef at The Lobster Trap, used to go to oyster-shucking tournaments, in which people competed to shuck the most oysters in a certain amount of time. Hundertmark was a champion oyster shucker. After returning from a competition in Boston back in 2006, he told Billy about a beer he had heard of there: an oyster stout.

"I had lost my overall obsession with homebrewing by that point. It wasn't because I stopped loving doing it, I just didn't have the time," Klingel says. "But there we were with a cooler with a dozen different varieties of oysters in it on any given day, and I thought, *Well, this is my chance.* Every homebrewer dreams about making the jump to having their own brewery. I had always had this vision that I would have this little pizza place, and we would make our own beer, and I might not be a millionaire, but I'd get by, and it would be great. I thought, *Well, it's not really the way my dream was written out, but it's certainly a great way to start.* So I got a little obsessed again."

Don't make the mistake of going to Oyster House and *not* having its oyster stout.
Erik Lars Myers

Over the next year, he brewed 60 or so batches of homebrew, and at least 50 of them were oyster stouts. He tweaked the recipe each time until he thought it was just right. He brought the final product in to his boss, Amy Beard, founder of The Lobster Trap. "At that point," says Klingel, "Amy was a Bud Select drinker. So for her to take a drink of something you can't see through and say, 'That's good!' was pretty great."

Klingel told Beard his plan and came up with a sample budget, and The Lobster Trap soon began making its own beer. He originally tried to find a three-barrel system in hopes that he could devise some way of fitting a small brewhouse and fermenters into the restaurant, but he ended up getting a half-barrel Brew Magic system built from half-barrel kegs—essentially an elaborate homebrewing system. He made about 12 gallons of beer at a time.

Klingel brewed on his small system three days a week, mostly making oyster stouts, and sometimes contracted out other styles at French Broad Brewing Co., brewing there about once a month to fill more kegs for the restaurant. Klingel kept this up for several years but still had a dream of opening his own place with more room. In 2013, that dream became a reality when Klingel opened his own stand-alone brewpub, Oyster House, on Haywood Road in West Asheville.

Oyster House's home is a small but striking brick building with outdoor seating for nice days. The inside is painted a bright blue that complements the beautiful silver tin ceiling. An L-shaped bar with oyster shells embedded in its top owns one corner of the space. Behind it are around nine taps pouring Oyster House draft beer, in addition to one or two cask offerings and guest taps. Through windows in the back corner, visitors can see Klingel's compact brewing room with its five-barrel system and fermentation vessels (each named after a famous female soul singer).

Klingel makes many more styles than oyster stout. Visitors will find IPAs, a Scottish ale, a blonde ale, and other beers to tempt their palates. However, the Moonstone Oyster Stout is undoubtedly the pub's crown jewel. Each batch contains about 100 oysters, added at the end of the boil. While Klingel has experimented with different varieties of oysters, he's not sure they make a significant difference. The main factor, he says, is the size. Some oysters are big and some small. So while the flavor might not change much, the cost of the beer may vary dramatically.

Many people are skeptical of oyster stout, says Klingel. "They have a hard time trying it. But I tell them, 'It doesn't taste like oysters. The only reason you know there are oysters in there is because I'm telling you in case you have an allergy to shellfish.'"

Klingel's story is one of persistence and refusing to be discouraged: "One day, I looked out here [The Lobster Trap], and this was probably a few months after we started making beer, and the whole bar was full, all the seats were taken, and everybody at the bar except for two people had a pint of stout. This was old, young, men, women. And I thought, *I have just won.*"

Visitors to Klingel's charming and delicious brewpub will certainly agree.

EXPANSION BREWERIES

For those inside North Carolina, it's been clear for some time that the state is a great place to be if you're in the beer industry. But in 2012, the rest of the country found out as a new class of craft brewery came to exist in North Carolina: expansion breweries.

Dale Katechis has two passions: beer and mountain biking. When he opened Oskar Blues Brewery in Colorado in 1997, mountain biking was a large part of the corporate culture there. So when he was looking at the possibility of expanding, North Carolina seemed like a natural fit. Some of Katechis's favorite mountain biking trails are in North Carolina's Pisgah National Forest, the entrance of which is right down the road from what is now the Brevard branch of Oskar Blues.

That was just the beginning. Soon afterward, Sierra Nevada Brewing Company announced an expansion in Mills River, North Carolina, which opened in 2014. New Belgium followed suit with a brewery in West Asheville that will be in full production in 2016. Not only are these breweries creating a smaller carbon footprint by reducing the need to ship beer across the country, they're providing jobs and economic growth in North Carolina. They're also serving as a beacon for beer tourism, as beer fans arrive to visit the new facilities of these popular breweries.

They won't be the last. More large craft breweries are exploring the idea of opening in North Carolina, drawn by the state's location—right in the middle of the Atlantic coast—its excellent water supply, its quality of life, and, of course, its outstanding beer culture.

ASHEVILLE PIZZA AND BREWING COMPANY

Merrimon Avenue location:
675 Merrimon Avenue
Asheville, NC 28804
828-254-1281
Hours: Daily, 11 A.M.–midnight

Coxe Avenue location:
77 Coxe Avenue
Asheville, NC 28801
828-255-4077
Hours: Monday–Thursday, 11 A.M.–midnight;
    Friday, 11 A.M.–2 A.M.; Saturday, noon–2 A.M.;
    Sunday, noon–midnight

Hendersonville Road location:
1850 Hendersonville Road
Asheville, NC 28803
828-277-5775
Hours: Daily, 3 P.M.–10 P.M.

Website: ashevillebrewing.com
Head Brewer: Doug Riley
Opened: 1999

DOUG RILEY CAME TO ASHEVILLE IN 1998, making the move from Portland, Oregon, where he had been a brewer for Nor'Wester Brewing Company. He came east to help start a brewery, but it wasn't his own. Rather, it was the third brewery to open its doors in Asheville—Two Moons Brew and View, located on Merrimon Avenue not far from UNC-Asheville.

A year later, the owners sold it to Riley and his partners, Mike Rangel and Leigh Lewis. They merged the operation with Asheville Pizza Company, creating the successful brewpub—and now brewery chain—that has been a staple in town for over a decade.

"It's your typical brewpub movie theater," jokes Riley about Asheville Pizza and Brewing's original location. "We show second-run films and serve pizza and beer." The movie theater is what patrons would expect from a small venue—the wide white screen, the ruffled-curtain walls—but instead of rows of low-slung,

A view of fermentation vessels past the brewhouse at Asheville Pizza and Brewing
Company
Erik Lars Myers

upholstered movie seats, tables and chairs face the screen. It's the perfect place
for a pizza and a beer while watching a movie.

The operation was so effective that in 2006 the partners opened a second
location closer to downtown, on Coxe Avenue. That Asheville Pizza and Brewing is a bright pizza parlor with a light wooden motif, a long L-shaped bar, and
an outdoor patio. It is similar to the first location but without the movies. The
second location meant that Asheville Pizza doubled its brewing capacity, rather
than giving itself twice as many locations to dispense the same amount of beer.
"We were in pretty high demand for our beer," Riley explains, "so we expanded
out of necessity. There's a second full brewery on Coxe Avenue, with about as
much room in the back of the brewery as there is in the front."

In 2012, Asheville Pizza expanded again, opening a carry-out and delivery
location on Hendersonville Road in the South Asheville area.

Asheville Pizza started packaging its beer in 22-ounce bottles statewide but
eventually put a canning line in place to help expand capacity. "We thought that
a canning line would be a lot better—more environmentally friendly. Our beer
can get into state parks, at the beach. With Asheville being such an outdoorsy
town, it just made sense," Riley says.

After witnessing the Asheville brewing scene grow up around his brewery,
Riley has one word: "*Crazy*. It's a small town, and it supports a lot of breweries,
but we all make different types of beer, and I think there's enough for everybody
to go around."

HI-WIRE BREWING

South Slope:
197 Hilliard Avenue
Asheville NC 28801
828-575-9675
Hours: Monday–Thursday, 4 P.M.–11 P.M.;
    Friday, 2 P.M.–2 A.M.; Saturday, noon–2 A.M.;
    Sunday, 1 P.M.–10 P.M.

The Big Top:
2 Huntsman Place
Asheville NC 28803
828-575-9675
Hours: Monday–Thursday, 4 P.M.–10 P.M.;
    Friday, 4 P.M.–midnight; Saturday, noon–midnight;
    Sunday, 1 P.M.–10 P.M.

Email: info@hiwirebrewing.com
Website: hiwirebrewing.com
Founders: Chris Frosaker, Adam Charnack, Matt Kiger
Head Brewer: Luke Holgate
Head of Specialty Brewing: Johnathan Parks
Opened: 2013

NORTH CAROLINA IS A STATE THIRSTY FOR CRAFT BEER, which means that if one brewery closes, it isn't long before another rises to take its place. When Asheville's Craggie Brewing Company shut its doors in December 2012, Chris Frosaker, Adam Charnack, and Matt Kiger saw an opportunity for new beginnings, and Hi-Wire Brewing was born.

Although Hi-Wire took over Craggie's South Slope location and brewing equipment, its approach to beer is decidedly different. Hi-Wire Brewing's aesthetic is circus-themed, as is apparent from its beer names: Bed of Nails, Lion Tamer, Strongman, etc. But while those names may sound dangerously daring, most of the recipes are not. In fact, one of the adjectives the founders use to describe their core beers is *approachable.* The eponymous Hi-Wire Lager, one of the flagships, is a straightforward American-style lager designed to appeal to craft and non-craft drinkers alike, while brown ale, pale ale, and IPA round out the core styles. These beers, distributed in six-pack bottles, have created Hi-Wire's buzz in the beer market, while seasonal and specialty beers entice drink-

The Hi-Wire Big Top is an impressive expansion, just a couple of years after opening.
Erik Lars Myers

ers to its funky taproom on Hilliard Avenue.

Hi-Wire's original building is a small brewery with a taproom carved out of the front. On nice days, large garage doors and windows open the space to the sidewalk. The bar has a distressed, industrial feel, with wooden touches and a circus-themed décor to match the beer names.

However, it wasn't long before Hi-Wire outgrew its downtown location. In July 2015, it opened a larger 30-barrel production brewery and bottling plant closer to the Biltmore side of town. "The Big Top," as it is called, has a taproom area featuring brightly colored curved tables and 16 taps of Hi-Wire beer. When this facility opened, head brewer Luke Holgate moved over to run it, while Hi-Wire hired Johnathan Parks as its new head of specialty brewing. Parks is in charge of experimenting with recipes and has launched a new series, the Farmhouse beers, which will feature one-off rustic Belgian-style ales.

Just a few months after The Big Top opened, Hi-Wire's expansion enabled it to send its core beers farther afield, to South Carolina and Tennessee. This circus has found its wheels and is making a bid to become one of the biggest acts in the state.

THIRSTY MONK PUB & BREWERY

2 Town Square Boulevard #170
Asheville, NC 28803
828-687-3873
Email: hello@monkpub.com
Website: monkpub.com/biltmore-park
Hours: Monday–Thursday, 4 P.M.–midnight;
  Friday–Saturday, noon–2 A.M.; Sunday, noon–10 P.M.
Founder: Barry Bialik
Head Brewer: Norm Penn
Assistant Brewer: Ian Yancich
Opened: 2011

outside

FOR YEARS, THIRSTY MONK HAS BEEN ONE OF THE MOST RECOGNIZABLE NAMES in the Asheville beer scene. Its Patton Avenue bar opened in 2008 and gained a reputation as an outstanding place to get a beer. The ground floor of the building is dedicated to American craft beers, while the dark and cavelike basement bar focuses on European beers, primarily Belgians.

With two bars and a full bottle selection, Thirsty Monk had everything . . . except for beer of its own. That changed in 2011, when owner Barry Bialik got together with homebrewer and Thirsty Monk fan Norm Penn. Together, they came up with the idea for Thirsty Monk beers. Penn started brewing for Bialik on a one-barrel system located inside Thirsty Monk's Gerber Village location, which had been open as a bar since 2009. Penn's beers were used to complement the other craft beer selections. Their popularity created a demand that Penn struggled to fill on that small system.

Within three years of starting it, Thirsty Monk made some big changes to its brewing program. It upgraded to a four-barrel system, closed the Gerber Village taproom, and opened a new brewpub and taproom at Biltmore Park. The new facility has more brewing capacity and acts as the hub for Thirsty Monk beer. The public side is a bright and cheerful taproom with floor-to-ceiling windows that open onto a patio to create a seamless indoor-outdoor space on nice days.

Well known to beer drinkers: the bar at Thirsty Monk's originial location
Thirsty Monk Pub & Brewery

The bar pours 40 taps, a mix of the high-quality international craft beers Thirsty Monk is known for and beers brewed by Penn on the in-house system.

As the name suggests, Thirsty Monk's beers lean in one direction. "We began as a small bar in Asheville that only served Belgian and Belgian-style beer, and as we've grown those styles are still central to our mission," Vice President Chall Gray explains. The focus on Belgian-style beers doesn't mean Thirsty Monk doesn't experiment, though. For example, the Euro Monk lager is created by lagering with the house Belgian yeast strain. One of the brewery's challenges, Gray says, has been "figuring out how to balance the characteristics of Belgian yeasts with some of the flavor profiles that drinkers like and associate with American beer. We feel like we've found a happy medium, though, and our beers have been really well received."

Thirsty Monk has continued to find success. It now has a third bar location, at Reynolds Village in North Asheville and, according to Gray, is planning to expand again by building "a larger production brewery in 2016" at a two-acre location in Biltmore Village. For the moment, the Biltmore Village brewpub is the best place to find the Monk's own beers.

TWIN LEAF BREWERY

144 Coxe Avenue
Asheville, NC 28801
828-774-5000
Email: info@twinleafbrewery.com
Website: twinleafbrewery.com
Hours: Monday–Thursday, 4 P.M.–10 P.M.;
    Friday, 2 P.M.–midnight; Saturday, noon–midnight;
    Sunday, 1 P.M.–9 P.M.
Owners: Tim Weber, Stephanie Estela
Head Brewer: Tim Weber
Opened: 2014

LOCATED IN THE CENTER OF ASHEVILLE'S BUSTLING SOUTH SLOPE BREWERY district is Twin Leaf Brewery, a tasty stop on any beer drinker's tour of the town. Twin Leaf can be found inside a large industrial-looking brick building on the corner of Coxe and Banks Avenues. While the front of the building may look forbidding, the side entrance on Banks features an expansive wall of windows that allows passersby to look down on the brewery's shining stainless-steel tanks and friendly taproom.

Inside, the taproom has a comfortable feel, thanks to the warm wood paneling behind the bar and the casual layout. Sturdy picnic tables and barstools provide most of the seating. Patrons looking for entertainment will find a giant Jenga set, as well as an assortment of board games. On the wall behind the bar, small, colorful chalkboard signs announce the beers on tap that day.

Tim Weber, Twin Leaf's co-owner and head brewer, makes five year-round beers and a slate of rotating beers. Weber is a graduate of the American Brewers Guild and has a mechanical engineering background, experiences that help him with the technical and artistic sides of brewing. His regular productions run a gamut of styles, from an ESB to Belgian beers to the IPA 144 (code name: Juicy Fruit). The rotating beers may be seasonal, such as an Oktoberfest, or just fun, such as the Black Double IPA. The variety of styles ensures that any patron will find a beer to his or her taste.

Because the craft beer scene in Asheville is so outstanding, most breweries

Brewer Tim Weber empties the mash tun at Twin Leaf Brewery.
Erik Lars Myers

are rapidly expanding, and Twin Leaf is no different. Just a year after opening, it dramatically increased its seating space by enlarging its taproom and adding a large outdoor area. At the moment, its beer is only available in kegs and growlers at the brewery. It did bottle one special batch for its one-year anniversary, but Weber says that cans, rather than bottles, could be the way forward for Twin Leaf. However, he has no plans to enter a large distribution contract. His vision is a local brewery that draws visitors and serves as a community gathering spot for friends looking to relax over a tasty beer.

BURIAL BEER COMPANY

40 Collier Avenue
Asheville, NC 28801
828-475-2739
Email: info@burialbeer.com
Website: burialbeer.com
Hours: Monday–Thursday, 4 P.M.–10 P.M.; Friday–
    Saturday, 2 P.M.–10 P.M.; Sunday, noon–8 P.M.
Founders: Jessica and Doug Reiser, Tim Gormley
Head of Brewing Operations: Doug Reiser
Head Brewer: Tim Gormley
Brewing Staff: J. T. Murrett, Jason Cook,
    Bennett Campbell
Opened: 2013

TUCKED AWAY IN ASHEVILLE'S SOUTH SLOPE DISTRICT, Burial Beer Company inhabits a funky space that manages to be both industrial and welcoming. When patrons walk into the building, the first thing to catch the eye is the shining brewhouse that dominates the back of the room. A North Carolina flag hangs from one of the fermenters, announcing the brewery's pride in belonging to "the Southern State of Beer."

Closer to the front of the space, a bar stretches against the raw brick wall. The current beer list is written on the mirror behind the bar, while an eclectic mix of tap handles is fixed to the wall of the brewery's cooler. The tap handles are decorated with pieces of farm tools—a sickle, a pitchfork, a trowel—that represent Burial's focus on the cyclical nature of life as expressed in farming and brewing.

Cofounder Jessica Reiser traces the concept behind Burial to the jazz funerals of her former home, New Orleans. As she explains, in New Orleans, "when someone passes, they celebrate their life instead of mourning their death." Burial's brand art features this mixture of life and death. Its cans are adorned with intricate pictures featuring skulls, birds, and flowers.

The beer in those cans and on tap at the brewery is as creative as the art. Burial produces a mixture of Belgian and farmhouse beers, with occasional for-

Old tools and kitchen implements serve as rustic tap handles at Burial's taproom.
Erik Lars Myers

ays into big American-style ales. Ingredients such as Thai basil, coconut, honey, and locally roasted coffee are common in its beers. Burial also uses locally malted grain from Asheville's Riverbend Malt House.

Burial started as a small operation with a one-barrel pilot brewing system. The three founders—Jessica and Doug Reiser and Tim Gormley—divided the work among them.

However, staying small is not in Burial's business plan. It took only a year and a half for the partners to expand their team and upgrade to their current 10-barrel brewhouse. More growth is coming. According to Jessica, the next step is "to have a larger system to focus more on widespread packaging." With luck, more of Burial's rustically creative beers will be reaching the market in the future.

GREEN MAN BREWERY

27 Buxton Avenue
Asheville, NC 28801
828-252-5502
Email: beerisgood@greenmanbrewery.com
Website: greenmanbrewery.com
Hours: Monday–Wednesday, 3 P.M.–9 P.M.;
    Thursday, 3 P.M.–10 P.M.;
    Friday–Saturday, noon–11 P.M.;
    Sunday, 1 P.M.–9 P.M. (Hours may change seasonally.)
Owner: Dennis Thies
Brewmaster: John Stuart
Opened: 1997

GREEN MAN IS ASHEVILLE'S SECOND-OLDEST BREWERY, having opened just a couple of years after Highland. It has been through an enormous amount of change and is currently in the middle of its third expansion.

For years, Green Man was part of Jack of the Wood, a downtown tavern and launch point for some of Asheville's most successful breweries. Brewers from Jack of the Wood have gone on to work at—or start—French Broad Brewing Company, Lexington Avenue Brewery, and Wedge Brewing Company.

In 2010, Green Man was bought by Dennis Thies, a beer industry veteran. Under Thies, Green Man found new independence from Jack of the Wood and has expanded operations, though it still brews beer for the pub. In the time it took to relicense the brewery, Thies and the team at Green Man remodeled. They also worked through the entire beer lineup with Green Man's original brewer, John Stuart, with an eye on quality and consistency, taking beers that were already great and fine-tuning them for excellence.

By the end of 2010, Thies had doubled Green Man's capacity and opened its tasting room, Dirty Jack's, which provides a relaxed atmosphere for enjoying Green Man beer and whatever soccer game is on television. He also started Next Generation Beer Company, an accompanying distributor that is in charge of getting Green Man beers—as well as a host of others from around the country—to the market.

Patrons enjoy themselves just feet away from where the beer Is made at Green Man Brewery.
Erik Lars Myers

Now, Green Man's flagship beers can be found in six-packs statewide, as well as in Tennessee, South Carolina, and Florida.

WICKED WEED BREWING

The pub:
91 Biltmore Avenue
Asheville, NC 28801
828-575-9599
Hours: Monday–Wednesday, 11:30 A.M.–11 P.M.;
Thursday, 11:30 A.M.–midnight;
Friday–Saturday, 11:30 A.M.–1 A.M.;
Sunday, noon–11 P.M.

The Funkatorium:
147 Coxe Avenue
Asheville, NC 28801
828-552-3203
Hours: Monday–Thursday, 4 P.M.–10 P.M.;
Friday, 4 P.M.–midnight; Saturday, 1 P.M.–midnight;
Sunday, 1 P.M.–10 P.M.

Email: info@wickedweedbrewing.com
Website: wickedweedbrewing.com
Founders: Walt and Luke Dickinson; Rick, Denise, and
Ryan Guthy
Head of Production: Eric Leypoldt
Director of Sour Production: Richard Kilcullen
Opened: 2012

outside

HISTORIANS ARGUE ABOUT WHETHER OR NOT ONE OF ENGLAND'S TUDOR KINGS declared hops "a wicked and pernicious weed." However, it is indisputable that Wicked Weed Brewing, named after that quote, is one of the best-known breweries in Asheville. Since its opening in 2012, Wicked Weed has expanded to three locations and has an astonishing number of different beers available at any given time.

Wicked Weed's rapid expansion is due to the vision and drive of brothers Luke and Walt Dickinson and their financial backers, Rick, Denise, and Ryan Guthy. Like most craft brewers, Walt and Luke got their start homebrewing. Luke took his interest and turned it into a career, doing a stint with Dogfish Head Brewing in Delaware. Walt pursued other opportunities, keeping beer as his hobby. In 2009, the brothers got together and floated the idea of a brewery of

In the short time it's been open, Wicked Weed has already made a name for itself in barrel aging and sours.
Erik Lars Myers

their own. Pooling their expertise, Luke and Walt started making a business plan and developing recipes. Financial backing from the Guthy family gave the brothers the push they needed to make their plan reality. They opened their brewpub on Biltmore Avenue in December 2012.

The Dickinson brothers designed Wicked Weed with two areas of focus: Belgian beers and West Coast American styles. So it is no surprise they're best known for funky sours, creative blends, and big IPAs. In 2014, the brewery brought home a gold medal from the Great American Beer Festival in the Specialty Honey Beer category for its limited-release Mompara. The following year, it was awarded a silver for Pernicious, an American-style IPA.

In 2014, Wicked Weed opened its second location, the Funkatorium, dedicated to its barrel beers. At this point, two of Wicked Weed's facilities—the pub and the Funkatorium—are open for visitors. Its large production facility (opened in 2015) is currently closed to the public, but tours and a taproom may be added in the future.

When visitors enter the pub or the Funkatorium, they'll notice the planning and careful polish. The pub is a multilevel restaurant and bar with a bottle shop where patrons can pick up Wicked Weed swag and beer to go. The Funkatorium, located on Coxe Avenue, has a darker, more cavelike feel, which is appropriate for a space dedicated to barrel-aging and blending beers. Both locations serve food from menus designed to match the atmosphere—upscale burgers and appetizers at the pub and European-style cured meats and cheeses at the Funkatorium.

With its new production facility just completed, Wicked Weed is poised to grow its distribution and reach in the craft beer market.

ONE WORLD BREWING

10 Patton Avenue
Asheville, NC 28801
828-785-5580
Email: oneworldbrewing002@gmail.com
Website: oneworldbrewing.com
Hours: Monday–Friday, 4 P.M.–midnight;
    Saturday, noon–midnight; Sunday, noon–10 P.M.
Founders: Jason and Lisa Schutz
Head Brewer: Jason Schutz
Opened: 2014

VISITING ONE WORLD BREWING FEELS LIKE DISCOVERING A SECRET CLUB.
The brewery's entrance is down an alley alongside the historic Leader Building on Patton Avenue in Asheville. A large, barrel-shaped overhang shelters the dark door and its small porthole window. It feels like the kind of door you'd need a password to enter. But all craft beer fans are welcome to descend the stairs to this underground bar.

One World is in the basement of what was at one time, according to the bartender, an old department store. The elegantly curved wooden bar is backed by the building's old, sweeping double staircase, which now ends at the room's roof. The dark-paneled room is dominated by a large table crafted from the floor of the building's old elevator, the gate from which stretches across the corner of the room by the bar. Other, smaller tables are scattered around the sides of the room. Darts and *sjoelbak* (a Dutch shuffleboard game) provide opportunities for friendly competition. Behind a low wooden wall at the back of the room sits One World's 1.5-barrel stainless-steel brewing system. The fermentation takes place in a separate room, where windows allow patrons to see the brewery's fermenters, highlighted by colored lights.

Jason Schutz co-owns One World with his wife, Lisa. Jason was a carpenter and a stonemason who homebrewed as a hobby. However, when the recession hit his business hard, he started to think about ways to turn his hobby into a new career. The transition wasn't immediate—it takes time and money to find a

One World's basement taproom is a beautiful hardwood homage to its department-store past.
Erik Lars Myers

location and start a brewery—but Jason's dream became reality in the spring of 2014, when One World opened for business.

When Jason describes One World, the word he turns to is *community*. His taproom is designed to be a gathering spot where friends bond over one (or more) of the 10 beers on draft. The taps are a mix of One World's original recipes and guest beers from around the state. Drinkers can expect to find hoppy offerings such as an IPA or a pale ale, a saison, and a dark beer or two.

The small brewing system allows Jason flexibility but also makes it hard to keep up with demand and to allow growth. It's likely that growth would mean opening a second production facility while keeping the Patton Avenue location as the central taproom and community spot.

LEXINGTON AVENUE BREWERY

39 North Lexington Avenue
Asheville, NC 28801
828-252-2827
Email: bookings@lexavebrew.com
Website: lexavebrew.com
Hours: Monday–Wednesday, 11:30 A.M.–midnight;
  Thursday–Saturday, 11:30 A.M.–2 A.M.;
  Sunday, noon–midnight
Owners: Steve Wilmans, Mike Healy
Head Brewer: Jonathan Chassner
Opened: 2009

STEVE WILMANS AND MIKE HEALY ARE NOT TYPICAL BAR OWNERS.
Wilmans, a recording-industry veteran, was a partner in Seattle's Stepping Stone Studios when such acts as Pearl Jam, Soundgarden, and Modest Mouse were on their way up—that is, he was until a Microsoft executive made him an offer he couldn't refuse. After a year of travel, Wilmans found himself in Los Angeles agreeing to help Healy, a longtime friend, pick up and move across the country to Asheville. There, Wilmans fell in love with the local vibe and ended up opening a new recording studio, Echo Mountain Studios.

At the same time, Wilmans and Healy pooled their resources and bought a space downtown. It had always been Healy's dream to open a pub, and it seemed fitting that his pub in Asheville would feature a brewery. After three full years of renovations, that space became LAB—Lexington Avenue Brewery.

To brew the beer, they hired Ben Pierson, a veteran of the Asheville brewing scene. Ben had brewed at Jack of the Wood (now Green Man) before leaving to become a brewery consultant who helped open breweries around the Southeast. This project, in a town where he had seen so much success, pulled him back. Pierson spent three years establishing LAB as a go-to beer spot before moving to South Carolina, where he opened Swamp Rabbit Brewery. These days, Jonathan Chassner is the brewer responsible for crafting LAB's creative and food-friendly beers.

Lexington Avenue was conceived as more than a regular brewpub. It is a gastropub—a pub that pairs high-quality food with its beers. It also places an emphasis on live music. LAB features two stages—an acoustic stage in the dining area and a stage in the back of the brewpub that's soundproof, so it can host live shows without disturbing dining patrons.

The sweeping, curved bar and the dining area are lavishly beautiful. The outdoor patio seating blends seamlessly into the brewpub's main dining area. And all of it is lit by the spectacular light show in the brewery, where colored lights are cast against the stainless-steel fermenters. Through the fermenters, the beautiful 15-barrel copper-kettle brewhouse is barely visible, allowing patrons to see shadows of movement while brewing is happening.

The bar at Lexington Avenue Brewery
Erik Lars Myers

FRENCH BROAD
BREWING COMPANY

101 Fairview Road #D
Asheville, NC 28803
828-277-0222
Email: andy@frenchbroadbrewery.com
Website: frenchbroadbrewery.com
Hours: Daily, 1 P.M.–8 P.M.
Owner: Andrew Dahm
Brewmaster: Aaron Wilson
Opened: 2001

ANDY DAHM HAS ALWAYS LOVED BEER. After a career in printing and graphic arts in and around the Southeast, he settled in Asheville and started Asheville Brewing Supply in 1994. Seven years later, when friend and local brewer Jonas Rembert decided to move on from his post at Jack of the Wood and start his own brewery, Dahm jumped aboard, though to this day he's not sure why. "I have no recollection," he says of the decision to start a brewery, "but it's a safe bet that alcohol was involved."

French Broad Brewing—one of Asheville's first breweries, opening just a few years behind Highland—set out to make distinctive European-style lagers. It did that well and soon began expanding its repertoire. The brewery first operated as a production-only facility. In 2004, it opened a 25-seat tasting room that has made it a popular destination, especially because of the constant schedule of live music. The intimate setting attracts some of Asheville's most popular musicians. French Broad now boasts music five nights a week.

Dahm speaks of founding brewer Jonas Rembert: "The music offerings reflect the interests of a lot of people in our company, but I'd have to say that Jonas really made the listening room part of our business happen, and we're grateful to him for getting that done."

Being one of the oldest breweries in town has given French Broad the ability to watch the Asheville brewing scene grow up around it, an experience Dahm calls "gratifying." Still, French Broad remains one of the smaller breweries in

The tiny bar inside French Broad Brewing Company
Erik Lars Myers

town, despite the fact that it distributes throughout the state. "We're probably working with less share capitalization than most breweries in town, and we've become a very resourceful, quality-obsessed organization because of it," says Dahm.

Since Rembert left the company, French Broad has had several head brewers. The man currently in that role, Aaron Wilson, started as an assistant at French Broad and moved to the head brewer position when Chris Richards left to join the team at Sierra Nevada. Wilson was—like every brewer who has ever worked at French Broad—a homebrewer. He met Dahm through Asheville Brewing Supply and worked briefly for him there before transitioning to brewery work. As head brewer, Wilson has shepherded French Broad through its most recent changes. The company had been bottling its flagship beers since 2006 but in 2013 made the decision to switch to easier-to-distribute cans. French Broad started selling its cans just in the local market but is now moving them into all of its existing markets in the Southeast.

Despite this new packaging, French Broad remains a small business with a relaxed approach to growth. The brewery will take the future as it comes, says Dahm. "We figure that moving forward is going to happen whether we plan for it or not."

WEDGE BREWING COMPANY

37 Paynes Way, Suite 001
Asheville, NC 28801
828-505-2792
Email: info@wedgebrewing.com
Website: wedgebrewing.com
Hours: Monday–Thursday, 4 P.M.–10 P.M.;
    Friday, 3 P.M.–10 P.M.;
    Saturday–Sunday, noon–10 P.M.
Owner: Tim Schaller
Brewmaster: Carl Melissas
Opened: 2008

WEDGE BREWING COMPANY IS IN THE RIVER ARTS DISTRICT, which is artsy and funky even by Asheville standards. It is an area known for its wide range of artists' studios. A simple sign painted on a beam leaning over the sidewalk reads, "Wedge In Back." There, a staircase leads down into a sculptor's wonderland of art and to Wedge Brewing Company.

The brewing company is named after the building it's in—Wedge Studios. Much of the building stands in tribute to its late owner, John Payne, a metal artist, sculptor, engineer, and inventor.

Wedge Brewing Company's owner, Tim Schaller, moved from Sag Harbor, New York, where he had worked as a contractor renovating historic houses. In Asheville, he saw opportunity. "I built some new houses down here," he says, "but I got out at the right time."

Always a fan of beer, he arrived in Asheville just after Highland Brewing Company opened its doors. "What got me into beer was beer," he says with a smile. "I like it. I've always been an entrepreneur of some sort, so I just took the idea of a brewery and ran with it. I usually sort of run with an idea until something comes up to stop me, but we didn't really run into any roadblocks."

He was good friends with Payne and talked to him about the possibility of the basement space. He speaks fondly of the River Arts District. "To me, this area is like the last frontier of Asheville—the last area where it's fairly local," he says. "And artists are interesting people to be around. I liked the idea of an old

The brewhouse at Wedge Brewing Company
Erik Lars Myers

man's democratic bar, where you sit around and just have conversations. And that was the idea."

Schaller found a local brewer—Carl Melissas, previously of Green Man Brewery—who was interested. He also located a good deal on equipment from a brewery in Florida. Payne, unfortunately, died a few weeks after the brewery opened.

The original idea for the basement space was that it would function primarily as a warehouse. But since the opening in 2008, it has turned into a community gathering space. Wedge Brewing Company is still trying to keep up with demand. For a time, Schaller says, Wedge distributed beer to 40 to 45 restaurants, but it has since pulled back. It's now down to six or eight. The company sells all the rest of its beer on-site.

Schaller sees Wedge as subsidizing the artists who continue to work in his friend's studios. "Wedge is able to pay twice the rent that the artists can, so it's still a good deal for them," he says. "We're in a transition time, and we're trying to steer it so that maybe we can get a restaurant down here or something, and that'll pay more rent again, so that maybe the artists can stay."

Aside from making Wedge even more community-friendly, Schaller has no plans for growth. "I'm 65," he said in a 2011 interview, "and I can make a living. We have a small system with no real room to grow in the space, so we're not looking at getting any bigger than this. People like our beer and like our scene, and that's the main thing to us."

Wedge Brewing Company lives up to its building's legacy. The beautiful space, used for produce storage in the 1930s, is now surrounded by metal sculptures, many built by Payne. The bar is small but warm and accommodating, and the expansive patio overlooks the railroad, where freight trains roll by bearing load after load of wood chips. ("There goes the Great Smoky Mountains National Forest," Schaller quips.) While mostly closed off from public view, the brewery still pokes its tall, skinny fermenters over the tops of walls inside the taproom. They look very much at home among the sculptures created by the brewery owner's dear friend.

HIGHLAND
BREWING COMPANY

12 Old Charlotte Highway, Suite 200
Asheville, NC 28803
828-299-7223
Email: info@highlandbrewing.com
Website: highlandbrewing.com
Hours: Monday–Thursday, 4 P.M.–8 P.M.;
    Friday, 4 P.M.–9 P.M.; Saturday, 2 P.M.–9 P.M.;
    Sunday, noon–6 P.M.
Founder: Oscar Wong
President: Leah Wong Ashburn
Visionary: John Lyda
Head Brewer: Hollie Stephenson
Opened: 1994

HIGHLAND BREWING COMPANY IS ONE OF THE OLDEST PACKAGING BREWERIES operating in North Carolina. The idea was that of John McDermott, who discovered beer as a homebrewer in the 1980s. After turning professional, McDermott worked at Catamount Brewing Company in White River Junction, Vermont; the Mill Bakery, Eatery, and Brewery, a now-closed chain of health-conscious brewpubs; and Dilworth Brewing Company. At that point, he set his sights on owning his own brewery.

Meanwhile, Oscar Wong was looking for a good business investment. Wong was living in Charlotte after a successful career as a completely different type of entrepreneur, having built his own engineering firm. When his company was bought out and the Charlotte branch closed, Wong was "coasting, cooking, and volunteering." A friend introduced him to McDermott, who needed backing to start his brewery. "I always appreciated beer," says Wong, "and I needed a hobby. My wife was glad to see me out of the house."

At the time, they felt the Charlotte market couldn't support another brewery, so they decided on Asheville as a startup location. They found a space beneath Universal Pizza and Barley's Taproom and set up shop, albeit slowly. The cramped location needed a fair amount of refurbishment, and city inspectors who had never dealt with a brewery gave them a hard time, but they eventually created Asheville's first legal brewery since Prohibition.

John Lyda was their first employee. He looks back at the early days with a shake of his head. "It was a big challenge, especially with sanitation. We were in the basement of a bar, so there was dust being kicked up all over the place."

Wong adds spice to the story: "Cleaning out the tanks by hand meant a brewer going shirtless. Somehow, visitors who saw the naked top half of a brewer would for some reason assume that he was fully naked. We weren't too quick to deny that."

In addition, they were using equipment not made for brewing beer. Their mash tun was a 35-barrel Sealtest ice-cream pasteurizer with steam pipes running through the middle of it for heat. Their fermenters were 2,000-gallon dairy tanks.

Wong has many stories of the initial challenges. He's particularly proud of Highland's Oatmeal Porter because "it was born under duress." After three 2,000-gallon batches of lager ended up in the sewer and a fourth was not quite up to par, the staff designed a dark beer to incorporate some of the lager. "We still had to dump most of it, because we didn't have sufficient sales," says Wong, but that porter developed into one of Highland's best-selling beers. Oatmeal Porter no longer contains any lager.

Highland started packaging 22-ounce bottles a couple of years after opening, but the process was less than ideal. "We didn't have equipment that gave us confidence in the filling process," Wong remembers, "so we pasteurized them in an open milk tank." He adds, "We would lose up to 40 bottles each time, and a good day was 12 or less."

Lyda joined the brewery with 10 years of homebrewing experience. His mother had bought him a kit at a church rummage sale when he was in college, and he fell in love with the process. His dream was to go to brewing school, but the Siebel Institute required three years of professional experience at that point, so he took the job with Highland to get it. His first brewery job proved to be his only brewery job. Upon completing the Siebel course, Lyda returned to Highland and, together with Wong, bought McDermott out of the brewery.

With Lyda and Wong at the helm, Highland continued to grow at breakneck pace. It quickly reached full capacity at its basement facility—about 6,500 barrels per year—and still had a hard time satisfying demand. It became obvious that the brewery needed a larger plant. But Lyda and Wong didn't want to move and immediately have the same capacity problems, so they shot big. They temporarily contracted out their bottle production while they started building a new brewery in a building that once housed Blue Ridge Motion Pictures.

Their brewery now resembles a large manufacturing facility, in sharp contrast to the old cobbled-together basement operation. The 50-barrel brewhouse has row upon row of 100-barrel tanks that tower throughout the giant warehouse. The constant rattle of the bottling line serves as a soundtrack as High-

A long time in coming: Highland's bottling line takes up an entire room, a far cry from the basement startup of 20 years ago.
Erik Lars Myers

land's crew fills case after case of beer, ready for distribution.

Highland's tasting room is bigger than many of the state's breweries. It has a long bar, hundreds of seats, and a stage for presentations and performances, all hemmed in by converted railroad cars that act as offices for some of the staff. In 2011, Highland added an outdoor stage, bar, and deck. In 2015, it completed an expansion of its production facility, including a room-sized bottling line. Up next will be an event space and a rooftop bar and deck.

Highland continues to be a family-driven business. In 2011, Leah Wong Ashburn, Oscar's daughter, joined the brewery. She has since taken on the job of president, while Oscar remains board chair. Leah's path to taking over the business was, as she likes to explain, anything but direct. In fact, Oscar refused to hire her when he opened the brewery. Several years later, he offered her the job she originally wanted, but this time Leah turned him down to focus on her own business. However, Leah always kept her eye on the brewery's growth and ultimately decided to leave her successful career to join Highland. At the time, Oscar was over 70. Though he had no plans to retire, the time had come to consider the future leadership of the company. Leah rose to the top of the candidate pool, and Highland became a second-generation brewery.

"The responsibility is great," Leah says, "but so is the team. And as Dad told me, only with risk comes opportunity."

Highland continues to expand its markets, finding success as a midsized regional brewery and a leader in the Asheville business community.

BLUE MOUNTAIN PIZZA AND BREW PUB

55 North Main Street
Weaverville, NC 28787
828-658-8777
Email: owner@bluemountainpizza.com
Website: bluemountainpizza.com
Hours: Tuesday–Thursday, 11 A.M.–9 P.M.;
    Friday–Saturday, 11 A.M.–10 P.M.;
    Sunday, 11 A.M.–9 P.M.
Founder: Matt Danford
Brewers: Joey Cagle, Mike Vanhoose
Opened: 2012

BLUE MOUNTAIN PIZZA AND BREW PUB IS A BUSTLING RESTAURANT on Main Street in the small town of Weaverville. The long, low building is fronted by a covered porch scattered with tables and chairs for outdoor dining. At night, lights line the entrance, welcoming visitors looking for a slice and a beer. Inside, the cozy space is packed with wooden tables and chairs. A small stage in the corner hosts live music. Murals line the wall next to the stage. Stretching across the opposite wall is the bar, a hanging shelf for glassware suspended above it. The décor is pleasantly cluttered—stars and hot-air balloons are repeated motifs—and reinforces Blue Mountain's reputation as a family-friendly, down-to-earth pizza place.

The restaurant has been around since 2004, but the brewery was added relatively recently, in December 2012. Blue Mountain's owner, Matt Danford, thought beer brewed on-site would add to the experience for the restaurant's regulars and attract new business from out of town.

The two-barrel system, installed in a side building, supplies the bar's three taps with a rotating lineup of beer styles. Because the system is small and the restaurant is busy, the beers change constantly. Former homebrewers Joey Cagle and Mike Vanhoose formulate the recipes and brew the beers.

It's possible that success could spell expansion for Blue Mountain Pizza and Brew Pub. But for now, visitors can look forward to a casual, low-key experience in this comfortable restaurant.

"Friends gather here," reads a sign behind the busy bar at Blue Mountain Pizza.
Erik Lars Myers

Volunteers pruning hops at Hop 'n' Blueberry Farm in Black Mountain
Van Burnette

HOP FARMING

Due to the growth of the craft beer industry, the state's farmers have increasingly looked toward hops as a crop, particularly as a potential replacement for tobacco. North Carolina's climate and latitude, however, pose some interesting challenges.

Van Burnette is the sole farmer at Hop 'n' Blueberry Farm in Black Mountain, one of the first hop yards in North Carolina to explore the possibility of growing hops commercially. Rather than growing an extensive variety or large acreage of hops, he works closely with the North Carolina Cooperative Extension and the North Carolina Hops Project. The project, a team effort of North Carolina State University's Departments of Soil Science and Horticultural Science, is designed to determine whether or not hops are a viable crop, what varieties can grow in the state, what the best possible geography is, what the best strategies are, and what problems (pests, diseases, nutrition) might arise in the state's climate. The project works with six farms around the state that grow a variety of hops. The farms serve as working labs for field researchers. For information about the North Carolina Hops Project, including some of its early results and the farms it has worked with, visit ces.ncsu.edu/fletcher.

Burnette grows about a half-acre of American varieties—Cascade, Chinook, and Nugget—which seem to do better in North Carolina than do European varieties. His farm is all-organic, which poses its own problems. Hops are susceptible to common garden pests and mildew. Still, those don't worry him. "It's not the heat or the humidity that hops really have a problem with down here," Burnette says. "It's the light."

Hops grow best between the 35th and 55th latitudes in both the Northern and Southern Hemispheres. North Carolina just barely falls within that range (34th to 37th latitudes). While hops have been successfully grown by hobbyists in all 50 states (which range as low as the 22nd latitude), most commercial hop farming takes place above the 45th latitude. That's because the higher latitudes have much longer days in the middle of summer than do the lower latitudes.

Hops grow incredibly quickly. The plants die back to the ground each winter and regrow their entire length—which can be upwards of 25 feet—each summer. In addition to water and nutrients, hops require an immense amount of sunlight to achieve such growth. Burnette has noted that his hops—especially second- or third-year hops—tend to start flowering before they've achieved their full length. "The days don't get long enough for the hops to achieve their full growth before they start flowering, so we end up with smaller harvests," he says.

On the other hand, long Southern summers mean multiple harvests. In other parts of the country, large commercial facilities cut hop bines down when the flowers are ready for harvesting. Since the bines are so tall, it is difficult and time consuming to harvest the hop cones from the plants. When they're cut down, the flowers are easily threshed from the bines. Burnette harvests the first set of cones from the bines, leaves the plants up, and then reaps a smaller late-season harvest. Using those techniques, he is able to get an overall harvest close to a commercial harvest north of the 45th parallel. But he's still not quite there.

All of Burnette's hops currently go to Pisgah Brewing Company in Black Mountain for its annual fresh hop ale, appropriately named Burnette's Brew. "It's a lot of fun to bring the hops down there and throw them straight into the kettle with the guys at Pisgah, even if it does mean an entire season's worth of work is gone all at once," he says.

Burnette hopes to find hops that grow better in North Carolina. In the coming years, he plans to try new varieties that are reported to grow well in southern latitudes, and he'll continue to monitor his current hops as they enter their third year of growth.

Interested parties can visit the farm and even volunteer to help with the hop yard. Burnette notes that it takes "about one person per acre of hops" working full-time to maintain a hop yard. He welcomes help. "I'm not getting any younger," he jokes.

There are now more than a dozen hop farms of various sizes in North Carolina. Some are similar to Burnette's and expend an entire production year in a batch of beer, but others are attempting large-scale production and seeing some success.

Although in its early stages, the state's hops industry is growing and will soon be a significant factor in North Carolina beer.

PISGAH BREWING COMPANY

150 Eastside Drive
Black Mountain, NC 28711
828-669-0190
Email: info@pisgahbrewing.com
Website: pisgahbrewing.com
Hours: Monday–Wednesday, 4 P.M.–8 P.M.;
  Thursday–Friday, 2 P.M.–9 P.M.; Saturday, noon–9 P.M.;
  Sunday, 1 P.M.–8 P.M.
Owner: Jason Caughman
Head Brewer: Jason Caughman
Opened: 2005

DAVID QUINN AND JASON CAUGHMAN, the founders of Pisgah Brewing Company, did not meet during business, but rather at a potluck dinner held by mutual friends in Charleston, South Carolina, where they were both living. As it happened, Quinn, a longtime brewer, brought a keg of his pale ale to the party. The two quickly became friends. Soon, their complementary skills—Quinn's homebrewing and Caughman's graphic design—led them to begin a business together. "It was a pretty typical entrepreneurial start," says Caughman. "I always wanted my own business, and to do something a little different to flee the corporate world."

The two found a small industrial space in Black Mountain. Theirs is a unique company that fits perfectly into the Asheville area's ethos. Up until 2013, most of Pisgah's beers were certified organic. Quinn and Caughman lost their certification when the USDA changed the governing rules, though their beer-making process did not change. Even when it isn't brewing organic, Pisgah sticks to a strong commitment to buying as many of its supplies and ingredients as possible from local vendors.

Pisgah has also become known as a music venue, hosting local, regional, and national acts including Steel Pulse, Lucinda Williams, and Grace Potter at both indoor and outdoor stages. "The music just came about," says Caughman. "I'm a music lover, so we just kind of went in that direction. We built a stage instead of buying more tanks."

The brewery is noted for its constantly rotating selection of small-batch beers. At times, a dozen or more beers are on tap in the brewery that can't be had anywhere else. "We're pretty small, but we have a tremendous amount of local support," says Caughman. "We have to continue to make new, exciting, different beers to stay engaged and stimulated. I think our customers appreciate being able to try 20 to 30 unique beers from us each year, too."

Pisgah is not easy to find. It's located in a small warehouse in an industrial park. Its hours vary depending on the season and whether or not it's a live-music night.

From the outside, Pisgah could be any other office space. Once inside, though, patrons see its true colors. The brewhouse sits tucked inside its own separate room around the corner from the bar. The rough, black-box space with a short wooden bar is backed by more than two dozen taps. The short stage opposite the bar promises music to patrons on most nights. While seating is absent aside from stools at the bar, the taproom offers plenty of space for patrons to stand and hang out. Outside, Pisgah has constructed a large, covered wooden stage in front of an expansive grassy area. The stage has hosted an impressive array of concerts on beautiful western North Carolina evenings.

The bar at Pisgah Brewing Company
Jim White

103 South Ridgeway Avenue
Black Mountain, NC 28711
828-357-5169
Email: info@lookoutbrewing.com
Website: lookoutbrewing.com
Hours: Monday–Thursday, 2 P.M.–9 P.M.;
   Friday–Saturday, 2 P.M.–10 P.M.;
   Sunday, noon–6 P.M.
Founder: John Garcia
Head Brewer: Chris Terwilliger
Opened: 2013

BLACK MOUNTAIN, NC

CRAFT BREWERIES HAVE A REPUTATION FOR REVITALIZING the areas they call home. In Lookout Brewing's case, it has taken two storefronts in an old strip mall and transformed them into a brewery and tasting room that draw visitors from the moment the doors open in the afternoon until the taps are turned off at night.

The taproom, which is at the end of the strip, is furnished with an eclectic selection of wooden tables and chairs, a set of shelves that hold board games, and a large projection screen. On nice days, the garage door is open and drinkers can enjoy the side patio, which holds a cornhole set and a fire pit. The shining, copper-topped bar, which cuts across one corner of the space, serves up at least eight different styles of Lookout beer. John Garcia, the owner, has broad tastes that are represented in the recipes. The taps are a mix of year-round beers such as Black Mountain IPA and Alison's Front Porch Pale (designed by Garcia's wife) and seasonal or experimental beers including White Chocolate Stout. One of Lookout's fermenters is dedicated to sours, so a sour offering is often on tap. Garcia and his brewer, Chris Terwilliger, have even experimented with catching and using wild yeast from the area around the brewery. The two men are also fans of wet hops—hops picked fresh from the vine and delivered to the brewery before drying—and use as many of them as possible during the hop harvest season.

Garcia intentionally started small. He renovated the space and installed his first half-barrel brewing system with the help of his parents, Richard and Patricia

Lookout Brewing makes an impressive amount of beer on a small system.
Erik Lars Myers

Jones, who later opened Good Hops Brewing in Carolina Beach. Garcia's small-batch brewing was successful enough that he was able to grow to a three-barrel system and hire more people, who can be seen at work behind the glass window separating the brewing room from the bar. Hidden behind a projector screen is a door leading into the rest of Lookout's space, which includes a cold room, a fermentation room, and a large storage room.

Garcia recently signed a distribution deal and envisions a 15-barrel brewing system and more fermentation space to meet demand for his tasty mountain-brewed beer.

DRY COUNTY
BREWING COMPANY

585 Oak Avenue
Spruce Pine, NC 28777
828-765-4583
Website: drycountybrewing.com
Hours: Wednesday–Saturday, noon–9 P.M.;
    Sunday, 4 P.M.–9 P.M.
Founders: Chad Mohr and Jennifer Rambo
Head Brewer: Chad Mohr
Opened: 2010

ONE OF THE LEGACIES OF NORTH CAROLINA'S PROHIBITION MOVEMENT is the dry towns and counties scattered across the state. Mitchell County is one of those, but with an exception: the town of Spruce Pine. In 2009, Spruce Pine legalized the production and sale of alcohol inside town limits. A year later, Chad Mohr and his wife, Jennifer Rambo, took advantage of that to open Dry County Brewing Company.

Dry County is a small brewing operation inside The Pizza Shop, a restaurant also run by Mohr and Rambo. Mohr developed his interest in beer as a home-brewer; it complemented his interest in food. When he and Rambo bought an existing pizza shop in Spruce Pine, Mohr decided to take his brewing skills and add them to the business. Now, he has a 10-gallon SABCO system on which he brews multiple times a week. The Pizza Shop bar pours six taps. Mohr's goal is to keep them filled with a range of beers in styles that will appeal to his broad customer base. Mohr doesn't gravitate toward one style but rather tries to keep all of his recipes well balanced, something he attributes to his background as a chef. Patrons of the restaurant can try sample flights of the beers or drink them by the pint as they enjoy the house-made pizza at one of the casual booths or tables.

The Pizza Shop and Dry County Brewing have become a popular destination for locals and tourists. The demand is high enough that Mohr doesn't distribute any of his beer, which all goes straight to the restaurant. He doesn't rule out future expansion of his brewing business, either through contracting or adding on to The Pizza Shop. But for the moment, he is content to sell his beer to

The bar and pizza oven at Dry County Brewing Company
Erik Lars Myers

the thirsty people in Spruce Pine. Curious drinkers will have to plan a trip to the mountains to sample this small-batch beer for themselves.

BLIND SQUIRREL BREWERY

4716 US 19E South
P.O. Box 173
Plumtree, NC 28664
828-765-2739
Email: blindsquirrelbrewery@gmail.com
Website: blindsquirrelbrewery.com
Hours: Friday–Saturday, 11 A.M.–9 P.M.;
    Sunday, noon–4 P.M.
Founders: Cleve and Robin Young
Head Brewer: William Young
Brewing Staff: Neil Kadala, Justin Tate,
    Gage Baldwin
Opened: 2012

outside

PLUMTREE'S BLIND SQUIRREL BREWERY IS PERCHED ON THE BANKS of the North Toe River at the edge of Pisgah National Forest. The brewery's building is an old processing facility that dates from Avery County's history as a center of mica mining and production, while the taproom is the former T. B. Vance General Store, built in 1919. Both buildings had fallen into disuse when they were picked up by the Young family, who renovated the old store into the Vance Toe River Lodge and transformed the other building into the Blind Squirrel Brewery production space.

Visitors to Blind Squirrel will find a welcoming, laid-back atmosphere. Head brewer William Young explains, "A small-batch, artistic, mountain approach drives all aspects of our business from food to beverage to lodging. Our facilities are historic, our employees are family, and our style is balanced."

Inside, the lodge still has the feel of a general store. To the left of the spacious room is a long bar serving up 12 taps of Blind Squirrel's beers, while a restaurant dominates the area on the right. Comfortable seating encourages guests to relax and enjoy their food and beer. The lodge sells bottles of Blind Squirrel beer to go, in addition to other merchandise. The building doubles as a bed-and-breakfast and private event space.

The Youngs entered the brewery business through homebrewing. As with

A brewpub, winery, and general store, Blind Squirrel lights up the mountain night with warmth and good times.
Erik Lars Myers

many other new homebrewers, some trial and error was involved. According to William, "After purchasing a 20-gallon all-grain system and attempting to brew a brown ale, we realized how little we originally knew about the brewing process."

Blind Squirrel's name came out of that early home experimentation. William remembers, "After our owner tasted the beer for the first time, he exclaimed, 'Well, boys, even a blind squirrel finds a nut every once in a while!' With that prophetic statement, our professional brewing operation of the future was named."

The Youngs produce a wide variety of beers, seven of which are bottled and distributed throughout North Carolina. The bottled beers range across a variety of styles. The taproom releases, even more inventive, include creative serving options such as a sprinkling of cinnamon sugar to sweeten the rim of a glass of dark holiday beer.

William describes statewide distribution as "a welcome challenge" that is pushing the brewery to increase its production and infrastructure. Blind Squirrel's main focus, though, is its corner of Avery County. According to William, a benefit of distribution is that "more and more folks are learning just how wonderful the High Country of North Carolina can be."

The Youngs look forward to welcoming many of those craft beer fans to their historic buildings in Plumtree.

BEECH MOUNTAIN BREWING COMPANY

1007 Beech Mountain Parkway
Beech Mountain, NC 28604
828-387-2011
Email: brewery@skibeech.com
Website: beechmountainresort.com/mountain/
    brewery/
Hours: Thursday–Friday, noon–7 P.M.;
    Saturday, 10 A.M.–7 P.M.; Sunday, noon–6 P.M.
Founders: Ryan Gavigan, Ryan Costin
Head Brewer: Ryan Gavigan
Opened: 2014

THE DRIVE UP TO BEECH MOUNTAIN BREWING COMPANY is one of the most scenic, and most vertical, in North Carolina. Beech Mountain is the highest town in the eastern United States. The ski resort where the brewery is located is reached by a series of switchbacks that give travelers panoramic views of the mountains and valleys of North Carolina's High Country.

The Beech Mountain ski resort opened in 1967 and has expanded over the years. In addition to winter skiing and snowboarding, the resort offers mountain biking and other summertime activities, making it a multiseason destination. The brewery was started to capitalize on North Carolina's thirst for craft beer and to add another reason for visitors to seek out Beech Mountain.

The brewery opened in 2014, spearheaded by Beech Mountain's general manager, Ryan Costin, and Ryan Gavigan, the head brewer. Its three-barrel system, located in an attractive building in the middle of the resort's ski village, is open to the public during times when the resort itself is open. The shining, wood-paneled room has one corner dedicated to the brewing system and a separate room for fermentation. The small eight-tap bar fits into another corner, conveniently located next to a fireplace. Patrons can enjoy their beers inside or venture out onto the spacious deck for a view of the mountain slopes. In addition to the brewery building, the beer is served at other bar locations at the resort, including the 5506' Skybar at the top of the mountain.

Given the brewery's small system and resort demand, it's not surprising that

The perfect place to grab a pint after skiing the slopes: the brewery at the bottom of the mountain
Erik Lars Myers

Beech Mountain's beer isn't found at many off-site accounts. The brewery does occasionally participate in beer festivals. However, to get the full experience, drinkers should make the drive into the mountains to try this high-altitude beer whenever the resort is open.

FLAT TOP BREWING COMPANY

567 Main Street East
Banner Elk, NC 28604
828-898-8677
Email: info@flattopbrewing.com
Website: flattopbrewing.com/home/
Hours: Monday–Thursday, 2 P.M.–8 P.M.;
　　Friday–Saturday, 2 P.M.–10 P.M.;
　　Sunday, 2 P.M.–6 P.M. (Hours change
　　seasonally.)
Founder: Nathan Paris
Head Brewer: Michelle MacLeod
Opened: 2014

IN A LONG, LOW BUILDING ON THE EASTERN END OF MAIN STREET, visitors to Banner Elk will find Flat Top Brewing Company. The taproom feels like a cross between a living room and a lodge. A fireplace and a popcorn machine share space on one wall, while a shuffleboard table occupies another. Soft, comfortable seating is mixed with high wooden chairs that are grouped around tables and line the slate-fronted bar. More entertainment is provided by the television behind the bar and the pool table in a separate room out back. Patrons interested in the brewing process can look through the large windows above the shuffleboard table to see the 20-barrel brewing system and the fermenters that make the beer pouring from the taps.

Flat Top is the brainchild of Nathan Paris, a former homebrewer and stay-at-home dad who was convinced that Banner Elk should join many other towns in the mountains in having its own brewery. The road to opening was rocky. Paris planned to start his brewery in the new local business incubator, but the incubator was run and funded by Avery County, and the county board of commissioners voted against allowing a brewery to operate in the space. With the support of the town, Paris found a location on Main Street East, where he installed his brewery and taproom.

From the beginning, Paris has benefited from the fermentation sciences program at nearby Appalachian State University. His first brewers, Paul Thompson and Drew Gibson, were both graduates of the program, as is Flat Top's current head brewer, Michelle MacLeod.

The technical know-how of the ASU graduates and Paris's passion for the business have made Flat Top a young success story. The beers are mostly familiar styles brewed true to form, such as Flat Top's Rollcast Kölsch-style beer, one of its flagships.

At the moment, Flat Top is distributed only in kegs in the local area, but Paris is planning on moving his product into cans in the near future so more North Carolina drinkers can experience this "Refreshingly Elevated" beer.

Small location, big brewhouse: the brewery at Flat Top Brewing Company is a surprising find in the small mountain town.
Erik Lars Myers

LOST PROVINCE
BREWING COMPANY

130 North Depot Street
Boone, NC 28607
828-265-3506
Email: info@lostprovince.com
Website: lostprovince.com
Hours: Monday–Wednesday, 11:30 A.M.–10 P.M.;
    Thursday–Friday, 11:30 A.M.–11 P.M.;
    Saturday, 11 A.M.–11 P.M.; Sunday, noon–10 P.M.
Founders: Andy and Lynne Mason
Head Brewer: Andy Mason
Brewing Staff: Aaron Maas, Seth Hewitt
Opened: 2014

THESE DAYS, PEOPLE ARE USED TO CALLING THE NORTHWESTERN CORNER OF NORTH CAROLINA the High Country. But back at the end of the 19th century, there was another name for it: the Lost Province. The tall ridge of the Eastern Continental Divide separated Watauga, Ashe, and Alleghany Counties from the rest of the state, limiting economic and social contact and essentially isolating the area until roads and railroads were built in the early 20th century.

North Carolina's High Country is no longer "lost." Andy Mason, cofounder and brewer at Lost Province Brewing Company, sees a different meaning in the old name. "To us, the term Lost Province signifies a place that remains somewhat difficult to get to, that's perhaps hard to find, but is a place to be sought, and a place where you will find food and drink for your body and soul, relaxation, fellowship, and peace."

Lost Province opened in August 2014 in historic downtown Boone. Its building dates from 1939 and was originally a Chevrolet dealership. The building's long life had taken its toll. According to Mason, "We had to completely gut the building and rebuild it from the inside out." That effort was complicated by the fact that Mason wanted to slot a 10-barrel brewery and a full-service restaurant into the space, a process he describes as "trying to fit 10 pounds of stuff in a five-pound sack."

The pizza oven at Lost Province is designed to look just like a copper kettle in a brewery.
Erik Lars Myers

The end result is impressive. The front of the building is an attractive restaurant backed by a long, curving bar that separates the seating area from the kitchen. Visitors' eyes are almost immediately caught by the large, copper-sheathed, wood-fired pizza oven that anchors the left corner of the bar, advertising Lost Province's signature menu item. The atmosphere is bright, welcoming, and busy, especially on weekends during Appalachian State's football season. In the back of the building, out of sight of the main restaurant, is the neatly laid-out brewery, where Mason and his brewers, Aaron Maas and Seth Hewitt, craft Lost Province's beers.

Mason is a homebrewer with a background in chemistry, while Aaron and Seth have professional brewing experience, Aaron at Flat Top Brewing and Seth at Howard Brewing and Blowing Rock Brewing. Lost Province doesn't focus on one flagship beer. Instead, as Mason explains, it showcases "stylistically authentic beers from a diverse range of geographic locations—American, Belgian, British, French, and German—using the best stylistically correct ingredients and processes." That doesn't mean Lost Province never experiments, though. Several of its recipes include fruits or herbs, such as the Alpine Meadows Saison, which features chamomile, lavender, and orange peel. At any time, visitors will find around 11 Lost Province beers on tap at the restaurant.

In just its first year, Lost Province received local and statewide recognition. It won first place in the People's Choice Award competition at Asheville's 2015 Brewgrass Festival and gold, silver, and bronze medals at the NC Brewers Cup.

When asked about Lost Province's future, Mason reveals short- and long-term goals. "Our immediate plans include increasing our draft distribution both in the High Country of North Carolina and in other areas 'off the mountain,' " he says. "Eventually, we will pursue a separate production facility with packaging in bottles or cans and increase distribution of our beers statewide. Then? Who knows!"

APPALACHIAN MOUNTAIN BREWERY

163 Boone Creek Drive
Boone, NC 28607
828-263-1111
Website: appalachianmountainbrewery.com
Hours: Monday, 2 P.M.–10 P.M.;
 Tuesday–Thursday, 2 P.M.–11 P.M.;
 Friday, noon–11 P.M.;
 Saturday–Sunday, noon–10 P.M.
Founders: Sean and Stephanie Spiegelman
Director of Brewery Operations: Nathan
 Kelischek
Head Brewer: Christopher Zieber
Opened: 2013

THE TOWN OF BOONE'S FIRST EXPERIENCE WITH LEGALIZED FERMENTATION happened at the university level, when Appalachian State started its fermentation sciences program. Although the Ivory Tower Brewery, as the ASU system is known, doesn't sell beer in the market, it has made important contributions to the craft beer economy.

In 2013, when Boone's first legal retail brewery opened, ASU graduate Nathan Kelischek held the reins of the brewing operation. Appalachian Mountain Brewery, cofounded by Sean and Stephanie Spiegelman, is a 10-barrel brewery in the southern part of Boone. The Spiegelmans and Kelischek wanted to develop a brewery with strong ties to the local community and a focus on sustainability. As part of that vision, they donate a percentage of their tasting-room sales to local nonprofits. They have invested in solar panels to help power the brewery and in the ecological restoration of Boone Creek, which runs past their facility.

Appalachian Mountain Brewery's community focus also comes through in its taproom, a lively gathering spot for craft beer drinkers. From trivia to live music, something is happening almost every night in the small wood-paneled bar. Drinkers often find the brewery-owned Farm to Flame food truck parked out front. Of course, the beverages are the main focus. Appalachian Mountain has

The busy bar at Appalachian Mountain Brewery
Erik Lars Myers

three flagship beers—a porter, an IPA, and a blonde ale—and features between 10 and 14 of its beverages on tap at any time. Not all are beers, though. In 2014, the brewery expanded its license to include the production of ciders, which are also on tap at the bar.

The brewery is publicly traded, which is unusual in the craft beer business. It has seen fast growth since its opening. Appalachian Mountain Brewery began packaging its flagship styles in cans in 2014. Also that year, it won the Brewbound Start Up Brewery Challenge, a national event. It has since entered into a strategic partnership with the Craft Beer Alliance, another publicly traded brewing company, based in Portland, Oregon. The Craft Beer Alliance includes brands such as Kona Brewing Company, Redhook, and Widmer Brothers and is partially owned by Anheuser-Busch InBev. This partnership is expected to expand Appalachian Mountain Brewery's distribution reach, though it remains to be seen what will happen to its small Boone facility.

BOONESHINE BREWING COMPANY

BOONE, NORTH CAROLINA

Production facility:
246 Wilson Drive, Suite L
Boone, NC 28607
828-773-4851
Website: booneshine.beer
Hours: By appointment
Founders: Carson Coatney, Tim Herdklotz
Brewers: Carson Coatney, Tim Herdklotz
Opened: 2015

Taproom in Basil's Fresh Pasta and Deli:
246 Wilson Drive, Suite K
Boone, NC 28607
828-386-4066
Website: basilspasta.com
Hours: Monday–Wednesday, 10:30 A.M.–10 P.M.;
    Thursday–Saturday, 10:30 A.M.–11 P.M.
Owner: Patrick Sullivan

BOONESHINE BREWING, ONE OF BOONE'S NEWEST BREWERIES, is tucked away in a shopping center on the south side of town. Big glass windows give passersby a clear view of the 10-barrel brewing system and fermentation tanks inside the neat, compact brewing space. One look tells visitors that Booneshine is a production-only brewery. However, they need only walk one door down to Basil's Fresh Pasta and Deli, a restaurant and store that also acts as Booneshine's taproom. At Basil's shining wooden bar, craft beer fans can sample up to eight different Booneshine brews.

Friends Carson Coatney and Tim Herdklotz met while on fishing trips to the Outer Banks. They were both homebrewers and got excited by the idea of starting a brewery in Boone, which did not have one at the time. Carson was already a small business owner in Boone—he owns Stick Boy Bread Company and Melanie's Food Fantasy—and Tim had corporate experience. It took them several years to refine their recipes and put the business plan together, by which point Boone had opened its first brewery. However, the team persevered and opened Booneshine in the summer of 2015.

Booneshine Brewing's beers are available at the tasting room inside Basil's Fresh Pasta and Deli, next door to the brewery.
Erik Lars Myers

Booneshine's lineup features seven recurring beers and a variety of seasonal recipes. The styles run from light, easy-drinking ales to porters and stouts, so the taps are likely to appeal to a wide audience.

At the moment, Booneshine packages beer only in kegs and is focused on restaurant and bar accounts in the Boone area. However, the partners are not ruling out future expansion and are contemplating cans or bottles as a next step.

BLOWING ROCK
BREWING COMPANY

Blowing Rock Ale House:
152 Sunset Drive
Blowing Rock, NC 28605
828-414-9600
Hours: Monday–Tuesday and Thursday,
    11 A.M.–9 P.M.; Friday–Saturday, 11 A.M.–10 P.M.;
    Sunday, noon–9 P.M.

American Honor Ale House:
883 Highland Avenue SE
Hickory, NC 28602
828-855-9999
Hours: Sunday–Thursday, 11 A.M.–11 P.M.;
    Friday–Saturday, 11 A.M.–midnight

Email: info@blowingrockbrewing.com
Website: blowingrockbrewing.com
Founders: Jeff Walker, Todd Rice
Head Brewer: Ray Hodge
Brewing Staff: Josh Carlough, Jim Deaton
Opened: 2013

ALERT NORTH CAROLINA BEER LOVERS MAY LOOK AT THE OPENING YEAR
LISTED ABOVE and do a double take. They're not wrong. Beer has been packaged and sold under the Blowing Rock label since 2008. Blowing Rock's cofounders, Jeff Walker and Todd Rice, dreamed up the idea for a brewery in the first decade of the new century. Their plan was a brand that could represent North Carolina's High Country. To start their business, they opted for a contract brewing model, in which the company's recipes would be sent to another brewery, which would make and package the beer. Walker and Rice incorporated Boone Brewing Company and worked with the Lion contract brewery in Wilkes-Barre, Pennsylvania, to produce Blowing Rock's first beers, which hit the North Carolina market in 2008.

The Blowing Rock–branded ales were a success, prompting Walker and Rice to move forward with financing and opening a brewing facility in North

The home of Blowing Rock Brewing Company
Sarah H. Ficke

Carolina. In 2012, they partnered with Lisa Stripling and Rob Dyer to renovate the building in downtown Blowing Rock that opened the next year as Blowing Rock Ale House & Inn. Walker and Rice hired Ray Hodge, a veteran of many startup breweries, to man the five-barrel brewing system and create the new rotating Ale House series of Blowing Rock beers.

In 2014, the Blowing Rock team opened a 30-barrel production facility in Hickory and an associated restaurant known as the American Honor Ale House. That brewery, located in a renovated mill area, was designed to make and package Blowing Rock's longstanding Legacy series of beers—the ones originally brewed at Lion—as well as some larger-scale batches of the Ale House series beers. As a part of this move, Blowing Rock has switched from 12-ounce bottles to cans, which can be found throughout North Carolina.

BOONDOCKS BREWING

Taproom and restaurant:
108 South Jefferson Avenue
West Jefferson, NC 28694
336-246-5222
Hours: Sunday–Thursday, 11 A.M.–8 P.M. (January–
    March); Sunday–Thursday, 11 A.M.–9 P.M. (April–
    December); Friday–Saturday, 11 A.M.–11:30 P.M.
    (year-round)

Brew Haus:
302 South Jefferson Avenue
West Jefferson, NC 28694
336-846-7525
Hours: Open for special events and by appointment

Email: brewman@boondocks-brewing.com
Website: boondocksbeer.com
Founder: Gary Brown
Head Brewer: Gary Brown
Opened: 2012

GARY BROWN STARTED HIS CAREER IN CORPORATE AMERICA, but his heart belonged to beer. He tried to satisfy his interest through brewing at his home in Rocky Mount, North Carolina—an operation known to friends and family as Boondocks Brew.

However, Brown's passion for beer wasn't satisfied by homebrewing, so one day he decided to make a change: "I literally woke up the morning of June 11, 2012, went upstairs to my home office, pounded out a business plan for Boondocks Brewing Tap Room & Restaurant, walked downstairs several hours later, and told my wife I was heading up to West Jefferson to make an offer on a location to start Boondocks Brewing."

The Browns had vacationed in West Jefferson for years, so the choice of location was no accident. West Jefferson was originally a small railroad and manufacturing town and still has the distinction of being home to a Dr Pepper manufacturing and bottling facility. However, with the decline of manufacturing in North Carolina, the town has transformed itself into a tourist destination.

Looking down upon the brewery and event space at Boondocks Brewing
Erik Lars Myers

Brown prides himself on contributing to the economic revitalization of West Jefferson. Craft breweries tend to encourage growth, he says: "We have been the primary reason that several new businesses have opened in our area, and instead of being just another brewery or restaurant, we have become a destination."

Boondocks itself has expanded since its opening in 2012. The original location—a large building with two dining rooms, two fully-stocked bars, an extensive menu, and perhaps the best craft beer selection in the area—serves as a taproom and restaurant. It is often packed with locals and tourists enjoying a hearty lunch and a brew. Three or four of the taps in the restaurant are dedicated to Boondocks offerings, which rotate through a variety of styles.

In 2014, Boondocks opened the Brew Haus, a special-event space just up the street from the restaurant. The Brew Haus is a beautifully renovated building that started life as a Rhodes Furniture store in the 1940s and was most recently a pizza place. Now, it is a multilevel open room with a shining wooden bar made from the trunk of a tree and the siding from an old barn. It offers ample space for the parties, dinners, and comedy shows that are booked on a regular basis.

The brewing equipment was originally wedged into a corner of the restaurant. In 2015, Brown moved his three-barrel system down to the Brew Haus, where it adds visual interest to one side of the event space.

Brown is looking to increase his capacity to a five-barrel system and to expand his market reach. He plans to do this sustainably, though, with an eye on what is best for West Jefferson and the people he works with. "I spent the first 49 years of my life making a living," he explains, "and my hope is that the remainder of my life I can make a difference in the communities that we serve and in the lives of our employees."

FONTA FLORA BREWERY

317 North Green Street
Morganton, NC 28655
828-475-0153
Email: contact@fontaflora.com
Website: fontaflora.com
Hours: Monday, 5 P.M.–10 P.M.;
   Wednesday, 5 P.M.–9 P.M.;
   Thursday–Friday, 5 P.M.–10 P.M.;
   Saturday, 3 P.M.–10 P.M.;
   Sunday, noon–7 P.M.
Founders: Mark and David Bennett, Todd Boera
Head Brewer: Todd Boera
Opened: 2013

THERE'S NO QUESTION THAT TODD BOERA IS ONE OF THE MOST RECOGNIZ-ABLE PEOPLE in the North Carolina beer industry. With his long, flowing beard and colorful tattoos, Boera stands out even in an industry that specializes in bearded and tattooed men. However, it's Boera's beer, not his beard, that has put Fonta Flora Brewery on the national map. With two Great American Beer Festival gold medals to its name and numerous mentions in national publications, Fonta Flora is one of the best-recognized small breweries in North Carolina.

Visitors to Fonta Flora's brewery and taproom in Morganton will find the tap list a mixture of the familiar and the strange. People into traditional beer can look for the Hop Beard West Coast–style IPA or the gold-medal-winning Dry Irish Stout. However, the true Fonta Flora experience comes from drinking the experimental beers, such as its other GABF winner, a beet saison named Beets, Rhymes and Life, or its carrot IPA.

Boera and his business partners, Mark and David Bennett, are committed to working with farms and foragers to source as many of their ingredients as possible. It isn't unusual to find the likes of lemon balm, ramps, dandelions, kiwis, and honey listed on Fonta Flora's board. Boera's vision when he left his job as head brewer at Catawba Brewing Company was to build a brewery that celebrated the local agricultural community and created beers unique to the Morganton area and its history. In fact, the brewery is named after a historic African American community that was flooded by a power company in 1916 to create Lake James.

Fonta Flora releases some of its beers in 22-ounce bottles, but the releases

Mad scientist Todd Boera at work in Fonta Flora's cozy brewery/taproom
Erik Lars Myers

are always fairly limited, due to Boera's small brewing system and high demand. The best place to find Fonta Flora beers is at its cozy brick taproom and brewery, located at the intersection of North Green and North Sterling Streets in downtown Morganton. The curved wooden bar features 10 to 12 Fonta Flora and guest beers on tap, listed on a colorful chalkboard sign. Visitors can enjoy their beers outside on the patio or at the wooden tables lining the taproom. No matter where they sit, they have a good view of the brewing system, which occupies the left side of the space, separated from the bar by only a low curb that keeps the brewing water away from the taproom's floor. A separate special-events room also doubles as Boera's barrel storage area for his aged beers.

Fonta Flora's small, local aesthetic doesn't lend itself to rapid regional expansion, and that's fine with Boera. He is much more interested in expanding his partnerships with local farmers, restaurants, and other producers. To that end, he's started the State of Origin craft beer festival in Morganton, a small event featuring only beers brewed with North Carolina ingredients. While Fonta Flora may continue to gain a national reputation, its heart is rooted in the agricultural and artistic community of western North Carolina.

CATAWBA BREWING COMPANY

Morganton:
212 South Green Street
Morganton, NC 28655
828-430-6883
Hours: Monday–Tuesday, 5 P.M.–9 P.M.;
  Wednesday–Friday, 5 P.M.–10:30 P.M.;
  Saturday, 1 P.M.–10 P.M.; Sunday, noon–7 P.M.

Biltmore Village, Asheville:
63 Brook Street
Asheville, NC 28803
828-424-7920
Hours: Monday–Thursday, 4 P.M.–9 P.M.;
  Friday, 3 P.M.–10 P.M.; Saturday, 2 P.M.–10 P.M.;
  Sunday, 2 P.M.–9 P.M.

South Slope, Asheville:
32 Banks Avenue
Asheville, NC 28801
828-552-3934
Hours: Monday–Thursday, 2 P.M.–10 P.M.;
  Friday–Sunday, noon–10 P.M.

Website: catawbabrewing.com
Owner: Scott Pyatt
Head Brewer: Kevin Sondey
Opened: 1999

SCOTT PYATT DIDN'T PLAN TO OPEN A BREWING COMPANY. He used to home-brew with his brother, Billy, back in the 1990s. "It was something that we did on the weekends, just to hang out," he says. "Then people start telling you that your beer is great, and you just get this idea in your head. Honestly, he really wanted to do it more than I did. I wanted to get into manufacturing, but not into malt beverages." But he helped his brother get a brewery off the ground before Billy took a corporate move out of state. Scott stayed home, finished the facility, and started operations in Glen Alpine, just west of Morganton.

Catawba Valley Brewing Company began as a one-man operation in the basement of an antique mall. After a year or two, Pyatt could afford to ditch his

Catawba Brewing Company's South Slope taproom is its third location.
Dave Tollefsen, NC Beer Guys

'69 GMC pickup and buy a van as he started driving and selling more beer.

He looks back at those beginnings with a grin. "If I would have known then what I know now, I never would have tried to do what I did with what I had," he says. "We started off with pure junk. It was just stuff we cobbled together. We were both fairly accomplished engineers, so we purpose-built stuff, and we'd take stuff that we liked and convert it into something that we could use. A lot of people probably couldn't make good beer with what we had, and I'm glad we don't have to make good beer on it anymore, because it was a whole lot of work."

Fortunately for Pyatt, the late 1990s were rough for the craft beer industry, so he was able to pick up good used equipment from breweries that were closing in other parts of the country. As he did, Catawba was able to grow.

Almost a decade later, that growth took him out of the basement brewery and down the road to Morganton. The brewery moved into a much larger space with its own interesting history. In the 1950s, the warehouse space had served as a showroom for Heritage-Henredon Furniture Industries' collection of Frank Lloyd Wright–designed furniture, known as "the Taliesin Ensemble." In the 1970s and 1980s, it was a "Wild West nightclub" called Slick Willy's.

In 2007, when Catawba Valley Brewing Company moved in, Pyatt managed to incorporate the best aspects of the building's long history into its new life as a brewery. The facility is not just a brewery but also a large tasting room and bar. Tables and chairs take up most of the available space in the warehouse. A long bar reaches from the brewing area in the back toward a row of garage doors that stand open on warm evenings. The brewery space is compact and efficient. Tall fermentation tanks are lined against the back wall of the brewery, natural light from the old wire-framed windows spilling over them.

Catawba Valley Brewing Company became a community hangout and a place to hear good live music. Pyatt put effort into building a full stage opposite the bar. "If I get interested in something, I like to support it, so we have a great music program," he says. "We have better equipment here than most bands do. We try to make it a pleasure to put on a show here."

The Morganton brewery offers an open mic night every week and has welcomed regional and national acts. It also plays host to a large number of community events such as birthday parties and weddings. "I guess we've done everything here except for a wake," says Pyatt.

But what is most important to Pyatt is his team. "One of the things that happens that really shows me that I'm doing something right is when you look at your employees, and you've got employees who are getting married, they're raising families, they're buying cars, they're buying houses, and you're expanding your brewery family. Having employees that can count on you and work not just for you but with you. You know you're really making it then."

The Catawba team made some big changes between 2013 and 2015. The brewery was rebranded to Catawba Brewing Company and started canning its core beers. Catawba also hired a new head brewer, Kevin Sondey, and opened tasting rooms in the Biltmore Village and South Slope areas of Asheville. The South Slope location has a brewing system as well, and the original Catawba facility in Morganton is also seeing expansion to match the company's growth.

LOE'S BREWING COMPANY

1048 Harper Avenue
Lenoir, NC 28645
828-754-3652
Email: info@loesbrewing.com
Website: loesbrewing.com
Hours: Thursday–Sunday, noon–9 P.M.
Owners: Stephen and Robert Loe
Brewmaster: Stephen Loe
Opened: 2010

LOE'S BREWING COMPANY IS ONE OF THE FEW TRULY FAMILY-OPERATED BREWERIES in North Carolina. Robert Loe has been homebrewing for about 40 years, said his son Stephen in a 2011 interview. "I'm 33, so I've been helping him homebrew since I was pretty little." Stephen himself got into homebrewing around 2006. A Culinary Institute of America graduate, Stephen credits that experience for pushing him toward the brewing industry. "Culinary school helped me develop my palate," he says, "and we were starting to make some pretty good beers, so I kind of went ahead with it."

Stephen put out "maybe 75 to 100 applications" to different breweries around the country, hoping his experience as a homebrewer and his Culinary Institute degree would get him in the door somewhere. But he didn't hear back from any of them, so he decided that doing it himself—or rather, with his family—was the way to go.

Today, three members of the Loe family—Robert, Stephen, and Bobby—run the brewery, all using skills they picked up through different careers to help the operation grow. All three take time on the kettle.

The original Loe's brewery, located in Hickory, was tiny—just a few hundred square feet of space, with a small bar and barely enough room for the family to do the brewing on a 1.5-barrel system. The Loes constructed most of that brewery themselves.

"The idea was to partner up with the restaurant next door," says Stephen. "We were moving from a 1,000-square-foot restaurant to a 6,000-square-foot restaurant, and I was going to lease space for a brewery. The space was set up as a nightclub, and we had to spend three days in there with a jackhammer remodeling."

In 2011, Stephen outlined the family's future plans: "We definitely want to grow. We're starting to do some hand-bottling now to get into stores, and we've considered doing some contract brewing in the future until we can get our own 20-barrel system or something."

In 2012, that "or something" emerged: a new brewpub in downtown Lenoir, just half an hour down the road from their old town of Hickory. Now, Stephen gets to put his culinary skills to use crafting tasty food options to pair with the brewpub's beers, as well as with the guest taps Loe's regularly brings in. The casual, warm, family-friendly atmosphere and the recipes inspired by a variety of food traditions are great reasons to seek out this small brewpub.

The cozy taproom and restaurant of Loe's Brewing Company
Erik Lars Myers

HOWARD BREWING

1001 West Avenue NW
Lenoir, NC 28645
828-572-4449
Email: info@howardbrewing.com
Website: startabrewmance.com/home
Hours: First Wednesday of the month and Thurs-
    day–Friday, 5 P.M.–11 P.M.;
    Saturday, 3 P.M.–11 P.M.
Founder: Jason Howard
Brewer: Jason Howard
Opened: 2012

SCANNING THE SHELVES OF BEER STORES IN WESTERN NORTH CAROLINA, curious drinkers might notice cans with a boldly blocked *H* on the front and energizing names such as Action Man and Trail Maker. These beers are the flagships of Howard Brewing, the first brewery in the town of Lenoir.

Howard Brewing is named for its founder and operator, Jason Howard, who launched himself into the craft beer business after 10 years as a homebrewer. Since he was already a self-employed business owner, Howard felt confident in his ability to open and run a business. But he had less experience in the art of professional brewing. In an interview with Glenn Cutler and Dave Tollefsen as part of their "NC Beer Buzz" series, Howard credited local craft breweries including Catawba and Olde Hickory for inspiration and guidance as he got ready to start his own brand.

When looking for locations, Howard considered multiple towns. Lenoir didn't have a craft brewery, but it did have open warehouse space and the potential for growth, two things that excited Howard.

When he opened his facility on West Avenue, it was just a 15-barrel production brewery with no taproom. Howard focused on packaged sales, but customer demand soon changed his mind, and he carved a taproom out of the corner of his brewery in 2013. Now, drinkers can visit three afternoons and evenings a week to sample the beers at their source. The taproom is a small wood-paneled room with a short bar and lots of tall stools and barrels converted into high-top tables. In addition to serving beer to locals and visitors, the taproom hosts a once-a-month Wednesday charity night called Ales for Trails, which helps raise money to build and improve a local trail.

Unlike many other North Carolina brewers, Howard is not trying to push the envelope with the number of beers he puts out or the styles he brews. Instead, his attention is on consistency and quality, the two characteristics guaranteed to bring drinkers back to his beers again and again. In addition to the four year-round beers he cans, Howard produces two seasonals a year in 22-ounce bottles: his Mistletoe brandy-barrel-aged robust raspberry porter (for winter) and General Lenoir's Old Ale (for spring). That ale is based on a 1795 recipe written by General William Lenoir, making it an interesting throwback to North Carolina's historic beer culture.

Howard's cans and bottles are currently distributed only in the western part of the state. His plans are grounded in gradual expansion, so as to maintain the quality he is so proud of. Hopefully, Howard's beers will one day be available throughout North Carolina.

GRANITE FALLS
BREWING COMPANY

47 Duke Street
Granite Falls, NC 28630
828-212-1222
Email: Mario@granitefallsbrewing.com
Website: granitefallsbrewing.com
Hours: Monday, 11 A.M.–10 P.M.;
    Tuesday, 5 P.M.–10 P.M.;
    Wednesday–Thursday, 11 A.M.–10 P.M.;
    Friday–Saturday, 11 A.M.–11 P.M.;
    Sunday, 11 A.M.–4 P.M.
Founders: Mario Mastroeli and Larissa Mastro
Head Brewer: Joseph Ackerman
Brewing Staff: Jacob Rice
Opened: 2013

outside

GRANITE FALLS BREWING COMPANY IS ONLY A FEW YEARS OLD, but its warehouses have been the site of beverage bottling for over 112 years. The original owners were the Bolick brothers, who founded Granite Bottling Works, a soda-bottling business that remained in operation until 1978, when it was sold to the Pepsi-Cola Bottling Company of Hickory.

When Mario Mastroeli and his wife, Larissa Mastro, purchased the buildings to start their brewery, they were aware of the history but weren't expecting the surprise they found during renovations. "During an expansive buildout and adaptive reuse," Mario explains, "we discovered the 1903 two-story brick Bolick's Bottling Plant preserved behind the 1962 Granite Bottling Works block walls. There is even a hidden attic that stands as it did in 1903." As he puts it, this discovery was "eerie." But it also provided a fascinating connection between the town's history and this modern craft brewery.

The couple's renovations have transformed the old warehouses into a functional production brewery and a bright, cheerful restaurant and bar. The signature Granite Falls blue color can be found on the triangular brick façade and accenting the multiroom restaurant. Booths, tables, and two bars—including, according to Mario, "the longest tasting counter in North Carolina"—give ample room for customers to enjoy the restaurant's expansive food and beverage op-

The beautiful, long tasting counter at Granite Falls Brewing Company
Granite Falls Brewing Company

tions. A wall displaying old-fashioned beer cans reminds visitors of America's beer history, while the taps pour fresh offerings from Granite Falls and other craft breweries.

Granite Falls has almost 40 different beers (and counting) in its repertoire, eight to 10 of which can be found at the restaurant. It has also started bottling some of its year-round beers and distributing them to bottle shops and grocery stores. While the year-round beers follow familiar styles—IPA, blonde ale, Scottish ale—Granite Falls is not afraid to experiment with more elaborate recipes, including such offerings as a peanut butter ale, strawberry jalapeño beer, and beers made with sprite melons, spicebush, and oatmeal cookies.

The response has been enthusiastic. Mario has his eye on growth, with plans to expand his fermentation and bottling capacity in order to reach new markets in the Southeast. However, he also wants to increase traffic to the restaurant so people can experience the beer in its hometown of Granite Falls.

Olde Hickory Taproom:
222 Union Square
Hickory, NC 28601
828-322-1965
Hours: Daily, 11 A.M.–2 A.M.

Amos Howards Brew Pub:
2828 US 70 SW
Hickory, NC 28602
828-323-8753
Hours: Monday–Thursday, 11 A.M.–11 P.M.;
　　Friday–Saturday, 11 A.M.–midnight;
　　Sunday, noon–10 P.M.

Olde Hickory Station:
232 Government Avenue SW
Hickory, NC 28602
828-322-2356
Hours: Daily, 7 A.M.–2 A.M.

Email: info@oldehickorytaproom.com
Website: oldehickorybrewery.com
Owners: Steve Lyerly, Jason Yates
Brewmaster: Steve Lyerly
Opened: 1994

IT'S IMPOSSIBLE TO GO TO HICKORY AND NOT RUN ACROSS OLDE HICKORY somewhere—whether it's the taproom in Union Square, the old brewpub Amos Howards on US 70, or the brewery itself on Third Street. All have become iconic locations in this old textile center.

Steve Lyerly returned to North Carolina in 1994. He had spent years in Missouri during high school and then college, but a job at North Carolina State University enticed him back, and he moved to Hickory to establish residence before applying for the position. He never had that chance.

An avid homebrewer, Lyerly was excited to learn a brewpub was coming to town. He visited before it even opened its doors to ask about volunteering.

Olde Hickory Brewery
Erik Lars Myers

The brewpub, Amos Howards, already had a brewer, a local man by the name of Jim Walker, who was also a homebrewer. In fact, Walker ran something of a homebrew supply shop out of his basement.

As it turned out, being a full-time brewer wasn't in the cards for Walker. He already held a full-time job, and he and his wife had just had twins. "The job was sold to him as, 'You can just come in on Saturdays and make some beer,' but it just doesn't work that way commercially," says Lyerly. "So Jim got frustrated very quickly and decided that it just wasn't what he wanted to do. I just ended up being the only person left standing in the building who knew anything about beer, and I talked the ownership into giving me a shot."

The brewery didn't exactly have the best equipment. In fact, the owners of Amos Howards had bought reclaimed dairy equipment from Highland Brewing Company in Asheville—the same equipment John McDermott, Highland's first brewer, had adapted for use in its initial facility. Some of it still resides at Amos Howards today.

Soon after Amos Howards opened, Lyerly met the person who would eventually become his business partner. Jason Yates was an engineer at a textile mill in nearby Morganton, where, Lyerly says, "they had a huge boneyard full of stainless-steel tanks perfect for a brewery." The two started planning a joint venture in which they would open their own operation not as a brewpub but as a packaging brewery. The owners of Amos Howards, however, caught wind of the plan and made an offer instead. Almost a year after Amos Howards opened, Lyerly and Yates bought it from the original six investors. They had their brewery.

Soon after the purchase, the pair also bought a little deli in a historic building in downtown Hickory's Union Square and started renovating it. After about a year and a half of remodeling, they opened Olde Hickory Taproom. Today, the taproom, which occupies a prominent location on the square, is often filled with happy patrons. It's a warm, welcoming environment with one room of comfortable tables and booths and a long, dimly lit bar featuring a couple of dozen taps, liquor, and rows of pewter mugs hanging ready for the regulars they belong to.

Opening the taproom, Lyerly says, completely drained their capacity at Amos Howards. That's when the partners started looking to expand into a production facility. They found another space and opened a packaging facility on Third Street in 2000, starting with used equipment from the Middlesex and Pilgrim brewing companies in Massachusetts.

The production brewery is like many others: lined with tanks. In fact, it has more than most breweries of its size. Olde Hickory's production facility also contains its own little taproom, an array of equipment that could almost serve as a brewery museum, and barrels. Barrels are everywhere, stacked high wherever there's room for them. Not only does Olde Hickory barrel-age its own beers—its barleywine, its Irish Walker, and some of its imperial stouts—it also ages Olde Rabbit's Foot, the collaborative blend it releases each year in conjunction with Foothills Brewing and The Duck-Rabbit Craft Brewery.

Olde Hickory has expanded its production in recent years and has grown its distribution around the state, switching from 22-ounce bottles to six-packs of 12-ounce bottles for most of its core beers. In addition, Lyerly and Yates opened a fourth location in Hickory in June 2013, remodeling the old train station to create a combination bakery/deli/café that features 50-plus taps of craft beer—many of them, of course, from Olde Hickory itself.

CHARLOTTE AREA BREWERIES

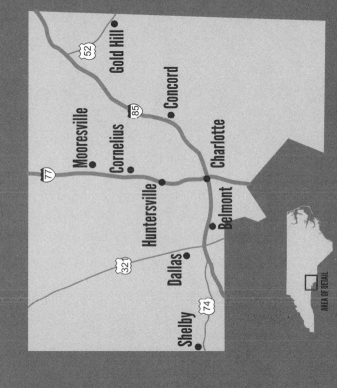

N

Shelby
Newgrass Brewing Company

Dallas
Ole Dallas Brewery

Belmont
Rivermen Brewing Company

Huntersville
Primal Brewery

Cornelius
Bayne Brewing Company
Ass Clown Brewing Company
D9 Brewing Company

Mooresville
Lake Norman Brewing Company

Concord
High Branch Brewing Company

Charlotte
The Olde Mecklenburg Brewery
Sugar Creek Brewing Company
Three Spirits Brewery
Triple C Brewing Company
Lenny Boy Brewing Company
Sycamore Brewing
The Unknown Brewing Company
Wooden Robot Brewery
Birdsong Brewing Company
NoDa Brewing Company
Free Range Brewing
Heist Brewery

Gold Hill
Morgan Ridge Vineyards & Brewhouse

AREA OF DETAIL

NEWGRASS BREWING COMPANY

213 South Lafayette Street
Shelby, NC 28150
704-937-1280
Email: info@newgrassbrewing.com
Website: newgrassbrewing.com/home
Hours: Tuesday–Thursday, 4 P.M.–10 P.M.;
    Friday, 4 P.M.–midnight; Saturday, 11 A.M.–
    midnight; Sunday, noon–10 P.M.
Brewery Manager: Jordan Boinest
Brewmaster: Lewis McCallister
Brewing Staff: Dustin Di Lorenzo, Devin Hollowell
Opened: 2015

DRIVING DOWN SOUTH LAFAYETTE STREET IN SHELBY, visitors will notice an eye-catching sign at the corner of East Arey Street proclaiming Newgrass Brewing Company. The storefront has a retro look, which is fitting for this building over 100 years old. Formerly Hudson's Department Store, it stood empty for a long time before Newgrass moved in. Now, freshly renovated, it acts as a food-and-beverage hub in the uptown district of Shelby.

A group of investors provided the money for the transformation, but the people driving Newgrass forward are Jordan Boinest and Lewis McCallister. Jordan, a Shelby native, and Lewis, who has family ties to the area, are deeply invested in what their brewery can contribute to the local area. The taproom is floored with wood from a local textile mill that used to employ a large number of Shelby citizens. Jordan and Lewis also work with a nearby farm to source ingredients for some of their beers (including their seasonal Belgian dubbel, made with pumpkins and figs) and with a local coffee roaster to make a coffee stout. Their beer names have a local focus, too, referencing North Carolina's trademark red clay and the Big Broad River.

Newgrass sends a few kegs to western North Carolina accounts, but most of its beer stays in the taproom, where a lively crowd keeps it moving. The two-level seating area has room to host convivial groups enjoying Newgrass's food and beer and the regular live music performed on the stage. Music is important to the Shelby area, as might be guessed by the Newgrass logo: the head of a guitar blended with a beer bottle. The brewery is located between two music-related venues named after famous local men: the Don Gibson Theater and the Earl Scruggs Center. Newgrass fills the niche as a music venue for local and regional acts not big enough to play the Don Gibson Theater—yet. Expansive windows behind the stage and the bar allow visitors a view of the brewing equipment and barrel storage, visually bringing together the different components that make Newgrass a unique location in Cleveland County.

OLE DALLAS BREWERY

136 Durkee Lane
Dallas, NC 28034
704-266-1472
Website: oledallasbrewery.com
Founders: Chris and Cliff Cloninger, Beau Nor-
    wood, Kyle Britton
Head Brewer: Beau Norwood
Opened: 2015

ALTHOUGH OLE DALLAS BREWERY DOES NOT HAVE A TAPROOM YET, it does have an amazing place patrons can go to try its beer over the summer months: the Gastonia Grizzlies' ballpark, which hosts the local collegiate summer baseball league. In the ballpark's beer garden, Ole Dallas features all the beer it can squeeze out on its half-barrel system, including the official beer of the Grizzlies: Chizz Ale, named after Chizzle, the Grizzlies' mascot.

The partners behind Ole Dallas Brewery are all born-and-bred natives of Dallas, North Carolina. It seems only natural that they would partner up to start a business. In fitting fashion, Chris Cloninger and Beau Norwood played baseball together in high school. In fact, all the partners knew each other in high school, grew up together, and call Dallas their home.

The brewery is a tribute to the town they know and love. Their beers are even named after local legends and locales—such as Old George's Porter, named after George Mifflin Dallas, the 11th vice president of the United States and the town's namesake, and Wildcat Wit, a nod to the North Gaston High School mascot.

In the baseball off-season, Ole Dallas's beers may be found at bars in town and increasingly in other accounts around the Gastonia area. The partners are working on creating Ole Dallas's new taproom location, which should open in 2016.

52 Ervin Street
Belmont, NC 28012
704-363-4698
Email: pat@rivermenbrewingcompany.com
Website: rivermenbrewingcompany.com
Hours: Sunday–Thursday, 11 A.M.–9 P.M.;
    Friday–Saturday, 11 A.M.–10 P.M.
Owner: Pat Brennan
Brewers: Pat Brennan, Jonathan Fulcher
Opened: 2015

CHARLOTTE IS KNOWN FOR ITS GROWING BEER SCENE. But west of the outer loop, the town of Belmont is also riding the craft beverage wave. In 2011, Muddy River Distillery opened in an old mill complex. Rivermen Brewing Company joined it in the late spring of 2015.

Rivermen opened in the same building complex as Muddy River, a deliberate decision by Rivermen's owner, Pat Brennan, who figured that a building zoned to allow a distillery would also be able to accommodate a brewery. He was right about that and was soon able to install his small brewing system and a taproom in his leased space.

Brennan's background is in banking, but his two longtime hobbies were whitewater paddling and brewing beer at home. Conversations with his paddling friends over beer led Brennan to the idea that he could turn one of those hobbies into a busy and fulfilling career. With encouragement and support from those friends, he launched himself into the world of professional brewing.

Rivermen started as a small operation. It brews in two-barrel fermenters and keeps about five beers on tap in its small taproom, in addition to sending kegs to bar and restaurant accounts in the area. The local response has been enough to keep Brennan busy. Luckily, he has help on the brewing side, thanks to Jonathan Fulcher, his co-brewer. Fulcher has a longer history in Charlotte beer. He was the brewer and one of the founders of Four Friends, a craft brewery that operated from 2010 to 2014. Fulcher's original background was in IT. Like Brennan, he jettisoned an unsatisfactory career and turned his homebrewing into a profession. Now, the two men spend their time crafting brews for the thirsty people of Gaston County.

At the moment, Rivermen rotates through about seven different recipes. Though its beers are in familiar styles, it highlights the ones that might be less common in the market: Scottish ale and black IPA, for example. Rivermen also stands out in the market because it makes and bottles its own nonalcoholic root beer, which it sells at the taproom and in local stores.

Though less than a year old as of this writing, Rivermen is riding the craft beer wave and already working on an expansion. It's planning to move out of the old mill complex and into a larger space closer to the heart of Belmont, which is set to open in the spring of 2016.

PRIMAL BREWERY

16432 Old Statesville Road
Huntersville, NC 28078
704-947-2920
Email: info@primalbrewery.com
Website: primalbrewery.com
Hours: Tuesday–Thursday, 4 P.M.–10 P.M.;
    Friday–Saturday, noon–11 P.M.;
    Sunday, noon–8 P.M.
Founders: Ray Steimel, David Hoy
Head Brewer: Dan Scheifen
Opened: 2014

VISITORS LOOKING FOR PRIMAL BREWERY IN HUNTERSVILLE will have an easy time finding it. The brewery is right on a main road, and a bold sign with Primal's eye-catching logo sits proudly next to the street.

Primal's welcoming vibe continues inside the taproom, which has a cozy living-room feel. One section of the room features a stone-lined fireplace fronted by comfortable leather couches and chairs, while the other contains light wood tables and a bar serving up 10 to 12 taps of Primal's beer. There are no televisions, which keeps the taproom's focus on friendly conversations and family get-togethers, as founders Ray Steimel and David Hoy intended.

Steimel and Hoy found their way to brewing through friendship. Steimel coached Hoy's daughter in soccer, and the two men started talking. Neither was a homebrewer at the time, but Hoy adopted the hobby, Steimel started brewing with him, and the hobby grew into something more. As Steimel explains, "We love beer. After home-brewing with friends for years, we decided to share the craft with all of Huntersville."

They applied their business experience to starting their new venture and found the funding to get Primal off the ground. As part of their plan, they hired Dan Scheifen as head brewer to help them scale up their recipes for their new three-barrel system.

Primal's beers range across a variety of classic styles, including American lager, IPA, pale ale, and porter. Flavors such as hazelnut and caraway sometimes put in an appearance in their recipes, but beers containing those ingredients don't dominate the list. Fresh, drinkable beer is Primal's goal.

Primal Brewery's cozy fireplace creates a comfortable environment to enjoy a pint.
Erik Lars Myers

With two successful years of business under its belt, it looks like Primal has the people of Huntersville and the surrounding area on board with what it's doing.

BAYNE BREWING COMPANY

19507 West Catawba Avenue
Cornelius, NC 28031
704-897-6426
Email: baynebrew@gmail.com
Website: baynebrewingcompany.com
Hours: Thursday–Friday, 4 P.M.–10 P.M.;
    Saturday, 2 P.M.–10 P.M.;
    Sunday, noon–8 P.M.
Founders: Chris and Sean Bayne
Head Brewer: Chris Bayne
Opened: 2014

CORNELIUS, A SMALL TOWN NORTH OF CHARLOTTE, is developing its own independent craft beer scene. The opening of Bayne Brewing Company in December 2014 brought the number of breweries in town to three.

Chris Bayne was inspired by the success of the other Cornelius breweries, Ass Clown and D9, to take his homebrewing hobby and launch a career of professional brewing. Chris and his brother, Sean, are the official founders of the company, but Bayne Brewing is a family business in the truest sense, with Chris and Sean's family members pitching in to help run the public and business sides of the operation.

Bayne is a nanobrewery, making just two barrels of beer at a time. While it distributes kegs to a few local accounts, the best place to try its beer is at its taproom. Bayne's location is a storefront in an ordinary-looking shopping center, which drives home how much the craft beer movement these days is about local small businesses. A few parking spaces in front have been sectioned off to create a small outdoor seating area. Inside, visitors find a cozy neighborhood taproom. In one corner, a couch and some chairs are arranged around a coffee table, while other spots are filled with high-top tables and barstools. The metal-faced bar occupies another corner, with televisions hanging above it.

Wooden tap handles in a variety of shapes (including a beer bottle) pour Bayne's eight beers. Its core flavors are classic—pale ale, IPA, and brown ale—

The brewery equipment of this nanobrewery is on display behind the bar.
Erik Lars Myers

but its rotating selections branch out into smoked, coffee, coconut, and other flavors to tease more adventurous palates and showcase the range of Chris Bayne's tastes.

ASS CLOWN BREWING COMPANY

10620 Bailey Road, Suites E and F
Cornelius, NC 28031
704-995-7767
Email: matt@assclownbeer.com
Website: assclownbrewing.com
Hours: Tuesday–Thursday, 3 P.M.–9 P.M.;
 Friday–Saturday, noon–10 P.M.
Owner: Matt Glidden
Brewmaster: Matt Glidden
Opened: 2011

ASS CLOWN BREWING COMPANY HAS A NONTRADITIONAL STARTUP STORY in an industry built out of them. When the brewery opened, it was located in just about the last place anyone would expect: inside a mortgage company office, in a space labeled, "Interesting Mortgages." Visitors had no way to know that the first brewery in Cornelius was in operation.

"It was kind of a joke to begin with," says Matt Glidden of his brewing company's name. Glidden is a big fan of beer festivals, but he's always had one complaint: afterward, when people ask him what he liked, he can never remember anything specific. "I thought, *If these companies would focus more on some sort of whacked-out name that I can't forget, then my chances of remembering them would be better.*" The name came to him later. "I used to have a coworker who was a good buddy that used to call me an ass clown, and I'd kind of throw it back at him, and after a while we were just calling everybody ass clowns. It was kind of catchy, and I just thought I'd see how far we could go with it."

Like most small brewers, Glidden started out of his garage as a homebrewer. That was back in 2003. He used to share his beer with friends and neighbors. When he noticed the crowds getting bigger and bigger, he decided to give brewing a shot, mainly as an exploratory effort.

"When I started looking into making the jump, I kind of knew mortgages weren't going to be around forever, so I figured it would be nice to get slowly

The laughing visage of Ass Clown's logo greets people as they enter.
Erik Lars Myers

into brewing and see if I'd fall on my ass or if I'd be able to make a decent living out of it," he says.

Despite the "whacked-out" name, Glidden had serious plans for his company, and he's seen them come to fruition. Ass Clown no longer shares office space with Glidden's mortgage company. It now has its own comfortable taproom a few miles from its original site. The new location is in an industrial park, and it's much easier to find.

The laughing visage of the company's logo looks down over the brewery's front door. Inside, Ass Clown is warm and comfortable. Patrons are greeted by low, soft seating in front of an enormous Ass Clown tapestry. A collection of small tables leads to a bar with an impressive 31-tap lineup. The tap handles are creative and beautiful—a range of cooking utensils, handyman's tools, and Ass Clown's signature bicycle horn. Kitty-corner from the bar, a neatly curated display of bottles from other breweries makes for a beautiful reminder of the art of the craft-brewing industry.

The beer is as creative as the décor. As a brewer, Glidden likes to experiment. He counts Sam Calagione from Dogfish Head Brewery in Milton, Delaware, as an inspiration, even citing Calagione's startup model. "My niche is that I'm looking for an odd or a unique flavoring that's not out there. In my head, you don't really know what you might stumble across unless you try new things."

Originally, his brewery's small size allowed him room to experiment, but he now has a considerably larger system, brewing about 10 times as much on his 8.5-barrel system.

Although Glidden bottles and distributes some of his most popular beers in the Charlotte area, the best place to experience Ass Clown is right at the taproom, where you can relax and enjoy the quirky, yet delicious, experimentation taking place at this unique brewery.

GROWTH AND PLANNING

Because of the exponential and exciting growth of North Carolina craft breweries, many businesses are in development or temporarily closed for expansion or relocation. At the time of this writing, more than 60 breweries were in the planning stages in North Carolina. Many of them will open swiftly—and some before this book is even published!

Unfortunately, some successful breweries are not fully covered in these pages, since they were not producing beer at the time of this writing. They are:

- Bessemer City Brewing Company, originally located inside The Whiskey Mill, a popular restaurant in Bessemer City. As of this writing, the brewery was closed for expansion.

- New Sarum Brewing Company in Salisbury. As of this writing, New Sarum was undergoing a large expansion including a 30-barrel brewhouse, a range of 90-barrel fermenters, a canning line, and a tasting room.

- Barking Duck Brewing Company, originally located in Mint Hill, is seeking to open in a new location in 2016.

D9 BREWING COMPANY

11138-C Treynorth Drive
Cornelius, NC 28031
704-457-9368
Email: info@d9brewing.com
Website: d9brewing.com
Hours: Monday–Friday, 2 P.M.–10 P.M.;
    Saturday, noon–10 P.M.; Sunday, 1 P.M.–8 P.M.
Founders: Andrew Durstewitz, Aaron Burton,
    John Ashcraft
Head Brewer: Aaron Burton
Brewing Staff: Gregg Merryman, William
    Horlacher
Opened: 2013

LIKE MANY CRAFT BREWERIES, D9 STARTED WITH FRIENDS, a homebrew system, and a dream.

Andrew Durstewitz, Aaron Burton, and John Ashcraft began brewing beer together as a hobby and a break from their regular jobs. As word spread about their beers, the brewing parties in Durstewitz's garage got bigger—too big, it turned out. "Our HOA almost kicked us out of the neighborhood for how big our brewing parties had become," admits Durstewitz. "This, essentially, is what led to us starting a commercial location." They formulated a plan, rented a space, and named themselves D9 after District 9, the congressional district that serves the town of Cornelius.

D9's first licensed brewery was a small space in an industrial park right around the corner from another Cornelius brewery, Ass Clown. With its one-barrel brewing system, D9 was the definition of a nanobrewery. But its 2013 opening was successful, and the partners quickly planned a significant expansion. In 2014, they moved the operation to a much larger space and upgraded to a 10-barrel system.

The move, less than a mile in distance, was a huge step forward. Although the new space has the blocky, white façade of an office park, the striking two-story sign and stenciled designs on the windows signifying hops, malt, water,

The brewhouse at D9 Brewing Company
Erik Lars Myers

and other symbols of brewing lend the building a bold personality that matches D9's approach. Inside, a wooden-backed bar holds down the corner of the high-ceilinged taproom, while tables and chairs spread across the room to accommodate the craft beer fans seeking D9 beer at its source.

D9's list of "Fanatical Ales" is a mix of "unique and trusted styles," according to Durstewitz. IPAs are part of its year-round lineup, but D9's special kick is its wild and sour beer program, headlined by its Viking Fraoch Scottish sour ale. This beer and some others are bottled for sale in limited quantities. But the easiest way to find D9 beer is to get it on tap in the Charlotte, Asheville, Triad, and Triangle areas.

So far, brewing has been an adventure for the three founders. Durstewitz explains that "learning the business of beer" was a challenge for the team. "It's one thing to know how to brew, and yet another to know how to scale your brews. It's a completely different thing to know how to build a business around brewing."

However, if D9's early expansion is any indication, the three friends have faced that challenge head-on and are ready to take on the next ones as they come.

LAKE NORMAN

LAKE NORMAN BREWING COMPANY

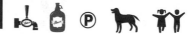

159 Barley Park Lane
Mooresville, NC 28115
704-660-1182
Email: mike@lakenormanbrewingcompany.com
Website: lakenormanbrewingcompany.com
Hours: Thursday–Friday, 4 P.M.–8 P.M.;
  Saturday, 2 P.M.–8 P.M.
Founders: Mike and Andy Prascak
Head Brewer: Sterling Smith
Opened: 2013

NOT FAR FROM THE SPRAWLING SHORES OF LAKE NORMAN lie the town of Mooresville and Lake Norman Brewing Company. It isn't the only brewing company near the lake, which stretches down to Huntersville and Cornelius, but it is the only one to take North Carolina's largest man-made lake as its inspiration. The Lake Norman name was first used for a brewery in the late 1990s. But that operation soon closed, and the name remained untapped until homebrewer Mike Prascak and his son, Andy, decided to launch their brewery in Mooresville.

Unlike Mooresville's former craft brewery, Carolina Beer and Beverage (which sold its craft beer brands to Foothills in 2011), Lake Norman Brewing Company has a small and local focus. When the brewery started, its system made less than a barrel of beer at a time, and it didn't have a taproom, just keg accounts in the area. Its growth has been slow and organic. In 2014, it opened a small taproom to sell pints and growlers to thirsty locals and visitors. And in the fall of 2015, it put in a five-barrel system. Andy left the company, and a new brewer, Sterling Smith, came on to take over the beers.

Lake Norman's recipes are designed to call out to recreational drinkers. Names such as Dockside Blonde, Outboard Amber, and Pontoon Pale Ale fit seamlessly with the brewery's laid-back atmosphere and its tap handles, which sport small propellers. About eight Lake Norman beers are on tap at any given time. Drinkers looking for strange or unusual styles won't find them here; Lake Norman's beers are all variations on classic styles. It is easy to picture them accompanying a relaxed fishing trip, a group hang-out, or a friendly game of cornhole (something patrons can enjoy at the taproom on a nice day).

More changes are on the horizon for Lake Norman Brewing. In January 2016, Mike Prascak announced he was selling the company to two investors, Darrin Jones and Robert Whitaker. Prascak plans to stay on with the company, helping it to expand beyond its current footprint and strengthen Mooresville's brewing culture.

HIGH BRANCH
BREWING COMPANY

325 McGill Avenue, Suite 148
Concord, NC 28027
704-706-3807
Email: info@highbranchbrewing.com
Website: highbranchbrewing.com
Hours: Friday, 4 P.M.–10 P.M.;
    Saturday, 2 P.M.–10 P.M.
Founders: T. J. and Maureen Creighton
Head Brewer: T. J. Creighton
Opened: 2015

HIGH BRANCH BREWING COMPANY HAS THE DISTINCTION OF BEING THE FIRST craft brewery in Concord, something owner and brewer T. J. Creighton is proud of.

High Branch is part of the redevelopment of an old mill building, Gibson Mill, and is just one of many businesses to call the space home. Visitors to Creighton's small, high-ceilinged space will find a rustic taproom that embraces the rough brick walls and exposed beams of the old building. The beer list behind the bar is made out of an old wooden pallet painted with chalkboard paint, each slat advertising a different brew.

At this point, High Branch serves five or six of its beers at any given time, all brewed on the 1.5-barrel system visible through a window in the taproom wall. Creighton, who owns High Branch with his wife, Maureen, is the man running the show. He's a homebrewer who taught himself the skills he needed to scale his recipes up to his nano-sized system.

Creighton is focused on building his local audience and developing his production schedule. While craft brewing is new to Concord, he knows he won't be alone for long—at least one other brewery is planning to open nearby. He finds that prospect exciting, figuring that more breweries will encourage beer tourism in Concord, just a half-hour from Charlotte.

Someday, Creighton hopes to reach beyond his taproom to outside accounts. But for now, a visit to Concord is in order for those wishing to try his artisanal beer.

THE OLDE MECKLENBURG BREWERY

4150 Yancey Road
Charlotte, NC 28217
704-525-5644
Email: info@oldemeckbrew.com
Website: oldemeckbrew.com
Hours: Sunday–Thursday, 11 A.M.–10 P.M.;
    Friday–Saturday, 11 A.M.–11 P.M.
Founder: John Marrino
Head Brewer: Carey Savoy
Brewing Staff: Brett Batista, Chase Petrovic
Opened: 2009

outside

JOHN MARRINO SPENT 16 YEARS IN A FIELD SOMEWHAT—but not completely—similar to beer. During his time in the water treatment industry, he traveled all over the world, from Los Angeles to Germany to London to Charlotte. It wasn't until after he left the business that he thought about getting into beer.

"I was actually camping with my family in Montana," he says. "I had picked up a paper and was reading an article about somebody up in New England working on rebuilding the old Narragansett brewery, and it struck me that there were no breweries in Charlotte. I told my wife that I'd go back to Charlotte and open a brewery, and that's what I did."

When Marrino got home, he began putting his business plan together, then started teaching himself about beer. He converted his garage into a brewery and "bought every book known to man" to figure out how to pursue his new career path. "I figured that if I was going to start a brewery, then I'd better learn how to make beer." A year and a half later, The Olde Mecklenburg Brewery opened its doors.

The brewery focuses on German-style beers, adhering closely to the Reinheitsgebot, the Bavarian Purity Law of 1516, which states that all beer should be made of just barley, water, and hops. "I lived in Germany for four years," says Marrino, "and I just like German beer." That plan proved ideal for his part of the state. Charlotte and Mecklenburg County are both named after Charlotte

Taps line up before a wall of glassware at Olde Mecklenburg Brewery's indoor beer garden.
Erlk Lars Myers

of Mecklenburg-Strelitz, who became Queen Charlotte when she married King George III of England. "It fits in with the character of the area," Marrino says of his German beers. He also notes that few breweries focus exclusively on German styles. "Most of the breweries you see out there are making either English- or Belgian-style beers, and I like to be a little different. That's just the way I am."

When it opened its first location, at 215 Southside Drive, The Olde Mecklenburg Brewery was the only craft brewery in Charlotte. The high quality of its beer and the welcoming atmosphere of its taproom and *Biergarten* built a broad and enthusiastic customer base. The taproom became a popular hangout for the burgeoning craft beer crowd in Charlotte. Popularity has led to growth. In 2014, the brewery moved down the block to a much larger facility, which has allowed it to significantly expand its production of kegs and bottles, as well as the taproom and *Biergarten*.

Throughout the growth, Marrino and the team at Olde Mecklenburg have kept their eyes on two goals: quality and freshness. The beer served at the taproom and in the *Biergarten* comes directly from cold serving tanks in the brewery. Out in the market, Olde Mecklenburg manages its own distribution with a fleet of refrigerated trucks that keep the beer at peak condition until it reaches retailers, so that it is "Always Cold, Never Old."

In 2012, Marrino's goal was "to continue to make Charlotte into a good craft beer location." The explosive growth of craft breweries since then suggests that his wish has become reality, and that Olde Mecklenburg's pioneering influence has led the way.

SUGAR CREEK
BREWING COMPANY

215 Southside Drive
Charlotte, NC 28217
704-521-3333
Email: info@sugarcreekbrewing.com
Website: sugarcreekbrewing.com
Hours: Monday–Wednesday, 4 P.M.–9 P.M.;
    Thursday, 4 P.M.–10 P.M.;
    Friday, 2 P.M.–10 P.M.;
    Saturday, 11 A.M.–10 P.M.;
    Sunday, noon–8 P.M.
Founders: Joe Vogelbacher, Eric Flanigan, Todd
    Franklin
Head Brewer: Todd Franklin
Brewing Staff: Justin Dovenmuehle, Andy Blake
Opened: 2014

CHOOSING THE LOCATION OF A NEW CRAFT BREWERY can be a tricky proposition. Owners have to consider zoning, size, accessibility, and a host of other variables. Luckily for the owners of Sugar Creek Brewing, their location came preapproved and even included its own brewing equipment. That's because Sugar Creek opened in the building formerly occupied by a Charlotte brewing stalwart, The Olde Mecklenburg Brewery, which relocated to a larger space down the street in 2014.

While the location and equipment are familiar to Charlotte craft beer fans, Sugar Creek is no copy of Olde Mecklenburg or any other brewery in the area. Instead, its distinctive branding and focus on Belgian beer bring a new dimension to the Charlotte craft scene.

Sugar Creek is the brainchild of two men: Joe Vogelbacher and Eric Flanigan. Vogelbacher's background is local—the house he grew up in was on the bank of Sugar Creek—though he joined the Merchant Marine Academy and traveled widely before settling back in Charlotte. Flanigan also traveled. As a member of the United States Marine Corps, he served in both Afghanistan and Iraq. Afterward, he settled in Charlotte and became involved in running the local restaurant and night spot Whisky River.

Sugar Creek Brewing Company's taproom offers views of its brewery and is overseen by a large balloon.
Erik Lars Myers

The opportunity to open Sugar Creek pulled both men into the world of professional brewing. The third member of their team is Todd Franklin, the head brewer. He got his start homebrewing, something he pursued as a hobby while a nuclear engineer for a shipbuilding company in Newport News, Virginia. Now, Todd applies that engineering experience to Sugar Creek's 15-barrel brewing system and to producing an array of high-quality beers.

Sugar Creek's name was inspired by Vogelbacher's childhood home on the creek, which was, as Franklin explains, "once the most polluted stream in Mecklenburg County." The fish in the brewery's logo is a clown trigger fish, which "represents the return of fish to Little Sugar Creek, as well as the restoration of natural beauty and cleanliness to the area."

Sugar Creek advertises itself as Charlotte's first Belgian-style brewery. Most of its beers are modeled after those brewed in farmhouses and monasteries in that country. When asked about the theme, Franklin says, "We fell in love with Belgian-style beers because there's room to break the rules and create a complex and magical experience for craft beer drinkers to discover." Two of Sugar Creek's core recipes are a Belgian witbier and an award-winning dubbel. It also serves occasional non-Belgian styles, including its pale ale and porter. Sugar Creek has recently added a bottling line, so some of its styles are available in 12- or 22-ounce bottles in Charlotte and select other parts of the state. It also sends kegs to local accounts.

A visit to the taproom is well worth the trip. Although they took over an existing taproom, the Sugar Creek team put their own stamp on the space. Blue tiles back the bar, picking up the blue-painted Sugar Creek name that decorates the wall above the windows separating the brewing area from the taproom. Hanging in the corner is a three-dimensional version of the brewery's striking logo. The logo—a hot-air balloon with a rowboat and a fish tied below it—was allegedly inspired by the poster for the 1988 movie *The Adventures of Baron Munchausen.* That logo suggests the heights Sugar Creek aspires to, as well as the whimsical and creative journey it hopes to take to get there.

Growing a brewery isn't easy, but Franklin and his partners are enjoying the ride. "Even in the daily, weekly, and monthly grind, we are fortunate to work in an industry that we are passionate about," he says. "Having just recently celebrated our first anniversary, we are so proud of how far we have come in just one year's time."

THREE SPIRITS BREWERY

5046 Old Pineville Road, Suite 110
Charlotte, NC 28217
980-207-4881
Email: threespiritsbrewery@gmail.com
Website: threespiritsbrewery.com
Hours: Thursday–Friday, 4 P.M.–8 P.M.;
   Saturday, 2 P.M.–8 P.M.
Founders: Jennifer and Mwatabu Terrell
Head Brewer: Mwatabu Terrell
Assistant Brewer: Matthew Thomas
Opened: 2015

MWATABU TERRELL, CO-OWNER OF ONE OF CHARLOTTE'S NEWEST BREWER-
IES, always thought he might start a brewery . . . later, after he retired from his
career as a doctor.

He had started homebrewing for fun, to give himself a mental break from
the demanding life of a medical student. And it remained just fun until things
changed. As Mwatabu—who usually goes by Tabu—explains, the brewery's
name and his career change were inspired by a classic story, Charles Dickens's
A Christmas Carol. The friendly Tabu doesn't seem to have much, if anything,
in common with Scrooge or the ghosts who haunt him. But he explains it this
way: "This is my second career, after being an emergency medicine physician.
And like Ebenezer, I found myself working for all of the wrong reasons, and I'm
now trying to get back to being the person I once was and putting my family first
again."

Tabu is also clear that he wouldn't be where he is without the support of his
family, especially his wife and co-owner, Jennifer. When Tabu first brought up
the idea of a brewery, "I thought she was annoyed, as she just got up and left the
room," he recalls. "But she came back with her laptop and the Siebel Institute's
homepage up." Tabu took time off over the next two and a half years to get his
degree in brewing. "My friends still joke that I am the only person with a professional degree to go back to school and get an associate's degree," he admits.
But it's an accomplishment he is proud of, and that pride has transferred to his
brewery.

A classy British pub façade makes getting a beer at Three Spirits even more enjoyable.
Erik Lars Myers

Like many North Carolina craft breweries, Three Spirits is located in an industrial building. But Tabu has added a façade designed to look like an English pub. It looks incongruous next to the rest of the building but suggests the welcoming interior visitors will find. The taproom is a long space that stretches to the back of the building, where a garage door lets out onto a small patio. Scattered tables and a substantial bar fill the spacious room, creating space for friendly conversations and convivial drinks while watching the current sporting event on TV.

The brewing side of Three Spirits is all business. The 10-barrel system and fermenters fit comfortably inside the large space. The brewery definitely has room to grow.

Three Spirits has four flagship beers right now: a porter, an IPA, a golden ale, and an amber lager. As Tabu explains, his goal is to brew "what we call comfort beers." His flagships and the seasonals he is planning promise to live up to this goal of being balanced and approachable. Three Spirits is also "a little less hop-driven than most other breweries."

Tabu is still ramping up his brewery. Looking forward, he is most interested in getting the word out about his venture. He plans to attend festivals, "to start to can our most popular beers, and to spread our footprint in the Charlotte area through distribution to bars and restaurants."

Look for a larger presence for Three Spirits beer—heralded by the reformed curmudgeon on its label—in the near future.

TRIPLE C BREWING COMPANY

2900 Griffith Street
Charlotte, NC 28203
980-585-1728
Email: info@triplecbrewing.com
Website: triplecbrewing.com/home
Hours: Tuesday–Friday, 4 P.M.–9 P.M.;
    Saturday, noon–9 P.M.;
    Sunday, noon–6 P.M.
Founders: Chris Harker, Chris and Christina
    Murphy
Head Brewer: Scott Kimball
Assistant Brewers: Sam Fonda, David Carey,
    Tyler Hamelin
Opened: 2012

PEOPLE WHO WANT TO KNOW HOW WELL CRAFT BEER IS DOING IN CHAR-
LOTTE need only look at Triple C Brewing to find their answer. Triple C opened
in 2012, during the first half of the Charlotte craft beer wave. In the short time
since, it's gone through one major expansion and is on the brink of another.
All of this says good things about Charlotte beer—and about the business at
Triple C.

Triple C was founded in 2012 by current owner Chris Harker and two of
his friends, Chris and Christina Murphy (hence "Triple C"). Harker and the
Murphys were homebrewing friends who made the shift to the professional
craft beer world. Although they had their own recipes and ideas, the founders
went looking for a brewer with professional experience to helm their brewhouse.
They found not another C, but rather Scott Kimball. Kimball had been brewing
professionally for three years, first at Fordham and Old Dominion Brewing in
Delaware (two breweries that merged in 2007) and later at Eddyline Brewing in
Colorado. He was ready for a change, and Triple C's offer seemed like the right
move.

A glance at Triple C's flagship lineup will confirm that its tastes tend toward
hoppy and light. Five of the seven beers fit into the realm of pale ales or IPAs.

The brewhouse peeks through the window into Triple C's crowded taproom.
Erik Lars Myers

Triple C has won acclaim for its hoppy beers. In 2015, its 3C IPA brought home a bronze medal from the Great American Beer Festival in the Strong Pale Ale category. It is also one of the few breweries in North Carolina to have a smoked ale as one of its core beers.

Triple C is located in a large brick warehouse at the intersection of Griffith Street and Fairwood Avenue. Patrons can enjoy the casual outdoor seating or the spacious, modern-looking taproom. The light wood tables and wall accents, the white paint, and the skeletal metal beams framing the ceiling all lend an upscale industrial air to the bar area. A brightly colored sign above the taps announces the menu of the day, while a wide window allows drinkers a view into the brewing area.

The brewing room is where Triple C has seen the most expansion. It still has its original 15-barrel system, but in the spring of 2015 it installed more—and larger—fermenters, a grain silo, and a canning line (it had already begun bottling in 22-ounce bottles). The goal of that expansion is to grow production so Triple C can widen its distribution area. Up next, according to recent news, is a physical expansion into a nearby warehouse that Triple C hopes to transform into a barrel-aging space, increased storage, and an event venue.

It is safe to say that Charlotte beer is booming.

LENNY BOY
BREWING COMPANY

2224 Hawkins Street
Charlotte, NC 28203
980-585-1728
Email: info@discoverlennyboy.com
Website: discoverlennyboy.com
Hours: Thursday–Friday, 4 P.M.–9 P.M.;
    Saturday, noon–9 P.M.; Sunday, noon–6 P.M.
Founder: Townes Mozer
Head Brewer: John Watkins
Opened: 2013

FERMENTATION CAN BE ABOUT MORE THAN JUST BEER.
Townes Mozer of Lenny Boy Brewing would certainly agree. Like many brewery founders, he started experimenting with fermentation at home. But in Mozer's case, the fermentation wasn't beer. It was kombucha, a nonalcoholic fermented tea made with a symbiotic culture of bacteria and yeast (known as a SCOBY). Mozer got interested in this probiotic beverage while in college at UNC-Wilmington, where he started learning to brew his own. Friends praised his kombucha, and Mozer realized he had the seeds of a business with potential, considering the popularity of kombucha and how quickly the market was growing. After graduation, he set about getting the experience he'd need to start his own kombucha business. In 2011, Mozer founded Lenny Boy as a kombucha brewery in Charlotte.

Lenny Boy focused strictly on nonalcoholic kombucha until 2013, when the business was certified organic and received its beer-brewing license (making it the only certified organic brewery in North Carolina at the time). At first, Mozer used the license to experiment with what he dubbed his Wild Ale series. These ales are not brewed like traditional beer. Some are made with unboiled wort, and some contain no grain at all, just a mixture of fruits, herbs, and sugar fermented with the kombucha yeast culture. In these cases, the fermentation is

Kombucha in fermentation at Lenny Boy Brewing Company
Erik Lars Myers

designed to produce alcohol, though the alcohol by volume of the Wild Ales is on average lower than that of most craft beer. It wasn't long until Mozer and his new brewer, John Watkins, started brewing more traditional craft beers such as a Belgian tripel, a pale ale, and a brown ale. Even their traditional beers are often brewed with a twist, though, either in the yeast or the ingredients.

At this point, kombucha is still Lenny Boy's main business. It can be found in bottles around North Carolina and in other states throughout the Southeast. Perhaps because of much more difficult beer distribution laws, its Wild Ales and traditional ales are available only in North Carolina, primarily in the Charlotte area.

To get the full effect of Lenny Boy's beverages, a visit to its Charlotte taproom is in order. Like many other breweries, Lenny Boy occupies a brick manufacturing facility that is bland on the outside but welcoming on the inside. Behind the wooden bar hangs a chalkboard sign declaring the beers and kombuchas pouring from the 14 taps. Curious drinkers in the mood to experiment can get a flight of six different options—both ales and kombuchas—to sip while they look through the large window into the brewing area, where the beer and kombucha processes are open to view.

Considering the boom in both kombucha and craft beer in the Southeast, it seems both of Lenny Boy's brewing systems will be kept busy for the foreseeable future.

SYCAMORE BREWING

2161 Hawkins Street
Charlotte, NC 28203
704-910-3821
Email: cheers@sycamorebrew.com
Website: sycamorebrew.com
Hours: Monday–Thursday, 4 P.M.–10 P.M.;
    Friday, 4 P.M.–11 P.M.; Saturday, noon–11 P.M.;
    Sunday, noon–7 P.M.
Founders: Sarah and Justin Brigham
Head Brewer: Andrew Viapiano
Brewery Operations Manager: Jordy Smith
Opened: 2014

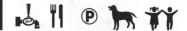

DRIVING DOWN HAWKINS STREET IN CHARLOTTE'S SOUTH END, it is hard to miss Sycamore Brewing. The large, blocky building has the brewery's name stenciled across it in large letters that pop from the red-brick background. The subtler sign of a sycamore leaf hanging from the building and the new-looking patio built to one side are also clues that visitors have arrived at one of the South End's newer breweries.

Inside, Sycamore is just as impressive. The long, narrow taproom has one wall paneled in rustic-looking wood, which also lines the front of the bar that runs along the other side. The light-colored walls and shining copper-topped bar make the taproom bright and friendly looking. The focal point is the bar, which offers an impressive lineup of 20 taps and television screens for people looking for their favorite games. Patrons can catch a glimpse of the brewing equipment through small windows on either side of the bar. But a better view of the brewing system is available from the outdoor beer garden, which features a fire pit, picnic tables, and a stage for live music. All in all, Sycamore is designed for groups of friends looking for a place to settle down and enjoy themselves.

Justin Brigham, co-owner with his wife, Sarah, has a background in the beer business—but not one people might expect. Justin grew up in Charlotte. While living in Colorado, he got a job with Coors, one of the biggest brands in the United States. He worked as a barley buyer while experimenting at home with his own beer recipes, reaching beyond the flavors Coors is known for. After returning to Charlotte, Justin and Sarah forged a path into the beer business. With

From the inside of Sycamore's brewery, patrons can catch a glimpse of the spacious outdoor patio.
Erik Lars Myers

the help of head brewer Andrew Viapiano and Jordy Smith, the Brighams have turned Sycamore into a successful young brewery.

The brewing team at Sycamore uses a 15-barrel system to crank out a variety of beers ranging across the style map. Patrons are just as likely to find a straightforward ESB as a coconut-infused red ale or a hoppy IPA. Sycamore's reputation got a boost in 2015, when its Southern Girl Lager won a bronze medal at the Great American Beer Festival in the American-Style Lager or Light Lager category. That medal brought Sycamore just two steps away from Justin's old employer, Coors, which took home the gold.

In its first year, Sycamore concentrated on keg and taproom sales, producing only a short run of special 22-ounce bottles. With 16 taps to fill (four of the bar taps are wine), there is plenty to keep the brewing team busy.

Sycamore has its eyes on a bigger future. In 2015, the Brighams were able to buy their building, and they're currently in the midst of planning an expansion that will add packaging capability on the production side and more seating on the public side. Their optimism is a symptom of how this neighborhood is quickly catching up to the NoDa district as a popular spot for Charlotte's craft beer lovers.

THE UNKNOWN
BREWING CO
LIVE WITHOUT BOUNDARIES

THE UNKNOWN BREWING COMPANY

1327 South Mint Street
Charlotte, NC 28203
980-237-2628
Website: unknownbrewing.com
Hours: Wednesday–Friday, 4 P.M.–10 P.M.;
    Saturday, noon–10 P.M.;
    Sunday, noon–8 P.M.
Founder: Brad Shell
Head Brewer: Brad Shell
Brewing Staff: Dave Morton, Tom Savage,
    Kyle Cox
Opened: 2014

A LIME GREEN STALK OF BARLEY CURVED INTO A QUESTION MARK, anchored by a hop cone at the bottom—that is the trademark icon of The Unknown Brewing Company of Charlotte's South End neighborhood.

Don't be fooled by the question mark. As it says on the brewery's website, "The Unknown is not about being mysterious. It's not that we couldn't come up with a name and gave up." Instead, it was a deliberate choice by owner Brad Shell to prompt his patrons to step beyond their comfort zone. "We encourage everyone to live without boundaries and never regret a day in your life," Shell explains. "We are a company that makes beer, but at the end of the day we want to be people that help a culture thrive."

Boasting 10 years of experience in the beer industry at nationally recognized brands including Sweetwater, Terrapin, and Rogue, Shell has had plenty of time to outline his philosophy of brewing and the culture he wants to create. That culture emerges in some of The Unknown's events, such as its weekly charitable Bike & Brew ride, and in Shell's boundary-challenging beer recipes.

When it comes to beer, Shell is an unabashed hophead. "Many of our beers are focused on IPA styles ranging from heavy-hitting double IPAs such as our Vehopciraptor at 9.9 percent to aromatic IPAs such as our Scratch N' Sniff at 4.8

The Unknown Brewing Company's massive brewhouse
Erik Lars Myers

percent. Our flagship that we hold near and dear to our hearts is our Over The Edge IPA. Sitting at 6.9 percent, this is what started it all."

That isn't to say that drinkers shy of hops won't find anything to tempt them at The Unknown. Porters, stouts, and a wheat beer brewed with ginger all make appearances on the brewery's tap list. In addition to its regular and recurring seasonal beers, The Unknown has a more experimental line released on its "Small-Batch Sundays" and sometimes pushes the envelope on a larger scale as well. Its second special bottle release, themed after Mexico's Day of the Dead, was an imperial Mexican lager brewed with agave, serrano peppers, and 99 real food-grade scorpions (added during the boil). As Shell says, "We live without boundaries when we make our beer!"

The Unknown's large brewing system enables it to brew and package a lot of beer. Some of its products are available in six-packs of cans, while others (such as the scorpion beer) are special bottle releases. Its beers are distributed by Tryon, a company with state-wide reach, The Unknown has even expanded its distribution to include South Carolina and Atlanta. In fact, Shell says, the scale of The

Unknown's production facility gives him a problem the opposite of that faced by many small breweries—he has to work to keep his beer list fresh and surprising. "It's been challenging to be able to brew enough small-batch stuff to stay ultra-chic and rare," he admits. "It's hard to do when each tank holds 13,000 pints!"

Shell has no problem attracting visitors to The Unknown's on-site taproom. The public area seems small in comparison to the expansive production floor and has a cozy feel. A stainless-steel wall of taps and bar faces a large glass wall showing off the brewery behind it. Chairs and tables fill part of the space, with other areas left open for standing groups. Visitors can also go into a roped-off area of the production floor to play games such as cornhole or venture outside, where they'll find a fire pit and casual seating.

And what is Shell's plan for The Unknown moving forward? "Whatever people are doing, do something different," he answers.

The future may be unpredictable, but Shell is ready for whatever comes.

HOW TO BUY BEER

It might seem silly, but buying beer isn't as easy as just picking a bottle off a shelf. Beer is a perishable product and can undergo considerable flavor changes over time. Unpasteurized craft beer (i.e., most of it) has a shelf life of about 90 days and should be kept cold at all times. Unfortunately, due to a lack of shelf space, most beer stores—even the really great ones—keep a lot of beer at room temperature, which can severely shorten its life span.

Here are some quick guidelines for making sure the beer you buy is (almost) always awesome:

1. Check for dates on bottles, and make sure you're buying something less than 90 days old. Some high-alcohol beers (over 6 percent), especially dark beers, can age exceptionally well. But as a general rule, beer should be consumed soon after it's made. Hop character diminishes quickly, so be sure to buy any hoppy beer as fresh as possible.

2. Never buy beer that has been sitting in direct sunlight. Sunlight (and many fluorescent lights) can cause a photochemical reaction in beer that creates an aroma similar to skunk urine. Professional tasters call such beer "lightstruck," but most people would use the term "skunky." Clear bottles and green bottles allow beer to become lightstruck in a matter of minutes. Brown bottles are more protective, but prolonged exposure can still cause damage to the beer they contain.

3. If you're unsure how old a beer is, hold the bottle up to the light and see what the beer looks like. If it contains flakes or large chunks, the bottle is probably old. Over time, proteins and calcium settle out of the beer and create unsightly flakes in the bottom of the bottle that are fairly easy to stir up. Some beers are meant to be hazy, and some are bottle-conditioned and contain yeast. Yeast should look like fine dust in the bottom of the bottle.

4. Check the area around the bottle cap for rust or lines of yeast. When beer is bottled, foam pours down the side of the bottle, and a cap is placed on top.

Beers on the shelf at a well-stocked bottle shop

A bottle that hasn't been well rinsed may have yeast or beer residue around the crown that can grow mold or bacteria, which in turn can infect the bottle through the seal of the cap and create unpleasant flavors. If bottles have been stored in a moist environment after bottling, caps can sometimes rust, leaving rust around the lips of the bottles.

5. Check the fill level in bottles. Bottling machines leave a wide variance in fill levels, but beer should always be inside the neck of the bottle. Exceptionally low fills can be dangerous because of built-up pressure within the necks of the bottles, or it can be a sign of a poor cap seal, which means that the beer has either leaked or evaporated from within the bottles and that the remaining beer is probably sour or infected.

WOODEN ROBOT BREWERY

1440 South Tryon Street #110
Charlotte, NC 28203
980-819-7875
Email: info@woodenrobotbrewery.com
Website: woodenrobotbrewery.com
Hours: Tuesday–Thursday, 4 P.M.–10 P.M.;
Friday, 4 P.M.–11 P.M.;
Saturday, 1 P.M.–11 P.M.;
Sunday, 1 P.M.–8 P.M.
Founders: Josh Patton, Dan Wade
Head Brewer: Dan Wade
Brewing Staff Member: Josh Patton
Taproom Manager: Tom Stanfel
Opened: 2015

DAN WADE AND JOSH PATTON HAVE BEEN FRIENDS SINCE MIDDLE SCHOOL. Although they parted ways when they went to college, their hobbies intertwined. Both found a love of beer and homebrewing despite their educational backgrounds in engineering and finance, respectively.

After college, Wade had doubts about his future career and found himself working for Swamp Head Brewery in Florida. He soon enrolled in a program in brewing and fermentation science at Heriot-Watt University in Scotland and traveled through Germany and Belgium in his free time. What he discovered there would shape his future.

After Wade returned to the United States and Swamp Head, he and Patton began talking in earnest about opening their own brewery. They considered other cities on the East Coast, but Patton had moved to Charlotte in 2009 to pursue a banking career and saw the enormous potential of the city's South End. Wade moved to Charlotte shortly thereafter. A few years later, Wooden Robot was born.

"The name Wooden Robot represents the blending of seemingly disparate elements into a wonderful union," says Patton. "The wood symbolizes the creative, artistic side of brewing, envisioning a novel concept and carefully craft-

Wood frames stainless steel in Wooden Robot's cellar. It operates the first foeder in Charlotte.
Erik Lars Myers

ing it by meticulously selecting the finest ingredients and honing the process to make the vision become reality. Meanwhile, the robot illustrates the scientific side of brewing: the intricate mechanical design of the brewing equipment, the endlessly complex chemistry of mashing, boiling, and fermentation, and the alluring microbiology of yeast and souring bacteria. Wooden Robot represents the combination of these two passions, art and science."

Inside their self-styled "urban farmhouse brewery," their naming aesthetic is reiterated. The warm, comfortable, wood-toned taproom offers views of the large stainless-steel fermenters, the tall wooden foeder for wild farmhouse fermentation, and the racks of oak barrels inside the production space. A long wooden bar runs along one wall of the taproom and leads to a patio filled with bright sunshine on beautiful days.

Wade and Patton have growth in mind. They're already planning for larger fermentation vessels—which they may need sooner than they think, as Wooden Robot was named one of "America's Best New Breweries in 2015" by *Beer Advocate* magazine.

Wooden Robot plans to start releasing limited bottle runs of special-release beers in 2016. But the best place to find its beer is in its inviting taproom in the South End, looking into its gleaming brewery.

BIRDSONG BREWING COMPANY

1016 North Davidson Street
Charlotte, NC 28206
704-332-1810
Email: jp@birdsongbrewing.com
Website: birdsongbrewing.com/web
Hours: Tuesday–Friday, 4:30 P.M.–10 P.M.;
   Saturday, noon–10 P.M.;
   Sunday, noon–8 P.M.
Founders: Chris and Tara Goulet, Chandra
   Torrence, Tom Gillam, Ben Cauthen, Jackie
   Mohrfeld, Michelle LeBeau
Head Brewer: Conor Robinson
Opened: 2011

BIRDSONG BREWING COMPANY WAS AN EARLY PART OF THE WAVE of craft breweries that have opened in the Charlotte area since 2009. It was the third brewery to open in 2011 (after Ass Clown and NoDa) and has gradually built its reputation as other craft breweries have started up around it.

Conor Robinson was a barely legal homebrewer when he met Tara Goulet. Robinson, a Johnson & Wales graduate, worked as a baker at Great Harvest Bread Company and liked to give his homebrew away to friends. Tara and her husband, Chris, were some of the lucky samplers of Robinson's brew, and it added spark to an idea they had: opening a craft brewery in Charlotte. Tara and Chris developed a business plan and together with five friends funded the brewery and offered Robinson the job of head brewer.

From Birdsong's beginnings, Robinson has been instrumental in developing the brewery's recipes and bringing them to life. He's one of a handful of brewers in the state with a professional culinary background, and it's a combination that works well. Robinson was also key in another way: he gave Birdsong its name. As the story goes, Robinson and some other founding members were on a beer vacation. In the middle of the night, someone woke to the sounds of chirping in the room. He started looking for the bird but instead discovered the sounds were coming from Robinson, who was fast asleep. "Birdsong" was born.

The brewery opened at the end of 2011 in the NoDa (North Davidson) arts district in a building next door to NoDa Brewing Company. Together, the

The impressive taproom at Birdsong's expansion location
Erik Lars Myers

two formed a delicious corner in the neighborhood. Birdsong's space featured a 10-barrel brewing system, an array of fermenters, and a small, friendly taproom dedicated to its beers. Birdsong brews four beers year-round, including its popular Jalapeño Pale Ale, made with fresh, deseeded peppers. It also puts out regular seasonal beers and has a specialty line called the Take Flight series that is notable for its catchy names (such as Turtles on Pterodactyls) and creative barrel-aged flavors.

Birdsong has been popular since its opening. Its steady success has already led to an expansion. In April 2015, it closed its original taproom and officially opened the doors at its new location farther up North Davidson Street. The new Birdsong has a 30-barrel system, many more (and larger) fermenters, and a shining new taproom where new and old fans can sample the beers. Like the old location, the new taproom doesn't serve food, but food trucks are frequently on-site on weekends, especially when there's live music or another event.

Along with its space expansion, Birdsong has gradually expanded its packaging options to include cans (for its regular beers) and 22-ounce bottles (for its specialty batches). It's still a self-distributing brewery. Most of its beer is sold in Charlotte, though it also has keg accounts in Asheville, the Triad, and the Triangle, and though some of its cans find their way into select bottle shops around the state. However, as the new facility ramps up, Birdsong is likely looking to send its beer soaring across more and more of the state.

NODA BREWING COMPANY

Original taproom:
2229 North Davidson Street
Charlotte, NC 28205
704-451-1394
Hours: Wednesday, 4 P.M.–9 P.M.;
    Friday, 4 P.M.–9:30 P.M.; Saturday, noon–10:00 P.M.

NoDa North End:
2921 North Tryon Street
Charlotte, NC 28206
704-900-6851
Hours: Monday–Tuesday, 4 P.M.–8:30 P.M.;
    Wednesday–Thursday, 4 P.M.–9 P.M.;
    Friday, 4 P.M.–9:30 P.M.; Saturday, noon–10 P.M.;
    Sunday, 1 P.M.–6 P.M.

Email: info@nodabrewing.com
Website: nodabrewing.com
Founders: Todd and Suzie Ford
Head Brewer: Chad Henderson
Opened: 2011

NODA, SHORT FOR NORTH DAVIDSON, IS CHARLOTTE'S ARTS DISTRICT—and the scene of a wave of craft beer. NoDa Brewing Company, the first of four breweries to open in NoDa, has led the charge.

Todd and Suzie Ford always enjoyed good craft beer but rarely had time to enjoy it together. Suzie was a banker in Charlotte and Todd an airline pilot. He flew for Pan Am until the airline ceased operations and then started moving freight for Airborne Express. Todd had been homebrewing since 1995, so when the banking industry took a downturn and Suzie found herself out of work, a possibility arose that they had never considered.

"I didn't ever think about going pro," says Todd about his brewing. "Like the airlines, it's a difficult job to get into and make any money, so you obviously have to like what you're doing. We both enjoyed this, and we've been looking forward to the opportunity to run a business together and spend more time with

The view from the brewhouse at NoDa's expansion facility
Erik Lars Myers

each other." Todd finally resigned from flying in July 2011 to dedicate himself full-time to the brewery.

Their story is a familiar one. "We started having house parties every six months, and we would give away our beer, and more and more people would tell us, 'You need to start selling this. You need to open a brewery,' " says Suzie. "For the first couple of years, we kind of laughed it off, and then we started thinking, *Well, why not?* So we took our retirement, jumped in with both feet, and haven't looked back."

Finding a place for the brewery ended up being a challenge they hadn't anticipated. They searched for months for the right spot, looking at dozens of potential locations. They had a hard time finding a place that met the criteria set by the city of Charlotte regarding the proximity of churches, schools, and residences. They kept coming back to one site in particular for a variety of reasons: good location, nice feel, lots of room, and only one nearby residence that would alter how they laid out their taproom.

Their brewery is directly across the street from CenterStage@NoDa, a popular theater venue. It is also near the original location of Birdsong Brewing, which was just a few months behind NoDa Brewing in starting up. The

Fords believe their brewery fits into NoDa perfectly. "We feel that brewing is an art," says Suzie, noting that they couldn't have found a more perfect community.

What's more, they were excited to be part of the growing Charlotte beer scene. Shortly after they opened, Todd predicted that a craft beer wave was coming to Charlotte—a prediction that has since come true. "We're not the youngest people to start a brewery," says Todd. "Everybody gets involved in the industry for different reasons, but we really enjoy the craft beer industry culture—enough so that we basically dumped relatively well-established careers to do it. We both understand that it's going to be a big challenge, and that we're going to make less money at this than what we did before, but we're both dedicated to doing this. It's our passion, and—God willing—I think we'll have some success. I think Charlotte's ready, and all of North Carolina is ready, for some new, unique beers."

The Fords assembled a formidable team for their young brewery, hiring George Allen—formerly a brewer for Carolina Beer & Beverage and Red Oak in North Carolina and Bison in California—as their brewery manager, as well as two other brewers, Chad Henderson and Matt Virgil. Allen left to pursue other opportunities, and Henderson stepped into the role of head brewer, leading Virgil and a talented brew crew. NoDa early on developed a reputation for good beer. This was reinforced in 2012, when it was awarded a silver medal at the Great American Beer Festival for its Coco Loco porter, and again in 2014, when it won a gold medal at the World Beer Cup in the extremely competitive American-Style IPA category for its Hop Drop 'N Roll. After that medal, sales of Hop Drop 'N Roll exploded. Even now, it is hard for stores to keep it on the shelves.

Thanks to its success, NoDa has recently completed its first expansion: a 32,000-square-foot brewery and taproom space on North Tryon Street. The new facility has a 60-barrel brewing system (compared to the 15-barrel system NoDa started with) and an upgraded canning line. The Fords hope to use the new capacity to push more beer into the market and slowly expand their distribution range.

FREE RANGE BREWING

2320 North Davidson Street
Charlotte, NC 28205
980-201-9096
Email: info@freerangebrewing.com
Website: freerangebrewing.com
Hours: Wednesday–Friday, 5 P.M.–11 P.M.;
    Saturday, 1 P.M.–11 P.M.;
    Sunday, 1 P.M.–7 P.M.
Founders: Jeff and Jason Alexander
Head Brewers: Jeff and Jason Alexander
Opened: 2015

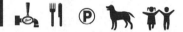

VISITORS DRIVING DOWN NORTH DAVIDSON STREET ON THE HUNT for Free Range Brewing will know they've arrived when they see a well-worn tractor proudly parked outside a brick warehouse. The concrete patio that will likely be crowded with beer fans is another clue. Upon climbing the stairs to the patio, patrons will see the shining three-barrel brewing system behind a large glass window that used to be, in the building's previous incarnation, a garage door. Inside, they'll find more reclaimed wood and vestiges of old buildings from the NoDa area reincarnated in this neighborhood bar.

As the taproom suggests, Free Range Brewing is all about taking the old and transforming it into something new and exciting. Brothers Jason and Jeff Alexander, the masterminds behind Free Range, spent years developing the business ideas that eventually led to their craft brewery. Neither was a homebrewer at the outset, but they were craft beer fans and believed that a brewery was the kind of small, community-oriented business they wanted to be in. As part of their planning process, they learned how to brew at home and started developing recipes they could bring to market.

Free Range's tagline is "Let your taste buds roam," and that is just what Jason and Jeff do with their beers. There are no flagship beers at their brewery, though some, such as their cream ale, appear more often than others. Farmhouse ales and wild ales make frequent appearances on their menu, as do beers that celebrate local ingredients. The Alexanders partner with farms to source ingredients

This vintage tractor welcomes visitors to Free Range Brewing.
Erik Lars Myers

including strawberries for a wild wheat beer, muscadines for a saison, and herbs for a gruit (an unhopped ale). Although there's no telling what will be on tap any given day, creative drinkers will certainly find something exciting to try.

Keg distribution may be in the future for this young brewery. But for now, the brothers are focused on building community in their taproom. Thanks to the innovate beer, the outdoor patio, the indoor kids' area, and the separate event space, beer lovers have plenty of reasons to make Free Range a regular stop.

HEIST BREWERY

2909 North Davidson Street
Charlotte, NC 28205
704-375-8260
Email: info@heistbrewery.com
Website: heistbrewery.com
Hours: Monday–Wednesday, 11 A.M.–midnight;
   Thursday–Saturday, 11 A.M.–2 A.M.;
   Sunday, 10 A.M.–midnight
Founder: Kurt Hogan
Head Brewer: Eric Mitchell
Opened: 2012

CRAFT BREWERIES ARE COMMON IN CHARLOTTE NOW, but brewpubs are thin on the ground. Breaking the mold is Heist Brewery, Charlotte's first non-chain brewpub. Heist opened in 2012, the brainchild of Kurt Hogan. At that point, the NoDa district was starting to become a craft beer center, with NoDa Brewing and Birdsong just down the street. Hogan took an old mill building and transformed it into a modern-feeling restaurant with unique touches including a wood-burning oven and light wood accents that contrast with the rough brick walls.

When Heist opened, its beer production was spearheaded by Zach Hart, formerly the award-winning brewer at The Mash House in Fayetteville. Hart's specialties were light-bodied lagers and classic styles (his GABF medal in 2001 was for an English-style IPA). Heist was a welcome addition to the craft beer scene in Charlotte, but Hart's classic beers didn't always match up with the assertive flavors coming out of Heist's kitchen. In 2014, Hart moved from Heist to the new brewery Granite Falls, and Hogan promoted Eric Mitchell to the role of head brewer. Mitchell had a background in homebrewing and started at Heist as the brewer in charge of the Not So Small Batch series of experimental beers. After becoming head brewer, he took on the task of reformulating Heist's brands and brought in Josh Johnson, formerly of Monday Night Brewing in Atlanta, to help with the experimental beers.

Now, visitors to Heist will find a variety of traditional and nontraditional styles on tap, ranging from an American pale ale to farmhouse-style beers and

The boil kettle and mash tun at Heist Brewery
Erik Lars Myers

big stouts. The Not So Small Batch releases continue on Sundays, keeping the beer lineup interesting and fresh.

Although the beer scene in Charlotte is changing rapidly these days, the Heist team is committed to keeping its operation at the top of the craft brewpub list.

Vineyards & Brewhouse

MORGAN RIDGE
VINEYARDS & BREWHOUSE

Vineyards and brewhouse:
486 John Morgan Road
Gold Hill, NC 28071
704-639-0911
Hours: Wednesday–Sunday, 11 A.M.–7 P.M.

Morgan Ridge Vineyards at the Village
834 St. Stephens Church Road
Gold Hill, NC 28071
704-984-8699
Hours: Thursday–Sunday, noon–5 P.M.

Email: morgan.ridge@gmail.com
Website: morganridgevineyard.com
Founders: Tommy and Amie Baudoin
Head Brewer: Tommy Baudoin
Brewing Staff: Vanita Edwards
Opened: 2013

BEER AND WINE ARE OFTEN PLACED IN OPPOSITION TO EACH OTHER, but not at Morgan Ridge Vineyards & Brewhouse.

Morgan Ridge started as a vineyard when owners Amie and Tommy Baudoin decided to convert her family's farmland to grape cultivation. The vineyard's first vintage dated to 2007; the beer was a later addition. Tommy and Amie's tastings were a success with the wine crowd, but they noticed that sometimes family and friends of their wine drinkers wished for beer instead. And so they added brewing to the Morgan Ridge repertoire.

Beer-focused visitors will find six beers on tap, with some rotation in the menu. The experience is definitely influenced by wine-tasting culture. People are encouraged to get flights of four or six beers to try, much as they might try a selection of wines.

Although the tasting room is open from Wednesday to Sunday, some advance planning will help visitors make the most of the experience. For example, the vineyard serves lunch or brunch during the days it is open, but visitors wanting to eat should call for reservations ahead of time.

Morgan Ridge's newest addition is a second retail location in the historic village of Gold Hill. Gold Hill was the site of North Carolina's gold rush in the early 1800s and was a booming town by the 1840s. Now, it boasts tourist-friendly shops and a park with walking trails winding through the old mining sites. Morgan Ridge's village location, a rustic-looking building made from dark wood, offers both wine and beer for sale.

TRIAD BREWERIES

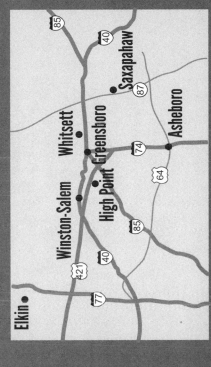

AREA OF DETAIL

Elkin
Skull Camp Brewing

Winston-Salem
Hoots Roller Bar & Beer Company
Foothills Brewing
Small Batch Beer Company

High Point
Liberty Brewery & Grill

Asheboro
Four Saints Brewing Company

Greensboro
Pig Pounder Brewery
Preyer Brewing Company
Gibb's Hundred Brewing Company
Natty Greene's Pub & Brewing Company

Whitsett
Red Oak Brewery

Saxapahaw
Haw River Farmhouse Ales

SKULL CAMP BREWING

2000 North Bridge Street
Elkin, NC 28621
336-258-8124
Email: info@skullcampbrewing.com
Website: skullcampbrewing.com
Hours: Friday, 2 P.M.–8 P.M.;
    Saturday, noon–6 P.M.
Owners: Kari Heerdt, Ken Gulaian
Head Brewer: Jeff Leftwich
Opened: 2012

THE YADKIN VALLEY IS KNOWN FOR ITS WINERIES. But beer and wine are not mutually exclusive here. Skull Camp Brewing is one of several North Carolina craft breweries affiliated with wineries, others being Morgan Ridge in Gold Hill and Andrews Brewing/Calaboose Cellars in Andrews.

Skull Camp opened as an offshoot business of Mount Airy's Round Peak Winery, named for the mountain that acts as a backdrop for the winery's scenic vineyards. Skull Camp started brewing on a half-barrel system tucked into the winery's buildings. The business grew organically from the Round Peak staff's fascination with homebrewing. In 2012, the winery also became licensed as a brewery and started to sell its beer in the Round Peak tasting room. The beer was a hit.

Two years later, Skull Camp expanded to a much larger building and a 10-barrel brewing system in the town of Elkin, 20 minutes away. After completing renovations, Skull Camp moved the brewery and taproom into part of a large, two-story building that used to be a restaurant. It has plans to open the rest as a smokehouse restaurant sometime in 2016.

The larger system has allowed Skull Camp to distribute to a wider area that includes cities such as Winston-Salem. In addition to finding Skull Camp in local bars and at the brewery in Elkin, drinkers can still sample it at the Round Peak Winery tasting room, where, in addition to Round Peak's classic dry styles, they'll find a line of Skull Camp wines that lean toward semi-dry or semi-sweet flavor profiles.

Skull Camp has made a wide variety of recipes in the past and doesn't publicly embrace any flagship styles, so drinkers will always be in for a surprise when they track down its beers.

NORTH CAROLINA CRAFT MALTING

Malting is incredibly important to beer.

Malting is the process through which barley is prepared for beer production. Barley kernels are roasted, caramelized, or otherwise treated to give brewers the sugar base—and thus the alcohol—and a large portion of the flavor in their beer, particularly the caramel, toffee, or chocolate notes.

Until recently, malting was the domain of large corporations located in the largest grain-growing centers or oldest brewing cultures in the world: the American and Canadian plains, Germany, and England, among other places. The idea of a brewery using local grain was unheard of unless it happened to be located near a maltster. But as the craft brewing industry has grown, so have related industries.

When they first met, partners Brent Manning and Brian Simpson were environmental consultants. They had a common question in mind: why was none of the barley grown in North Carolina fit for brewing beer? The answer turned out to be simple: because people grew barley for feed, not for beer.

The partners took themselves to a professional malting school and started working with a few local farmers. In 2010, they opened North Carolina's first maltster, Riverbend Malt House—a "micro-maltster," they call it—using traditional floor-malting techniques. Since then, they've seen their business grow exponentially. They now supply brewers around the state. Some of the state's largest breweries have used their malt or rye in special batches available around the country.

As they work to increase their capacity, they're also adding equipment, including roasting equipment. Still, despite their quick expansion, they can't hope to supply the entire industry in North Carolina at its size and rate of growth.

Soon, they'll be joined by other micro-malters in other parts of the state that will add more malt to the local supply. Epiphany Craft Malting in Durham will use new, innovative malting equipment from the owner's home country, Germany. And there are rumors of at least one maltster in the works in eastern North Carolina. Together, these malt houses will allow breweries to serve, and for drinkers to drink, a true taste of North Carolina.

HOOTS ROLLER BAR & BEER COMPANY

840 Mill Works Street
Winston-Salem, NC 27101
336-608-6026
Email: hootsbeercompany@gmail.com
Website: hootspublic.com
Hours: Monday–Thursday, 4 P.M.–midnight;
   Friday, 4 P.M.–2 A.M.; Saturday, noon–2 A.M.;
   Sunday, noon–midnight
Founders: Eric Swaim, Eric Weyer, Ralph Pritts
Head Brewer: Dave McClure
Opened: 2013

VISITORS LOOKING FOR HOOTS ROLLER BAR & BEER COMPANY on the west side of downtown Winston-Salem will find themselves turning down a short dead-end street that leads to a converted mill building. The building is the old Hoots Roller Mill, constructed in the 1930s to process grain into flour. The mill stopped operating in the 1950s and was used for a variety of businesses until recently, when it has been under redevelopment. Hoots Roller Bar & Beer Company is just one of the businesses revitalizing this corner of Winston-Salem.

The founders of Hoots all have backgrounds in music and an appreciation for what a lively neighborhood bar should be. The interior shows a great attention to detail, from the decorative wooden paneling on the wall to the shining brass and copper diver's helmet fixed in the center of the bar. Owls are a common theme in the décor, both inside and on the small patio, a nod to the name.

When Hoots opened, it was simply a bar, but the brewing system and house-made beer followed in short order.

The man behind the beer at Hoots is Dave McClure, a veteran of the craft beer industry. McClure got his start at Red Brick Brewing Company in Atlanta, where he was an award-winning head brewer. He left Red Brick in 2012 to move to Winston-Salem and take a position with Foothills Brewing, where he became

The gorgeous bar at Hoots Roller Bar
Sarah H. Ficke

brewery supervisor. Just two years after his move, McClure accepted the position of head brewer at Hoots, bringing his industry experience to the small startup.

Hoots Roller Bar has a strong local focus. It self-distributes its kegs in a limited area but concentrates mainly on developing the bar as a popular local hangout.

FOOTHILLS BREWING

Brewpub:
638 West Fourth Street
Winston-Salem, NC 27101
336-777-3348
Hours: Daily, 11 A.M.–2 A.M.

Production brewery:
3800 Kimwell Drive
Winston-Salem, NC 27103
336-997-9484
Tasting Room Hours:
    Wednesday–Thursday, 3 P.M.–8 P.M.;
    Friday, 3 P.M.–10 P.M.;
    Saturday, noon–8 P.M.;
    Sunday, noon–6 P.M.
Email: info@foothillsbrewing.com
Website: foothillsbrewing.com
Founder: Jamie Bartholomaus
Brewmaster: T. L. Adkisson
Opened: 2005

JAMIE BARTHOLOMAUS STARTED HIS BREWING CAREER AT A YOUNG AGE. He began homebrewing around 18, "maybe 19," as a sophomore in college. He got his start commercially simply by being a good customer. John Gayer, the owner of Blind Man Ales in Athens, Georgia, also ran a homebrew shop, and Jamie was one of his biggest customers. Eventually, he invited Jamie to help him brew. By the end of 1997—after Jamie graduated from college as an anthropology major—he was brewing at Blind Man full-time.

He still considers his time there to have been some of his most valuable. "It was like large homebrewing equipment. . . . We used to bottle out of homebrewing bottling buckets," he says with a laugh. "I learned a lot about what not to do, and how to get stuff done at all costs. Now, when stuff goes wrong, it doesn't really freak me out that much. It's probably happened before."

Jamie continued brewing at Blind Man and at Vista Brewpub in Colombia,

Barrels and kegs are neighbors at Foothills' Kimwell Drive facility.
Erik Lars Myers

South Carolina, but was on the lookout for a job with more room to grow.

He found it on a trip through North Carolina. Jamie stopped into Olde Hickory Brewery for a beer and by chance met the owners, Steve Lyerly and Jason Yates, who were looking for a brewer to help expand their production to meet the demands of their new taproom. Soon afterward, Jamie joined the team at Olde Hickory, took over production in its Amos Howards Brewpub, and helped build its production facility.

He worked at Olde Hickory for almost five years, helping the brand grow. Eventually, though, he found himself restless in the job. "Their timeline was different than my timeline," he admits. So when some friends had an idea to start a brewpub, Jamie eagerly signed on. Feeling it would be inappropriate to open a brewery near the one where he had worked, he took a job at Blue Ridge Brewing in Greenville, South Carolina, while his project got off the ground.

Finally, in 2005, he moved to Winston-Salem and opened Foothills Brewing, a big, open brewpub with two stories of expansive seating, event space, and a comfortable bar overlooked by tall windows through which customers can see the brewery. At Foothills, Jamie had a brand he could grow.

While the brewpub was the main focus, Jamie started self-distributing the beer. By the end of the year, he had footholds in beer markets around the state. The distribution and growth of the brand are his passion. "The challenges of getting it made often bring me back to the Blind Man days, where at any cost it's got to happen. It's a lot of fun to keep up with."

Foothills reached the point where it needed a production facility to meet demand. When Jamie went looking for it, he found an even larger opportunity in Carolina Beer & Beverage. Once the largest craft brewery in the state, boasting brands including Carolina Blonde, Carolina Strawberry Blonde, and Cottonwood (purchased from Boone's Cottonwood Brewery), Carolina Beer & Beverage had transitioned from beer to a lucrative side business—canning energy drinks and bottling progressive adult beverages such as Mike's Hard Lemonade for distribution.

When Foothills entered the picture, all the brands owned by Carolina Beer & Beverage were contract-brewed at Pennsylvania's Lion Brewery and merely distributed in North Carolina. Jamie simply wanted to buy the old brewhouse and fermenters Carolina Beer & Beverage had sitting around its warehouse. But Carolina Beer had a different idea. "We'll sell you the equipment," its owners said, "but you have to buy the brands, too." Jamie agreed.

At the end of 2011, Foothills completed construction on its new brewing facility. Between the production facility and the pub, Foothills produces a wide range of core beers (including many popular IPAs) and seasonals such as the popular, award-winning Sexual Chocolate Imperial Stout and Olde Rabbit's Foot, an annual collaboration with Olde Hickory and Duck-Rabbit. Along with all the Foothills brands he has been growing, Jamie also brews Carolina Blonde, Carolina Strawberry Blonde, and Cottonwood seasonal beers.

After 10 years as the Foothills brewmaster, Jamie handed over the reins to a new head brewer, T. L. Adkisson. Adkisson came to Foothills in 2010 from Ham's Restaurant & Brewhouse in Greenville (now closed). Now, Jamie focuses on growing the business while Adkisson continues to develop the high-quality beers Foothills is known for.

High-value, small-release beers such as Sexual Chocolate and Olde Rabbit's Foot are some of the best reasons to visit Foothills Brewing. On the date of the annual releases, beer aficionados from around the United States descend on Winston-Salem, attend the prerelease party at the brewpub to get a sample of the coveted brews, and often spend the night outside just to be the first in line to buy bottles of the beers the next day.

BREWING IN HIGHER EDUCATION

With the craft beer industry growing so robustly in North Carolina, it's no surprise that related industries are springing up around it, including hop farms, barley maltsters, keg suppliers, welding, and manufacturing. Education is another matter.

In a few short years, North Carolina has become the home of more college-level brewing programs than any other state in the country. Appalachian State University, Asheville-Buncombe Technical Community College, Blue Ridge Community College, Rockingham Community College, Wake Technical Community College, Southwestern Community College, and Nash Community College all feature education and some level of certification in brewing, distillation, and fermentation. The curricula in the state encompass hands-on experience on brewing systems; highly technical courses in microbiology, chemistry, and physics; practical skills such as sanitary welding, hydraulics, and pneumatics; and industry-specific courses in sensory evaluation and brewery and packaging maintenance.

The brewing, distillation, and fermentation program has been approved across the entire North Carolina community college system. It seems only a matter of time before it's offered in most, if not all, of the community colleges in the state.

SMALL BATCH BEER COMPANY

241 West Fifth Street
Winston-Salem, NC 27101
336-893-6395
Email: info@smallbatchws.com
Website: smallbatchws.com
Hours: Tuesday–Wednesday, 4 P.M.–10 P.M.;
    Thursday–Friday, 4 P.M.–midnight;
    Saturday, noon–midnight;
    Sunday, noon–10 P.M.
Founders: Ryan Blain, Cliff Etchason,
    Tim Walker
Head Brewer: Jamie Mingia
Opened: 2013

DRINKERS WONDERING ABOUT THE CONCEPT BEHIND SMALL BATCH BEER COMPANY don't need to look farther than its name. The brewery is committed to producing a frequently rotating lineup of creative beers that takes advantage of its one-barrel system. While some of its recipes mimic classic styles, Small Batch loves to play with spices, fruits, innovative hop varieties, and foods such as chocolate and nuts. Its website proclaims, "It's about quality. Not quantity." Thanks to its small size, it's able to source many of its creative ingredients locally.

The founders of Small Batch, Ryan Blain, Cliff Etchason, and Tim Walker, met through beer. As they experimented with homebrew recipes, they concocted a business plan to create a nano-sized brewery in downtown Winston-Salem. Blain, Etchason, and Walker funded a good part of the brewery themselves but turned to the online funding platform Kickstarter to raise the rest of the money needed to build out their bar. In June 2013, Small Batch became one of the several North Carolina breweries that have successfully received funding through Kickstarter. With that community support, Small Batch's founders were able to move forward with construction.

Small Batch's location on West Fifth Street was already familiar to the Winston-Salem community as the home of the Kopper Kitchen restaurant, which closed in 2011. The old Kopper Kitchen sign still crowns the roof, while

"Our Beer Lives Here"—a beautiful glass of beer at Small Batch Beer Company
Small Batch Beer Co.

a smaller Small Batch Beer Company sign swings at the corner of the building. Inside, the space has been renovated into a long, narrow room with a bar running the length of one side and small wooden tables lining the opposite wall. Visitors will find a small but varied food menu to pair with the beers or with the carefully curated list of cocktails.

As its name suggests, Small Batch is not looking for fast expansion and broad distribution. However, that doesn't mean the brewery has no growth plans. By 2015, it hired a new head brewer, Jamie Mingia, formerly with West-bend Brewhouse in nearby Lewisville. Mingia spearheaded a collaboration with Old Salem Museums & Gardens to brew a beer based on a historic recipe from Single Brothers' Brewery, one of the first breweries in North Carolina.

In addition to forging ties with the local community through beer, Small Batch is looking at related business opportunities. Cofounder Tim Walker is working on opening a sister restaurant called Burger Batch in the adjoining space. Small Batch's founders are hopeful that the new restaurant will contribute to the lively, growing community on Fifth Street.

LIBERTY BREWERY & GRILL

914 Mall Loop Road
High Point, NC 27262
336-882-4677
Email: libertyhp@hghosp.com
Website: libertysteakhouseandbrewery.com
Hours: Daily, 11 A.M.–2 A.M.
Owners: Mark Cummins, Jerry Scheer
Brewmaster: Todd M. Isbell
Opened: 2000

LIBERTY BREWERY & GRILL IS UNIQUE IN NORTH CAROLINA in that it is a stand-alone in a chain of restaurants. It is part of the Homegrown Hospitality Group, based in Charleston, South Carolina. A second Liberty Brewery & Grill is in Myrtle Beach, but the High Point location is special for a few reasons. For one thing, it is the sole member of Homegrown in North Carolina. The other thing that sets it apart is its location just outside High Point, "the Furniture Capital of the World." It stands alongside a mall, where visitors might expect to see an Applebee's, P. F. Chang's, Chili's, or other chain restaurant. Instead, at Liberty, they're greeted with well-made craft beer.

Liberty's first location—in Myrtle Beach—was opened by Josh Quigley in the mid-1990s in conjunction with the restaurant chain then known as T-Bonz. The chain soon expanded its brewing interest by opening a South Carolina packaging brewery called New South Brewing.

In the meantime, T-Bonz was working on another Liberty, this one in High Point. Needing a brewer, it hired Eric Lamb, an experienced packaging brewer from Mendocino Brewing Company in California. It was a change of pace for Lamb, who went from being a large plant packaging brewer to the sole person in a small brewery, creating his own recipes, managing his own procurement, and even helping out behind the bar when needed. Lamb's work ethic and fantastic beer meant that when Josh Quigley left Liberty in Myrtle Beach in 2007 to start

The brewhouse at Liberty Brewery & Grill
Erik Lars Myers

his own brewpub, Quigley's Pint and Plate, Lamb moved to Myrtle Beach to brew there, and a new brewer was needed in High Point. That was when Liberty found Todd Isbell.

Isbell had been around beer since he was a kid. His father worked for Miller Brewing Company in Fulton, New York, not as a brewer but as a production manager. Isbell remembers spending time around the brewery as a child.

He learned about beer while hanging out with his brother in high school. They had a ritual. Each weekend, they would pick up a six-pack of Milwaukee's Best and a six-pack of something they had never heard of—an import, a micro-brew, something that looked unique. "So, very quickly," he says, "I was able to learn that beer isn't what the Big Three tell you it is."

Isbell learned how to homebrew while he was in college. After that, he went into the army and was stationed in Germany, where his beer education really began. "I was able to learn all about German beer and to see how ingrained into society it was," he says. When he left the army and moved back to the United States, he started homebrewing again. In addition to holding a regular engineering job, he volunteered at Empire Brewing in Syracuse, New York.

"It wasn't much," he says, "just a couple of evenings a week and maybe a weekend day every week." He did that for close to a year and fell in love with it. "I had one of those epiphanies that I guess a lot of people don't ever have, where

I realized that money isn't everything and that you have to do what you love."

He immediately started saving up and put himself through the University of California–Davis's master of brewing program, graduating in 2004. He received job offers afterward, but not many he was interested in. "I couldn't just take an entry-level bottling-line position or anything," he says. "I still had bills to pay. I had all of these student loans from my first run at college."

His brother lived in Colorado. Knowing that many breweries were located there, Isbell moved. Two weeks later, he got a job at Rock Bottom in Westminster, Colorado. The next two to three years saw Isbell moving through a variety of part-time positions at breweries around Colorado, including Ironworks Brewery. "They never really had a consistent lineup of beers, so I got to play around with recipes," he remembers. "Fear of failure wasn't really present."

In 2007, longing to get back to the East Coast, he saw an advertisement for an open position at Liberty. He did a working interview alongside Lamb, took a look at the area, tried beer from the local breweries, and was sold on the job. By the end of the year, Isbell was brewmaster at Liberty.

As in his position at Ironworks, he has the ability to play around in the brewhouse. The Liberty locations in Myrtle Beach and High Point have the same names for many of their beers, but the recipes are those of the individual brewmasters. Isbell prides himself on a rotating seasonal selection that features a wide variety of styles.

Isbell has won dozens of medals at local professional brewing competitions in his years at Liberty. He has seen nothing but growth there. "We're officially undersized," he says proudly. "We can't make any more beer with the equipment that I have." In addition to his work at Liberty, Isbell is spreading knowledge to a new generation of brewers as a founding faculty member of the Rockingham Community College program in brewing.

The pub part of Liberty Brewery & Grill reflects its mall location, with its tiled floors and conservative black design. But nothing can take away from the gleaming beauty of the copper brewhouse attached to the side of the pub. Floor-to-ceiling windows let natural light flood the brewery, and sunlight glints off the fermenters and into the restaurant.

FOUR SAINTS BREWING COMPANY

218 South Fayetteville Street
Asheboro, NC 27203
336-610-3722
Email: joel@foursaintsbrewing.com
Website: foursaintsbrewing.com
Hours: Wednesday–Thursday, 4 P.M.–10 P.M.;
    Friday, 3 P.M.–11 p.m.;
    Saturday, 2 P.M.–11 P.M.;
    Sunday, 1 P.M.–6 P.M.
Founders: Andrew Deming, Joel McClosky
Head Brewer: Andrew Deming
Brewing Staff: Mark McKaughn
Opened: 2015

IN THE CENTER OF DOWNTOWN ASHEBORO, A CAREFULLY RENOVATED STORE-FRONT welcomes visitors to the Four Saints Brewing Company taproom. Inside, the space has an "Old World pub feel," in the words of cofounder Joel McClosky. To the right of the door, a fireplace offers cozy warmth in the cold months. An L-shaped bar topped in concrete sprinkled with bits of smooth brown glass stretches away to the left. Large and small wooden tables fill the space between the door and the back wall, where a small raised stage often plays host to live music on weekends. Behind the glass wall at the back, patrons can see the brewing system and production floor that supply the beer in their glasses.

The beer at Four Saints crosses national boundaries: an English-style ESB pours next to a Belgian-style dubbel and a German hefeweizen. In addition to a year-round lineup, Four Saints brews a variety of limited offerings in classic and nontraditional styles. The quality and variety of beers offered reflect cofounder and head brewer Andrew Deming's love of "the science and the creativity of brewing."

Deming and McClosky were homebrewing buddies, formulating recipes and boiling them up in a garage to share with friends. As they were tossing around the idea of starting a production brewery, McClosky says, "a friend dis-

A delicious and attractive flight of beer at Four Saints
Erik Lars Myers

covered four of the many patron saints of beer and brewing—Luke, Wenceslaus, Nicholas, and Augustine. Four Saints Brewing Company, as a name, was born."

Going from a name to an operating brewery was a long process. First, Deming and McClosky had to convince their wives, Amy and Kristen, that this wasn't just a pipe dream. They both took the same approach: a serious talk over the dinner table. According to McClosky, "Both wives listened. Both wives thought and/or prayed about it. Days later, both wives kissed their husband and said, 'I believe in you. Tell me what I can do to help make Four Saints Brewing Company a reality.'"

What it took, it turned out, was time, money, and hard work. Financial and construction setbacks slowed the brewery's progress, but McClosky and Deming persevered. "We kept our heads down and kept moving forward, no matter how hard we got hit," McClosky says.

The hard work has paid off. Two of their beers—the blonde and the hefeweizen—won awards at the 2015 NC Brewers Cup competition. And they're starting to think about expanding their distribution in the state and packaging some beers in 22-ounce bottles.

More importantly, the lively and comfortable taproom is fulfilling McClosky's dream "to help create a greater local community."

1107 Grecade Street
Greensboro, NC 27408
336-553-1290
Website: pigpounder.com
Hours: Tuesday–Thursday, 4 P.M.–9 P.M.;
    Friday, 3 P.M.–midnight;
    Saturday, noon–midnight;
    Sunday, noon–11 P.M.
Founder: Marty Kotis
Head Brewer: Sam Rose
Opened: 2014

MARTY KOTIS, OWNER OF PIG POUNDER BREWERY, already had a hand in Greensboro's food and beverage scene when he decided to open a craft brewery. In 2010, he bought and renovated Darryl's Wood-Fired Grill, a longtime Greensboro chain restaurant that had dwindled to one location and was on its last gasp. While Darryl's was a rescue operation of sorts, Pig Pounder was a fresh venture for Kotis. Craft beer wasn't a new phenomenon in the city (Natty Greene's opened its doors in 2004), but it was definitely seeing a surge of popularity in 2012 when Kotis started planning Pig Pounder.

Kotis's original plan was for Pig Pounder to supply beer for Darryl's and the other restaurants he'd opened in Greensboro. However, he ran afoul of North Carolina state alcohol law, which requires the three tiers of the alcohol system— producers, wholesalers, and retailers—to remain separate businesses. While an exception is allowed for breweries that want to operate restaurant retail locations (thanks to Uli Bennewitz and his groundbreaking brewpub, Weeping Radish), there was no way for an existing restaurant group with multiple restaurants to open, own, and operate a separate production brewery.

After Kotis worked out a rule exception with the state's Alcoholic Beverage Control, Pig Pounder finally opened in 2014. The brewery is located in a freestanding warehouse close to the intersection of Grecade Street and Battleground Avenue. Inside, visitors are treated to striking black-brick walls painted

The Pig Pounder logo peeks over the shoulder of a beautiful copper brewhouse in a brewery filled with pink.
Erik Lars Myers

with beer-related quotes in bright pink. The room isn't large, but the polished wooden rails that run around its perimeter allow for plenty of seating, as does the bar. A short hallway leads from the taproom to the brewery, which is notable for its bright pink floor—another nod to Pig Pounder's porcine theme. The bar pours an array of beers with pig-themed names. While the year-round beers are all English-inspired ales, the seasonal beers branch out into other style types.

Pig Pounder's beers can be found on draft around the Triad and Triangle. Some stores carry limited-release 22-ounce bottles of its rarer beers. Word has it that Kotis is planning to open a second, larger production facility in Eden, North Carolina, in the next year or two in order to expand Pig Pounder's reach.

PREYER BREWING COMPANY

600 A-B Battleground Avenue
Greensboro, NC 27401
336-256-9450
Email: info@preyerbrewing.com
Website: preyerbrewing.com
Hours: Tuesday–Wednesday, 4 P.M.–10 P.M.;
    Thursday–Friday, 4 P.M.–midnight;
    Saturday, noon–2 A.M.; Sunday, noon–8 P.M.
Founders: Nicole and Calder Preyer, Britt
    Preyer, Will Preyer
Head Brewer: Calder Preyer
Opened: 2015

VISITORS TO GREENSBORO'S PREYER BREWING COMPANY will know they've arrived upon seeing the building's striking exterior. A framework of sturdy beams and stone encases this beautifully renovated spot on the corner of Battleground Avenue and North Eugene Street. Inside is a comfortably designed taproom that invites patrons to choose a seat from a cluster of armchairs, a long, cushioned bench, or the seats at the scattered wooden tables. Or they can pull up a chair at the bar, where a clear view through a wall of windows shows off the brewing system that makes Preyer's beers.

Preyer Brewing is a family business. Calder Preyer, the president and head brewer, discovered a love of local beer that led him first into homebrewing and then into a professional program at the Siebel Institute in Chicago. From that point, it took him about three years to plan and start Preyer Brewing in collaboration with his wife, Nicole, and his brothers, Britt and Will.

Calder is in charge of running the 10-barrel brewhouse and developing the recipes, which run heavily toward IPAs. However, Preyer isn't just for IPA fans. A blonde ale and a porter are part of the regular lineup, and the seasonal beers stray from traditional styles into ales made with fruits and spices.

As a brand-new brewery, Preyer has exciting growth in front of it. At the mo-

Preyer's taproom is beautifully designed and filled with delicious beer.
Erik Lars Myers

ment, it sells its beer in kegs and crowlers (32-ounce cans filled fresh at the bar). New recipes, packaging options, and partnerships are all in its future as part of Greensboro's growing craft beer scene.

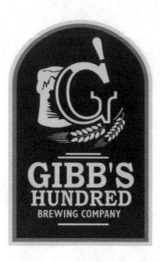

GIBB'S HUNDRED BREWING COMPANY

117 West Lewis Street
Greensboro, NC 27406
336-763-7087
Website: gibbshundred.com
Hours: Tuesday–Friday, 4 P.M.–midnight;
    Saturday, noon–midnight;
    Sunday, noon–10 P.M.
Founders: Mark and Sasha Gibb
Head Brewer: John Priest
Brewing Staff: William Brown
Opened: 2014

GIBB'S HUNDRED BREWING COMPANY IS TUCKED AWAY at the end of a dead-end street in downtown Greensboro. Its home is an old building that has been attractively renovated inside and out. Outside, patrons can choose a curving ramp or a more direct short set of stairs to climb to the front door. Inside, the spacious taproom has scattered wooden tables, comfortable soft chairs, and a long bar. The reclaimed wood floors and the brick wall that backs the bar suggest the historic nature of the building, while a wall of windows allows patrons to see into the shining, up-to-date brewhouse beyond.

The brewery's founders, Sasha and Mark Gibb, had beer in their relationship from the very beginning. Sasha remembers that "when we had our first date, Mark told me he was a certified beer judge. I completely thought he was kidding and called him out for what I was sure was a pickup line of sorts."

As she discovered, it was more than that. Mark took beer seriously. As their relationship developed, the couple started homebrewing together. Beer remained their hobby for the first 14 years of their marriage. Meanwhile, Mark worked a series of corporate jobs before landing at SMT Food & Beverage Systems, a manufacturing company with ties to the beer industry. As SMT started building equipment for craft breweries, Mark began thinking about a career change. In 2014, that plan became a reality when Sasha and Mark opened the doors at Gibb's Hundred.

The comfortable bar at Gibb's Hundred Brewing Company
Erik Lars Myers

The driving concept behind Gibb's Hundred is simple. "We brew what we like to drink," Sasha explains, "and strive to make every one a top-notch drinkable brew. We don't cut corners. If we can't get our hands on the right hops to make a great IPA, then we don't make any IPA this month."

The frequently changing lineup of beers at Gibb's is a mixture of flagship recipes, including Gibb's ESB, milk stout, and pale ale, and seasonals ranging from a Berliner weisse to a barleywine. Brewing the beers they like is a mixed blessing. "A lot of the styles we make aren't necessarily trendy," Sasha says. "It can be tough to get people to try a really well-crafted ESB instead of the latest experimental-hop IPA." Persuading customers to try the ESB has gotten easier, though, since Gibb's won a gold medal for that beer at the 2015 Great American Beer Festival, an impressive feat for a brewery so new.

Although Gibb's has gained national recognition, Sasha and Mark remain focused on growing their local beer community. The name Gibb's Hundred symbolizes their commitment. Sasha traces the brewery's name to the colonial idea of hundreds: "In colonial times, a hundred was a subdivision of a county or shire that supported about a hundred homesteads. Thomas Jefferson was a vocal proponent of the establishment of hundreds in the United States. He believed that the hundred was the perfect size for self-government and education, but small enough that everyone could know each other well."

Sitting in the taproom at Gibb's Hundred, it is easy to see its future as a gathering place for the people of Greensboro and craft beer lovers from around the state.

NATTY GREENE'S PUB & BREWING COMPANY

Elm Street location:
345 South Elm Street
Greensboro, NC 27401
336-274-1373
Hours: Daily, 11 A.M.–midnight
Brewmaster: Mike Rollinson
Opened: 2004

Lee Street location:
1918 West Lee Street
Greensboro, NC 27403
336-856-6111
Hours: Friday, 5 P.M.–9 P.M.
Brewmaster: Scott Christoffel
Opened: 2006

Email: general@nattygreenes.com
Website: nattygreenes.com
Owners: Chris Lester, Kayne Fisher

BACK IN THE EARLY 1990S, CHRIS LESTER AND KAYNE FISHER WERE STUDENTS and friends at UNC-Greensboro who dreamed of one day having their own brewery. In 1996, they finally started down that path when they bought Spring Garden Bar and Grill, a popular hangout for UNCG students. They renamed it Old Town Draught House and decided that great food paired with excellent craft beer available at few other locations in North Carolina would be a good fit. The place took off like wildfire.

In 1998, they expanded the idea into Winston-Salem, opening First Street Draught House. They followed that in 2002 with Tap Room in Greensboro. All three locations followed the same concept: great food, good prices, and excellent beer.

In 2004, they acted on their original dream of opening their own brewery. They found a building in downtown Greensboro and renovated it, and Natty Greene's—named after Nathanael Greene, the Revolutionary War general who ran the Southern campaign—was born. Although the building was old, it was

Natty Greene's Pub & Brewing Company
Erik Lars Myers

beautiful and perfectly positioned. Featuring high-quality food and a suite of beers created by brewmaster Scott Christoffel, the brewpub was an instant hit. Christoffel, a graduate of the Siebel Institute's World Brewing Academy, worked at Left Hand Brewing Company before arriving to create Natty's flagship brands.

The first floor has vaulted ceilings and an enormous dining area that greets patrons as they enter. A dark wooden bar leads toward the brewhouse, which is elevated and sits, gleaming, behind the stairs to the second story. The brewpub also features a quaint outdoor patio and a large event space in the loft, which is often used for private parties and business meetings.

It wasn't long before the brewpub started distributing its popular beers to outside accounts. In fact, Natty Greene's had a difficult time keeping up with production. Lester and Fisher decided it was time to expand. In 2006, they opened a full production facility, hiring classically trained German brewer Sebastian Wolfrum and Mike Rollinson—or "Uncle Mike," as he's known in the brewery. Christoffel moved to the production facility to continue brewing his flagship beers, Rollinson took over the brewpub, and Wolfrum worked as director of brewing operations. With a bottling line and talent in place, the brand exploded. Within three months of opening the production facility, Natty Greene's was the number-one craft beer in Greensboro, outselling all local and national brands.

Soon afterward, Lester and Fisher decided to expand again, this time in two places. First came another pub, in Raleigh in the Powerhouse Square building, the same location as the now-defunct Southend Brewery. The other expansion was of the production facility, which went from a 6,000-barrels-per-year operation to one that can handle up to 20,000 barrels a year. Unfortunately, the Raleigh pub location closed in August 2015 after the building changed landlords. But the production brewery expansion has dramatically grown the distribution reach of Natty Greene's. That success has prompted Lester and Fisher to plan an additional move and expansion, though the new location is undecided.

RED OAK BREWERY

6901 Konica Drive
Whitsett, NC 27377
336-447-2055
Email: office@redoakbrewery.com
Website: redoakbrewery.com
Hours: Monday–Friday, 9 A.M.–5 P.M.
Owner: Bill Sherrill
Brewmaster: Chris Buckley
Opened: 1991

IN 1979, ON A DIRT ROAD ACROSS THE STREET FROM GUILFORD COLLEGE, Bill Sherrill started his first restaurant. Called Franklin's off Friendly, it was Greensboro's inaugural fine-dining establishment, offering the freshest possible food and a million-dollar wine list. Shortly afterward, Sherrill began opening a chain of restaurants around central North Carolina. Spring Garden Bar and Grill had locations in Greensboro, Winston-Salem, Charlotte, and Chapel Hill. The effort proved to Sherrill that the trend toward casual dining was far outstripping fine dining.

Sherrill was no stranger to beer, as he had lived a large part of his youth in Europe, graduating from high school in Switzerland and spending time in Cologne, Germany. After college, he experienced the Pacific Northwest and saw firsthand the initial microbreweries opening their doors.

He decided to switch Franklin's off Friendly to casual. He closed the restaurant in 1988 and began renovations. Sherrill turned the piano bar into a brewhouse and renamed the establishment Spring Garden Brewery. Its flagship beer was Red Oak, a Vienna-style amber lager created by the original brewmaster at Red Oak, Christian Boos. It was so popular that by 2002 the name of the brewpub was changed to Red Oak.

Chris Buckley, Red Oak's current brewmaster, grew up in Bonn, Germany, and has the perfect background to work at a brewery specializing in German-style lagers. Through an apprenticeship at one of the oldest breweries in Germany, he is a certified brewer and maltster. After his apprenticeship, he worked

The bottling line at Red Oak Brewery
Erik Lars Myers

at Paulaner for a couple of years, then moved to the United States, getting a job at Native Brewing Company in Alexandria, Virginia. That job eventually brought him to Red Oak. Both brewing companies used the same German brewing system, so Boos and Buckley were often in touch. In 2002, Boos left the industry to take care of a family medical emergency. When he moved back to his native Canada, Red Oak had to look for a brewer. It employed Henryk Orlik of Abita Brewing Company for a brief stint, but Orlik missed New Orleans and soon had an opportunity to start his own brewery, Heiner Brau, in Louisiana. Left with a German-style brewhouse, an incredibly successful brewpub, and no brewer, Sherrill contacted the brewhouse manufacturer for a recommendation. It put him in touch with Buckley at Native Brewing.

For Buckley, the timing was perfect. Native Brewing was in the process of moving to Delaware (becoming Fordham Brewing Company in the process), and it wasn't a shift he was sure he wanted to make. "I came down here and saw the potential for this brewery," he says. "I remember passing those same weathered signs on I-40 that people talked about for years, the ones that said, 'Future Site of Red Oak Brewery.' There was no plan at the time, no blueprints, but I took the job on the premise that they would follow through and actually open up their brewery here."

Buckley soon took over brewing operations at the brewpub. "The brewpub was a fun challenge for me, because I went from working at Paulaner, which was a high-tech, fully automated megabrewery, to Native in Alexandria, which was a semi-automated system, to Red Oak in Greensboro, the brewpub, which was entirely manual. We were doing 16 brews a week, every week. We had just under 1,100 square feet of brewing space, and we made close to 5,000 barrels per year in that facility."

Just a few years later, though, Buckley was able to design, from the ground up, the new Red Oak brewing facility where it had long been advertised. The move to the facility started in April 2007. By July of that year, Red Oak turned out its first batch.

Having closed the brewpub when it made the move, Red Oak now self-distributes around the state. It started bottling its beers shortly after the production facility opened.

Currently, the brewery bottles its flagship Red Oak lager and Hummingbird helles. It also has a rotating list of seasonal bock-style beers that are released on draft.

Buckley is excited about the company's growth. But the most exciting thing for him is simply working at Red Oak. "It's just such a great company," he says. "It's like a big family. We all take pride in what we do, and I think it shows. Running this state-of-the-art brewery is just a dream come true."

HAW RIVER
FARMHOUSE ALES

1713 Sax-Beth Church Road
Saxapahaw, NC 27340
336-525-9270
Email: info@hawriverales.com
Website: hawriverales.com
Hours: Thursday–Friday, 4 P.M.–8 P.M.;
    Saturday, noon–9 P.M.; Sunday, noon–8 P.M.
Founders: Dawnya and Ben Woodward
Head Brewer: Nathan Gastol
Brewing Staff: Chais McCurry
Opened: 2014

AN IMPORTANT PART OF BEER HISTORY IS ROOTED IN RURAL FARMING COMMUNITIES.

To get a glimpse of what that looks like for a new generation, beer lovers can travel to Saxapahaw to visit Haw River Farmhouse Ales. Haw River is the model of a contemporary farmhouse-style brewery. Its relationship with local farmers and food producers is deep. Like many other North Carolina breweries, it gets a portion of its malt from Asheville's Riverbend Malt House. But most of Haw River's more unique ingredients come from within 100 miles of the brewery. A tour through its ever-rotating beer list uncovers local vegetables such as carrots and beets, fruits such as hibiscus and peaches, and herbs or spices including ginger and angelica.

Haw River cofounder Ben Woodward explains that "playing with flavor combinations and unorthodox ingredients" is a core principle of his small brewery. "Since we're located in rural Alamance County, surrounded by beautiful farms and growers of all kinds, it just makes perfect sense that we'd try to work with farmers to supply as many of our ingredients as possible." The brewery's focus on sustainability practices such as harnessing solar energy and capturing and reusing CO_2 from its fermentation process is also part of its commitment to creating a responsible local economy.

Like many other aspiring craft brewers, Dawnya and Ben Woodward spent years homebrewing and developing their business plan. But Ben says they shared

The entrance to Haw River Farmhouse Ales, sandwiched between Haw River Ballroom and the Eddy Pub in historic and beautiful Saxapahaw
Erik Lars Myers

their plans early in the game. "Because my background is in marketing and graphic design, our journey to opening day was a rather public one," he admits.

That early community building paid off when the Woodwards ran a Kickstarter campaign to fund some of their sustainability plans—and were delighted to exceed their goal. Visitors to their brewery in the lower floors of a renovated cotton mill and dye house see the care they put into their new space, from the wooden barrel and welcome sign at the entrance to the cozy taproom and the shining steel brewing system that lies behind it.

Although the Woodwards have a 10-barrel modern brewhouse, their passion for old-fashioned means of fermentation is clear in the number of barrels lining one wall of their brewery. In addition to the barrels and stainless-steel tanks, Haw River sports oak foeders—large wooden fermentation vessels—used to age some of the beers. The barrels and foeders help give Haw River's beers the funky, oaky notes that are quickly becoming their signature. In the future, Ben looks forward to adding to the brewery's wooden fermentation and aging capability. "Most of our expansion will be in the form of oak," he explains, "as it's a lot more flexible, as far as our limited amount of space goes."

Although Haw River's beers are all inspired by Belgian- or farmhouse-style recipes and ingredients, that doesn't mean they are created the same. In fact, visitors pulling up a stool to the taproom's short bar will find 12 taps pouring a pale ale or an IPA and a stout or two, as well as the anticipated saisons and abbey styles inflected with Haw River's unique ingredients and approach. With so many unusual beers available, many patrons may be found in front of the taproom's solid-wood sample trays, where four small snifters of beer allow them to compare the flavors and choose their favorite of the day.

Ben admits that "keeping up with demand while simultaneously keeping the level of quality high" can be a struggle for a young craft brewery, especially one as experimental as Haw River. Working with local and seasonal ingredients demands a flexible approach, but so far it has met with success, and the Woodwards and their brewery team are excited for the future. According to Ben, the upcoming plans are "to package and bottle a greater variety of beer, with fun side projects and small-batch releases."

New recipes and releases are fun, but Ben points out that it always comes back to the human community for Haw River: "We just hope to continue having a great time making beer people enjoy."

TRIANGLE BREWERIES

N

AREA OF DETAIL

Bear Creek
Bear Creek Brews

Carrboro
Starpoint Brewing
Steel String Brewery
YesterYears Brewery

Chapel Hill/Pittsboro
Carolina Brewery

Chapel Hill
Top of the Hill Restaurant, Brewery, and Distillery

Hillsborough
Mystery Brewing
Regulator Brewing Company

Durham
G2B Restaurant and Brewery
Bull Durham Beer Company
Bull City Burger and Brewe'y
Fullsteam Brewery
Ponysaurus Brewing Company
Triangle Brewing Company

Holly Springs
Carolina Brewing Company
Bombshell Beer Company

Apex
Blueprint Brewing Company

Fuquay-Varina
Aviator Brewing Company
Fainting Goat Brewing Company
Draft Line Brewing Company
Lincoln Brewing Company

Cary
Fortnight Brewing Company

Raleigh
Lonerider Brewing Company
Gizmo Brew Works
Raleigh Brewing Company
Trophy Brewing Company
Boylan Bridge Brewpub
Crank Arm Brewing
Nickelpoint Brewing Company
Neuse River Brewing Company
Sub Noir Brewing Company
Lynnwood Brewing Concern
Big Boss Brewing Company
Compass Rose Brewery

Angier
White Rabbit Brewing Company

Wake Forest
White Street Brewing Company

Clayton
Deep River Brewing Company

Smithfield
Double Barley Brewing

Hillsborough
Chapel Hill
Carrboro
Pittsboro
Bear Creek
Apex
Cary
Holly Springs
Wake Forest
Durham
Raleigh
Fuquay-Varina
Angier
Clayton
Smithfield

85
40 85
1
64
95
95
40
70

BEAR CREEK BREWS

10538 NC 902
Bear Creek, NC 27207
919-200-3930
Email: Dave@BearCreekBrews.com
Website: bearcreekbrews.com
Hours: By appointment
Founder: Dave Peters
Head Brewer: Dave Peters
Opened: 2014

TRIANGLE-AREA BEER DRINKERS LOOKING FOR SOMETHING OFF THE BEATEN PATH should turn in the direction of Bear Creek Brews, a nanobrewery located southwest of Pittsboro in Bear Creek. Bear Creek Brews is a one-man operation. Founder and brewer Dave Peters set up his tiny system in a steel cargo container in what is essentially his backyard. Outside of the container, he's built a small beer garden where visitors can sit and sip his brews while watching the chickens peck away at the spent grain from that brewing day. It's a picture about as far from the bustle of a busy taproom or restaurant as you can get.

Peters, a Wisconsin native who started as a homebrewer, got his professional brewing permits in order to share his beer with a wider number of people. Visits to his brewing location are by appointment only, but he's easy to find out and about in nearby towns at events including Pittsboro's First Sunday and Sanford's Second Sunday local markets, food truck rodeos, and music festivals. Bear Creek's beers come packaged in bottles with labels featuring a distinctive image of Yosemite's Half Dome. On his website, Peters explains that the picture isn't a dig at North Carolina's scenery but rather a callback to his youth and the natural beauty that first inspired him.

Since Bear Creek is so small, one of the services Peters offers is custom-made beer for special events. Beer enthusiasts in the Pittsboro and Sanford areas looking for a few kegs in a style of their choice might consider reaching out to Peters to see if they can commission a beer of their own.

STARPOINT BREWING

Carrboro, NC
Email: info@starpointbrewing.com
Website: starpointbrewing.com
Founder: Tim Harper
Head Brewer: Tim Harper
Opened: 2012

SOMEWHERE IN THE WOODS OUTSIDE CARRBORO IS A SMALL BUILDING with a three-barrel brewing system.

This building in the woods is Starpoint, Carrboro's most secluded brewery. Starpoint opened in 2012 when Tim Harper, an award-winning homebrewer, decided he'd like to try making those blue ribbon IPAs on a larger scale. Although Harper loves brewing, he was wary of making it his full-time job, so he started Starpoint as a part-time business out of a building outside his home.

Harper's approach frees him from worrying about opening hours, taproom policies, dishwashers, and serving permits. For him, it is all about making the best beer possible and getting it into drinkers' hands. Luckily, Harper has some help in that area. In 2014, he signed a contract with Mims Distributing that took a load off his car, which he was using to self-distribute, and gave him more time to focus on the beer. Harper's approach has paid off. He's planning an expansion of his brewing system in the near future.

Starpoint focuses on big, bold ales that showcase the flavors of American hops. Drinkers who love pale ales and IPAs will enjoy hunting up their beers on draft or in 22-ounce bottles to test Harper's variations on those styles. People who aren't into hops may want to seek out Starpoint's Whiskeytown Imperial Milk Stout, a hefty dark beer aged in whiskey barrels.

No matter which Starpoint beer craft drinkers choose, it is guaranteed to pack a punch.

The brewhouse at Starpoint Brewing
Starpoint Brewing

NORTH CAROLINA NC CRAFT BREWERS GUILD

NORTH CAROLINA CRAFT BREWERS GUILD

The North Carolina Craft Brewers Guild is a not-for-profit 501(c)(6) tax-exempt organization comprised of brewers, vendors, retailers, and craft beer enthusiasts focused on promoting North Carolina beer and breweries.

The guild had its start in 2008, when founding members Jamie Bartholomaus of Foothills Brewing, David Gonzalez of Rock Bottom Brewery (now of Foothills), Paul Philippon of The Duck-Rabbit Craft Brewery, John Lyda of Highland Brewing Company, and Sebastian Wolfrum of Natty Greene's Pub & Brewing Company (now co-owner of Epiphany Craft Malting and cofounder of Bull Durham Beer Company) rallied brewers and brewery owners from around the state to a common mission of promoting North Carolina beer, cooperating on purchasing, exchanging knowledge and support among members, and backing—or fighting—legislative initiatives in the common interest of the state's breweries.

In addition, the guild supports and is supported by retail members (bottle shops, bars, and restaurants) and affiliate members (suppliers, vendors, and service providers for the craft brewing industry). It has also created its "Pint Hound" program for North Carolina craft beer fans.

Since its creation, the North Carolina Craft Brewers Guild has seen great success, hosting educational programs for brewers and North Carolina–based beer festivals, as well as pursuing legislative changes and protecting the legal rights of breweries and brewers throughout the state. For information, a constantly updated list of North Carolina breweries and their events, and all the latest North Carolina beer news, visit the guild's website at ncbeer.org.

STEEL STRING BREWERY

106A South Greensboro Street
Carrboro, NC 27510
919-240-7215
Email: info@steelstringbrewery.com
Website: steelstringbrewery.com
Hours: Monday–Wednesday, 4 P.M.–midnight,
    Thursday–Friday, 2 P.M.–midnight;
    Saturday–Sunday, noon–midnight
Founders: Will Isley, Cody Maltais,
    Andrew Scharfenberg, Eric Knight
Head Brewer: Will Isley
Assistant Brewer: Kord Scharfenberg
Opened: 2013

STEEL STRING BREWERY'S HOME IS A WEATHERED BRICK BUILDING in the heart of downtown Carrboro. Tables spill out onto a concrete patio that adds to the town's active sidewalk life. Inside, a bar fronted in corrugated metal curves away to the right, while the rest of the taproom space is filled with scattered wooden tables. Drinkers have a choice of 10 different taps, five to seven of them Steel String brews and the rest a selection of guest taps, often from other North Carolina breweries. Steel String has a few year-round beers, including its Rubber Room Session Ale, but most of its taps rotate through a variety of recipes. Its tap list is likely to feature big, hoppy IPAs and farmhouse or sour styles such as saison and gose.

Steel String's owners like to keep things funky and flexible. Two of them, Will Isley and Cody Maltais, first collaborated as musicians when they played bluegrass together in college. When Isley got into homebrewing, Maltais was an enthusiastic taster. Several years later when Maltais returned from a tour in Iraq, he and Isley joined with Andrew Scharfenberg and Eric Knight to open Steel String.

The name and the brewery's décor are inspired by the musical background of Isley and Maltais. Fittingly, live music is a frequent event at Steel String, along with other community crowd-pleasers such as trivia contests that pack the brewery's compact taproom.

Taps stand before the Steel String mural.
Erik Lars Myers

The relatively small size of Steel String's building makes growth a tricky proposition. For the moment, the partners have no plans to expand their brewing system but are growing their barrel aging program with the addition of wine barrels, which visitors can see stacked on racks against the taproom wall.

YESTERYEARS BREWERY

300 East Main Street, Suite C
Carrboro, NC 27510
919-904-7273
Email: info@yesteryearsbrewery.com
Website: yesteryearsbrewery.com
Hours: Monday–Thursday, 3 P.M.–midnight;
  Friday–Sunday, noon–midnight
Founder: David Larsen
Brewmaster: David Larsen
Assistant Brewers: Stephanie MacDonald,
  Bill Larsen
Opened: 2015

YESTERYEARS BREWERY IS LOCATED IN THE BUSY HEART OF CARRBORO right next to the popular music venue Cat's Cradle. However, founder David Larsen wants his patrons to be able to leave the hustle of modern life at the door. For Larsen, beer is a chance for people to stop and take a breath: "I wanted a place where people could come in and forget about the outside world and remember when life moved a little slower."

YesterYears is Larsen's way of combining his love for the science and process of brewing with his passion for family, friendship, and community. The brewery's branding is focused on the mid-20th century, a time when, Larsen says, technology didn't get in the way of friendly get-togethers. Larsen credits his father with teaching him "how to do something fully and without regret." He brings that attitude to his business. The brewery, Larsen says, is partly a memorial to his father, who passed away in 2014.

Starting out, Larsen experienced the same challenges as many homebrewers who turn professional: getting used to a big system and scaling up recipes to match. Although known for his IPAs, he launched a variety of styles and plans to keep experimenting with one-off and seasonal beers to tempt the palates of taproom visitors.

From the outside, YesterYears has a modern look, thanks to the shopping center that is its home. Inside, however, Larsen and his team have made the brewery into an inviting communal gathering space. As patrons enter the

The spacious brewing floor at YesterYears Brewery
Erik Lars Myers

taproom, a brick wall on the left is covered with the kind of collage-style frames that traditionally hold family photographs, while a glass door on the right provides a glimpse of the brewing equipment (also visible through the large front windows). Gray Squirrel Coffee Company, which shares space with YesterYears, offers beverage options for non-beer drinkers and adds an extra dimension to the already-attractive location.

For anyone looking for a relaxed place to enjoy "the good old days in a bottle," YesterYears Brewery has a stool waiting at the bar.

CHAPEL HILL & PITTSBORO, NC

CAROLINA BREWERY

Chapel Hill location:
460 West Franklin Street
Chapel Hill, NC 27516
919-942-1800
Hours: Monday–Thursday, 11 A.M.–midnight;
    Friday–Saturday, 11:30 A.M.–1 A.M.;
    Sunday, 11 A.M.–11 P.M.

Pittsboro location:
120 Lowes Drive #100
Pittsboro, NC 27312
919-545-2330
Hours: Sunday–Thursday, 11 A.M.–11 P.M.;
    Friday–Saturday, 11 A.M.–midnight

Website: carolinabrewery.com
Owner: Robert Poitras
Head Brewer: Jon Connolly
Opened: 1995

outside

HEAD WEST DOWN FRANKLIN STREET FROM THE FLAGSHIP CAMPUS OF THE UNIVERSITY OF NORTH CAROLINA in historic Chapel Hill and you'll find Carolina Brewery, the town's first brewpub, now a major area attraction for beer and food lovers alike.

From the outside, it might be any other restaurant on the west end of Franklin Street. The building features simple brickwork, and large maple and pin oak trees grow along the road and push up the brick sidewalk around the tables in the brewery's outdoor dining area. Inside, the proud copper kettle gleams as visitors walk in the door. On most days, the rich, sweet smell of a mash in progress wafts through the restaurant. A long granite bar winds its way around the brewpub just feet from the brewing equipment, so visitors can often listen to the bubbling of active fermentation while watching their favorite sports teams on the televisions above the bar. The upstairs portion of the brewpub is a mixture of comfortable booths, tables, and a private room where patrons gather for seasonal beer releases and other special events.

The mash tun being emptied at Carolina Brewery's
Pittsboro location
Erik Lars Myers

Owner Robert Poitras was a student at UNC–Chapel Hill when a study-abroad experience near Interlaken, Switzerland, introduced him to the concept of locally made, flavorful brews. "I was impressed with the sense of pride people had for their local beer," he notes.

During a summer trip to San Diego, Poitras noticed a similar local beer movement. He and his original business partner, Chris Rice (who has since moved on), thought Chapel Hill could benefit from a brewpub like the ones in San Diego. "I didn't want to be a banker, stuck up on the 57th floor, working nine to six, and stuck in traffic, and wearing a tie," Poitras realized. Over the next year, Poitras and Rice started doing research to make a Chapel Hill brewpub a reality.

His first brewmaster turned out to be a master stroke. Originally a mechanical and electrical designer, Jon Connolly knew he wanted to be involved in the beer business in some way since his first sip of a hoppy IPA in California in the

1980s. Connolly tried out homebrewing but was unsatisfied with the results. "Of course I was doing everything with syrups," he says. "Whoever thought that tasted anything like Anchor Steam didn't know anything about beer."

In January 1994, Connolly attended the Siebel Institute's concise course in brewing technology. Soon afterward, he was able to join Legend Brewing Company in Richmond, Virginia. When Legend's head brewer left less than a month later, Connolly was thrust into the position, where, he says, "I learned really fast everything I needed to learn to make a small brewery hum."

A year later, Poitras contacted him to gauge his interest in moving to Chapel Hill and helping start Carolina Brewery. Connolly had relatives in the area and had been to Chapel Hill on a visit. "I really fell in love with the town," he says. "It was a perfect fit." Connolly has been here ever since.

The brewery was a success from the beginning, winning medals in regional and national competitions and growing in leaps and bounds. It even started to sell beer to other bars and restaurants in the area. "It started off slowly at first," Connolly says. "A bar in town would just say, 'Please, can I just put your beer on tap?' And it just grew and grew."

To meet that demand, Poitras and Connolly opened a second Carolina Brewery in Pittsboro in 2007. Pittsboro, they thought, was an underserved location. Just off Highway 64, it is equidistant from Chapel Hill, Cary, and Apex—fast-growing parts of North Carolina's Research Triangle.

The Pittsboro location has proven another great success. It looks like an expanded version of the Chapel Hill location, with the same long granite bar. But Pittsboro also has a large dining room and a gorgeous outdoor patio. The brewing equipment is behind a glass wall to keep the noise from reaching the bar, but patrons can still watch the brewing process. They can also join in a weekly tour to see from the inside the bustling facility now producing beer for multiple states.

The Chapel Hill pub, which now brews only small-batch seasonals, continues to be a hub of activity for Carolina sports and beer fans. It remains a vibrant part of the West Franklin Street restaurant scene.

POP THE CAP

Until 2005, the definition of a malt beverage in the North Carolina General Statutes read as it had since Prohibition: " 'Malt beverage' means beer, lager, malt liquor, ale, porter, and any other brewed or fermented beverage containing at least one-half percent (0.5%), and not more than six percent (6%) alcohol by volume."

All beer in North Carolina was limited to 6 percent alcohol or less. This policy was instituted when the state legislature passed the Alcoholic Beverage Control Act of 1937. It was never revisited. North Carolinians had few options for beer in 1937, just four short years after Prohibition was repealed. Many business owners may have greeted a cap on alcohol in beer as a way to control drunkenness in their workers.

In the 1990s, in the midst of the craft beer revolution, the restriction had a stifling effect on the beer industry in the state. In-state brewers couldn't brew many of the popular styles being produced around the country and the world, and distributors were limited in the beers they could import into the state for resale.

Unfortunately, many people—even those interested in good beer—had no idea a limit was in effect.

Sean Lilly Wilson, past president of Pop the Cap, relates how he learned about the law: "A friend of mine from business school took me to a party at Duke back in 2002. In it, they were selling, for a dollar per pint—true pints—barleywines and 'Batch Number-Ones' and cork-and-caged bottles and things I'd never seen before in North Carolina. I just started asking, 'Why have I never seen this before?' And my friend said, 'Well, they're illegal in North Carolina.' And my reaction was, 'That's really stupid. What can we do about it?' So it kind of got into my head, and I started researching, and I realized that North Carolina was one of five states with this restriction, and it just got to me a little bit.

"That night was my craft beer epiphany. I was a craft beer enthusiast just starting to explore this world of craft beer that was unavailable in North Carolina. And up to that point, I thought I knew craft beer really well. You know, I had bought Sam Adams on sale at Harris Teeter, and I supported the few local breweries

that were here when I had the chance. But it was from that party that I thought, *Let's figure this out.*"

Wilson contacted Julie Johnson Bradford of *All About Beer* magazine, who helped organize the movement. By February 2003, some 35 beer lovers were meeting in the offices of the magazine with one goal in mind: lift the alcohol-by-volume cap on beer in North Carolina.

The effort took two and a half years. The nonprofit organization, named Pop the Cap, raised money from thousands of North Carolinians in order to hire lobbyist Theresa Kostrzewa, who eventually shepherded the bill through two House committees, two Senate committees, and both houses of the state legislature. The bill did not pass without argument. It met opposition by those who likened strong beer to "drinking straight vodka" and those who argued that beer with a high alcoholic content would lead to unwanted pregnancies and academic-related suicides.

In the end, the bill passed both the House and the Senate by comfortable margins and was signed into law by Governor Mike Easley on August 13, 2005—but not without a slight change. The original bill as filed removed the cap on alcohol completely. Yet by the time the bill passed the legislature, another artificial cap—of 15 percent—was imposed, ostensibly to keep the alcohol percentage of beer distinct from that of wine. (Unfortified wine, fermented naturally or with sugar, does not exceed 17 percent alcohol. Fortified wine, which usually has added brandy to stop the fermentation, exceeds 17 percent alcohol.) However, the new cap effectively limits only a handful of specific beers—mostly ultra-rare novelties—from entering the state.

"In a way, our 15 percent cap makes those rare high-alcohol exceptions all the sweeter to track down and enjoy," Wilson says.

TOP OF THE HILL
RESTAURANT, BREWERY,
AND DISTILLERY

TOPO

Chapel Hill, North Carolina

100 East Franklin Street
Chapel Hill, NC 27514
919-929-8676
Email: contactus@topofthehill.com
Website: thetopofthehill.com
Hours: Daily, 11 A.M.–2 A.M.
Owner: Scott Maitland
Brewmasters: Aaron Caracci, Chris Atkins
Opened: 1996

SCOTT MAITLAND, FOUNDER OF TOP OF THE HILL, credits his time in the military for pushing him down the path of entrepreneurship. His undergraduate schooling was at the United States Military Academy at West Point. "I was in the Gulf War," says Maitland, "and between my experience having the dumbest company commanding officer that I've ever met in the army and seeing my father get fired from his job after 19 and a half years at the same bank, it sort of cemented the idea in me that I never wanted anybody stupider than me to be in charge of me ever again. I wanted to run my own business because I realized that, societally, we were making this transition from that whole work-30-years-and-retire deal to where we're all kind of our own free agents."

Following advice from some entrepreneurs he met soon after leaving the army, he enrolled in law school instead of business school to get his start. After a stint as Ross Perot's Florida campaign manager in his 1992 run for president, Maitland returned to Chapel Hill. Construction had just started on a new building atop what used to be a gas station at the corner of Franklin and Columbia Streets. When the owner announced that the new building would house a TGI Fridays, Maitland balked. "I couldn't stand the thought of a chain restaurant dominating historical downtown Chapel Hill."

He tells his story about how he came around to the idea of a microbrewery: "So I'm studying law in what was then the only coffee shop in Chapel Hill, and

Top of the Hill Restaurant, Brewery, and Distillery in Chapel Hill
Erik Lars Myers

I'm reading a *U.S. News & World Report*, and it's about this company in Seattle, Washington, called Starbucks and whether or not they were going to make it, because they had taken this commodity and turned it into a consumer product. And the whole article was talking about how Mrs. Fields did it with cookies, Ben & Jerry's did it with ice cream, Starbucks is now doing it with coffee. You know in those magazines how they usually have the story inside the story? In there was an article that said, 'What's the next food to be gentrified?' And the answer was . . . I don't know. But everywhere these upscale coffee houses were going, this concept called a 'microbrewery' seemed to be doing very well.

"A half-hour later, the owner of the coffee shop comes out and says, 'Folks, I've got bad news. Tonight is actually my last night of business. But don't worry. Two upscale coffee houses are opening up in downtown Chapel Hill in the next two months.' And he used the same term as the magazine, and that's where I had the thought to do this.

"So I went home and—this being 1994 and there not really being an Internet to speak of—I ran a search on LexisNexis for every article written in the past five years mentioning 'microbrewery,' 'brewpub,' whatever."

His search returned 872 articles. After reading 864 of them, he found an article mentioning that the headquarters of *All About Beer* magazine had moved from Boulder, Colorado, to Durham. It was at that point he thought, *I'm going to do this.*

Soon afterward, Maitland teamed up with his best friend from high school, who was a restaurateur, and Daniel Bradford, the editor of *All About Beer*, to make his idea a reality. Over a couple of years, he raised $1.2 million, much of it from the community. A plaque just inside the main doors of the restaurant bears the names of all the original donors.

With Bradford's help, Maitland decided he wanted to focus on English-style ales for the brewpub. He took out an ad in the British magazine *What's Brewing*, a CAMRA (Campaign for Real Ales) journal, and was contacted by John Withey. Withey had started his professional brewing career at Greene King Brewery in Suffolk, England, before joining the iconic Whitbread Brewery. Over the next couple of decades, he worked his way up to head brewer at Whitbread's Sheffield brewery before leaving for a director's position with the Shepherd Neame chain, where he remained until 1991. After a brief run at a pub near Canterbury, where he installed a brewery, he followed the "gold rush" to American craft beer, bringing more than 30 years of brewing experience—as well as his own traditional recipes and even his own yeast—to Top of the Hill.

It is a beautiful restaurant that spans the entire third floor of the building. Light wood accents the dark, sweeping bar that greets patrons as they enter. Comfortable seating gives them a close-up view of the brewing operation, which is situated behind a glass partition along the entire restaurant. The most popular feature of Top of the Hill, however, is its balcony seating overlooking Franklin and Columbia Streets. That intersection is often packed during festivals, holidays, and, of course, NCAA basketball championship runs. "I love beer and I love food, but my primary driver here is downtown Chapel Hill," Maitland says. "I love it."

In early 2010, Maitland added another dimension to Top of the Hill by opening the Back Bar inside the same building, in a space previously occupied by the Carolina Theater. While still showcasing the sleek design of Top of the Hill's brewpub, the Back Bar has much more in common with a traditional British pub. It's a hangout offering finger food, pool tables, dartboards, foosball, televisions, and, as would be fitting in any British pub, cask-conditioned ales. Two beer engines—hand-drawn pumps that pull beer from casks stored at cellar temperature beneath the bar—serve up ale the way it has been done traditionally in the UK for centuries.

Top of the Hill was the first North Carolina brewery to put its beer in cans. In 2004, at the Craft Brewers Conference in San Diego, Maitland met with a company called Cask, which was just starting to manufacture small canning machines for microbreweries. He was immediately enthralled. "I hate growlers," he says. "I think growlers are an abomination. Why anybody would want to treat their beer like that is beyond me. But cans, I thought, *Fantastic!* I thought, *This will be the replacement of the growler.*"

The brewery at Top of the Hill had some extra capacity, so despite the skepticism of his brewing staff, Maitland decided to get a small canning machine. What he later discovered was that the minimum order at that time was 160,000 cans. Having already bought the canning line, he felt he had to make the jump. The brewery created a new brand for it: Leaderboard Trophy Lager. Maitland wasn't immediately interested in getting into grocery stores. Feeling that shelf space was already growing tight for craft beers, he decided not to compete for that space. Instead, he wanted to shoot for a niche where he had noticed a consistent lack of good beer: golf courses.

The effort was extremely successful—so successful, in fact, that the brewery went through all its excess capacity and ended up falling behind on demand.

"That is what led me to get into distilling," says Maitland. He had decided he needed to build another brewery to handle the canning operation. But as he put the business plan together, he realized the profit margin on a packaging brewery was much smaller than on a brewpub. So if he was going to make that jump, he wanted to do so with a much larger brewing facility than he was currently operating. Of course, since it would take awhile for his sales and marketing to catch up with his new production volume, he needed a plan to deal with any excess beer he might have during initial production. He therefore started looking at distilling.

Maitland soon realized that, while all kinds of people are making craft beer now, few are doing craft distilling, so he shifted gears and left the idea of a brewery expansion behind. He started working on his idea for a microdistillery in 2006. After years of navigating long-untouched laws and regulations, TOPO Distillery finally opened in 2012, distilling vodka, gin, and whiskey using local and organic agricultural products.

Sadly, those spirits are off-topic for this book. But beer drinkers seeking out Top of the Hill for the beer might also enjoy slipping down the street for a tour of TOPO Distillery.

MYSTERY BREWING

Production brewery:
437 Dimmocks Mill Road, Suite #41
Hillsborough, NC 27278
919-MYSTERY

Taproom:
230 South Nash Street
Hillsborough, NC 27278
919-245-1325
Email: publichouse@mysterybrewing.com
Website: mysterybrewing.com
Hours: Monday–Tuesday, 4 P.M.–10 P.M.;
    Wednesday–Thursday, 4 P.M.–11 P.M.;
    Friday, 2 P.M.–midnight;
    Saturday, noon–midnight;
    Sunday, noon–10 P.M.
Founders: Erik Lars Myers, Andrew Turner,
    Meg Notaro, Raffaele Notaro, Brian An-
    derson, Patrick Clapp, Grace Webber
Head Brewer: Erik Lars Myers
Opened: 2012

16 ounce   outside

"Beer does not make itself properly by itself. It takes an element of mystery and of things that no one can understand."—Fritz Maytag

WHEN PATRONS WALK ONTO MYSTERY BREWING'S SPACIOUS PRODUCTION FLOOR, Fritz Maytag's words dominate one of the walls. That quote, from one of the forefathers of the craft beer movement, resonates with founder Erik Lars Myers. But his choice of the name Mystery Brewing has a longer history than Fritz Maytag and Anchor Brewing Company. "*Mystery* is the traditional word for the art or craft of a trade," Myers explains, "and the first recognized guild of tradespeople in England was a guild of brewers, dedicated to protecting the art and mystery of brewing."

Although Mystery has a traditional name, its business plan is anything but. For one thing, Mystery was the first brewery project to successfully fund through the online platform Kickstarter. The amount wasn't enough to cover all the opening expenses (breweries are not cheap), but it helped launch the brand

A band rocks out on the small stage at Mystery Brewing's Public House.
Erik Lars Myers

and started creating the supportive community any small business needs. For another thing, Mystery Brewing is the world's first seasonal-only brewery. Instead of making one or two flagship beers year-round, Mystery brews four beers for each season: a session ale, a hoppy beer, a saison, and a dark beer. Myers describes the unusual approach this way: "Most people are seasonal beer drinkers. No one drinks the same beer every week year-round. So I'm brewing beer the way people drink beer."

In addition to the core four seasonal beers, Mystery frequently releases one-off recipes, has a barrel aging program, and has a track record of interesting collaboration beers. Some are with other breweries, such as 2014's North Carolina Craft Brewers Guild collaboration, NC Gose West, which included ingredients ranging from the mountains to the coast. Some are with local restaurants, including La Place Louisiana Cookery in downtown Hillsborough. Others are with local music groups such as Raleigh band Jack The Radio, Mystery's house band, the Wiley Fosters, and Hillsborough's Yep Roc record label. All of these collaborations encourage Myers to stretch his creative muscles to make beers that capture the spirit of everyone involved.

Myers's approach to beer combines artistic license with chemical science. He spent over 13 years experimenting with interesting recipes at a homebrew level before taking himself to the Siebel Institute for its concise course in brewing. As a result, Mystery's recipes include a wide variety of atypical ingredients such as jasmine flowers, muscadine grapes, cayenne peppers, and even whole pumpkin pies. Meanwhile, in the on-site lab, co-owner and scientist Andrew Turner grows yeast, runs cell counts, and tests the scientific possibilities of the ideas Myers has for new beers.

Most of the time, the science works, but there have been occasional bumps along the way. One of Myers's favorite stories involves a nasturtium beer that stopped fermenting almost as soon as the petals touched the liquid. "It turns out that nasturtium is a natural antifungal," Myers laughs, "so of course it stopped the yeast as soon as it got into the solution." Careful coaxing restarted that beer, and it became a success story, like most of Mystery's unusual brews.

Mystery's other specialty is historical beer. La Querelle, its take on seefbier-style ale, won a silver medal at the 2014 Great American Beer Festival.

Although Mystery's production facility has a small five-tap bar that is open during tours, the best place to find its beer is at its taproom on Nash Street, which usually has 15 to 17 Mystery beers on tap, in addition to guest beers and local cider. Upon entering the taproom, visitors might notice the striking concrete-topped bar. Its metal facing, crafted by local artist and blacksmith Jim Adams, is made from an old Hillsborough water tower that used to stand above the brewery. The walls act as an art gallery for work by other local artists. At the back of the room is a bookcase stuffed with paperbacks and hardbacks waiting to be borrowed and read. The bookcase ties into another Mystery Brewing theme: literature and history.

All the beer names written on the wall are literary or historical references, and each has a story behind it. Some of the names come from well-known literary classics, such as Six Impossible Things, the chocolate breakfast stout inspired by Lewis Carroll's *Alice* books, in which the White Queen says, "Why, sometimes I've believed as many as six impossible things before breakfast." Other Mystery beer names dig deeper, such as Jack Thorne porter, which honors David Bryant Fulton—pen name Jack Thorne—an African-American author born in Fayetteville in 1863.

While Myers refuses to choose a favorite beer from his creations, one has special significance: Evangeline, the summer saison. The name comes from Longfellow's poem about the expulsion of the French from Canada. "My family is French-Canadian" Myers explains, "and when I was growing up, my grandparents lived on Evangeline Street." The summer saison is special for another reason, too. It features a yeast Myers cultivated back in his homebrew days that mutated to the extent that it became a recognizably different strain. That yeast is currently banked with White Labs as a proprietary strain and goes into all of Mystery's saison recipes.

After almost four years in business, Mystery is working on an expansion that involves more fermentation tanks and a canning line at the production facility and more seats, improved outdoor furniture for the dog-friendly patio, and a small restaurant kitchen at the taproom. The expansion will allow Mystery to broaden its reach in retail accounts across the state while also enhancing the experience for visitors to the pub looking to enjoy drinks, games, music, and conversation.

REGULATOR BREWING COMPANY

Hillsborough, NC
919-589-BREW
Email: regulatorbrewing@gmail.com
Website: regulatorbrewing.com
Founders: Ryan Dobbs and Anna MacDonald
Dobbs, Stephanie and Dustin Williams
Brewers: Ryan Dobbs and Anna MacDonald
Dobbs, Stephanie and Dustin Williams
Opened: 2015

WHEN TRYING TO DESCRIBE REGULATOR BREWING COMPANY, the word *hyperlocal* comes to mind. Regulator is Hillsborough's first nanobrewery, making just one barrel of beer at a time. Why so small? Because Regulator is committed to making "Beer from Here," using at least 75 percent local ingredients in every batch.

Regulator is a local product by every definition of the word. Dustin Williams likes to describe how the team first connected "on Mystery Brewing's production floor at the first meeting of the Nash Street Homebrew Club" in 2012. Ryan Dobbs and Anna MacDonald Dobbs were excited to find another homebrewing couple in Hillsborough to swap ideas with, and it wasn't long before the four were experimenting with new recipes.

Going professional was not their original plan, but enthusiastic feedback from fellow beer drinkers and a first-place win at the 2013 Homebrew for Hunger event in Carrboro inspired them to take the step. "It was amazing to have so many people ask us, 'Where can we buy this?' " Dustin recalls. "For us, that was the biggest compliment we could ever receive."

From the beginning, Regulator's focus has been on local ingredients and becoming part of "a thriving local food system," Dustin says. Regulator is a member of the Carolina Farm Stewardship Association and Got to Be NC and is forging connections with local hop growers and maltsters. Although relying on small local suppliers "requires a lot of flexibility," Dustin explains that "we believe that products grown by local farms are better for us and our beer." Those products go into three flagship beers—an IPA, a Kölsch-style ale, and Hazelnut Brown—as

The compact setup at Regulator Brewing Company
Regulator Brewing Company

well as seasonal offerings such as a pale ale brewed with jalapeño and cayenne peppers.

The company's name, also local in origin, is an homage to the War of the Regulation, a colonial rebellion in the country surrounding Hillsborough. The Regulators were colonists and farmers who banded together to protest unfair taxation and fees. The rebellion culminated in May 1771 with the Battle of Alamance, when Governor William Tryon overpowered the Regulator forces. After the battle, six of the captured rebels were taken to Hillsborough and hanged. Regulator Brewing looks back on those rebellious small farmers as early champions of a local, fair economy, the kind they hope to (peacefully) contribute to as their business grows.

Currently, Regulator operates on a small scale. Its compact brewing space is not open for tours or tastings, and it distributes kegs only to select accounts in Hillsborough.

The beer may be harder to track down than others, but visitors to Hillsborough should definitely keep their eyes peeled for this local treat.

G2B RESTAURANT AND BREWERY

3211 Shannon Road, Suite 106
Durham, NC 27707
919-251-9451
Website: g2b-restaurant.com
Hours: Tuesday–Thursday, 11:30 A.M.–1:30 P.M.,
    5 P.M.–9 P.M.;
    Friday, 11:30 A.M.–1:30 P.M., 5 P.M.–10 P.M.;
    Saturday, noon–3 P.M., 5 P.M.–10 P.M.
Founder: Shane Ingram
Head Brewer: Paul Wasmund
Opened: 2014

WHEN VISITORS ARRIVE AT THE LARGE BRICK OFFICE BUILDING that houses G2B Restaurant and Brewery, they might wonder if they've found the right location. The square, uncompromising façade doesn't project the feel usually associated with a gastropub or microbrewery.

Those questions vanish once they enter the sleek, modern dining area and see the impressive beer list. G2B's menu offers a well-curated and creative selection of seasonally appropriate dishes using local ingredients and, of course, beers that pair well with all of the food.

Shane Ingram, chef of Durham's acclaimed Four Square Restaurant, opened G2B (shorthand for Gastropub to Brewery) in 2011. At the time, the focus was on upscale pub food and high-quality beer brewed around the state and the world. Regular beer dinners pairing a local beer with a special menu helped build the restaurant's reputation as a beer destination. However, the lure of creating its own beers to pair with the menu was irresistible, so a small nanobrewing system was installed in the space in 2014.

Now, visitors to G2B find an array of creative house-brewed beers sharing the menu with other craft beers. The G2B beers stand out because of their focus on unusual and food-friendly ingredients including ginger, honey, persimmons, peanut butter, and pumpkins. The small size of G2B's brewing system means that the beers on tap change frequently to reflect the season.

The restaurant's commitment to craft beer doesn't stop with the brewery.

Secret entrance: around the back of an office building, patrons will find the blue awning and an incredible selection of food and beer.
Sarah H. Ficke

Many, if not all, of G2B's staff are Cicerone certified beer servers, a certification achieved through a test that requires knowledge of the ways to store, serve, and describe beers of various styles. This certification raises the bar for G2B employees and helps ensure that patrons enjoy a good craft beer experience, whether they're coming in for a casual lunch, a full-scale dinner, or just a taste of the latest G2B brew.

409 Blackwell Street
Durham, NC 27701
Email: info@bulldurhambeer.com
Website: bulldurhambeer.com
Hours: Open during Durham Bulls home
　games
Founders: Michael Goodmon, Sebastian
　Wolfrum
Head Brewer: Tate Little
Brewing Staff: Garrett Eder
Opened: 2015

BEER AND BASEBALL ARE A NATURAL COMBINATION, and nowhere is that more clear than at Durham Bulls Athletic Park, home of Bull Durham Beer Company Boasting a small production facility inside the ballpark itself, Bull Durham Beer Company has one of the most unusual locations and business models of any brewery in North Carolina.

Beer has long had a place at the Durham Bulls' ballpark. As the craft beer movement expanded in North Carolina, traditional ballpark beers such as Bud Light started sharing space with offerings from local companies including Carolina Brewery and Foothills. However, Bull Durham Beer's founders, Michael Goodmon and Sebastian Wolfrum, had a bigger idea: building a craft brewery right on the concourse. Thus, the Durham Bulls became the only minor-league team with a brewery of its own.

Of course, this idea came with a unique set of problems. Because of space constraints, the brewing system is small and there are a limited number of fermentation tanks. At the same time, the demand for the beer is high. Even though the ballpark continues to sell a variety of craft beers, it's hard to resist brews concocted only feet away from home plate. Wolfrum admits that "the challenge from day one has been to keep up with demand."

The demand for Bull Durham Beer's pints is not based only on proximity. Its focus is on classic, approachable beer styles. "Our desire is to be the gateway to craft beer for the uninitiated," Wolfrum says. "Because our brewery is situated

The view from the ballpark: Bull Durham's small brewery is on the concourse directly behind home plate at Durham Bulls Athletic Park.
Bull Durham Beer Company

in a baseball park, we feel we are uniquely suited to this task." Bull Durham Beer launched the 2015 baseball season with two beers: Water Tower Wheat and Lollygagger Kölsch. The light, refreshing styles seem appropriate for nine innings played under a hot North Carolina sun.

However, Wolfrum and his team are not planning to stop there. Soon, they hope to have their beer available in cans at retail locations. They also have plans to build a year-round taproom on Blackwell Street next to the ballpark. In order to keep up with the increased market, they hope to expand into a larger production facility at Rocky Mount Brewmill in 2017.

But for now, the only way to experience Bull Durham Beer Company is to take yourself out to a ball game, where you can peer through the large windows at the shining steel brewery while drinking a crisp pint of freshly brewed beer.

BULL CITY BURGER AND BREWERY

107 East Parrish Street
Durham, NC 27701
919-680-2333
Email: moocow@bullcityburgerandbrewery.com
Website: bullcityburgerandbrewery.com
Hours: Monday–Thursday, 11:11 A.M.–10 P.M.;
  Friday–Saturday, 11:11 A.M.–11 P.M.
Owner: Seth Gross
Head Brewers: Luke Studer, Seth Gross
Opened: 2011

THE BULL STARTS HERE.

That sentence is painted on the floor just as patrons walk in the door of Bull City Burger and Brewery, or BCBB. A big red line leads from the front door, guiding visitors between the small brewery (behind glass on the right) and the brightly lit bar and Enomatic wine machine (on the left). Rustic wooden tables are lined up neatly across the restaurant as patrons walk up to the counter, where they can order some of the best burgers imaginable. To the right of the counter, a ramp leads out the back of the building to a patio full of sturdy picnic tables that find themselves full of patrons on sunny afternoons.

Almost everything here is made in-house. The meat is ground on-site every day. BCBB makes its own sauerkraut and pickles and cures its own bacon. It even makes its own buns. And of course, it makes all the beer.

Seth Gross, the owner of Bull City, didn't start his career as a brewer. His college degree was in microbiology and genetics, but his passion was cooking. After graduating from the Culinary Institute of America, he moved to Chicago and began cooking in five-star restaurants. But something was happening nearby on Clybourn Avenue in a brand-new brewpub called Goose Island, now one of the most successful such operations in the country.

"Like every other guy in there, I spent a lot of time bothering Greg Hall, the brewmaster, and I guess he took a liking to me," Gross recalls. He started working as assistant brewmaster at Goose Island, and his entire career path changed.

The welcome sign at Bull City Burger and Brewery
Erik Lars Myers

He used his college training to do cell counts and maintain yeast health. Meanwhile, his knowledge of cooking helped him come up with new flavors for beer.

He looks back at the experience with fondness. "That period was some of the most rewarding, backbreaking work I have ever done in my life," he says.

After his tenure at Goose Island, Gross started exploring the world of wine, was certified as a sommelier, and ultimately became one of the owners of Wine Authorities in Durham, a successful store. "I love wine, but the thing about wine is that I really couldn't make it myself of any quality," he says. "We don't really have the climate for it here in North Carolina, plus I don't really have the patience to wait five years for a red to sort of come around."

Wine Authorities helped Gross find his way back into beer. He sold his share of the store to his business partner and used the proceeds to start Bull City Burger and Brewery.

From the beginning, Gross was committed to a business model focused on local food and sustainability. "For the most part, startup was pretty easy," he says. "What really surprised me was how difficult it was to source local pasture-raised beef." That's when he found Farmhand Foods, a local company whose sole purpose is to connect farmers with restaurants and retailers interested in using pasture-raised beef. It was win-win. Gross has continued to expand his relation ship with local farms and his sustainable practices. In 2014, Bull City became the first certified B-Corp restaurant and brewpub in North Carolina, a designation Gross is particularly proud of.

Finally, there's the beer. Gross notes that his tenure at Goose Island taught him authenticity. "It was a time in the early '90s when that's what people were trying to do: brewing authentic English-style ales. And we did it well. At that time at Goose Island, we were brewing 40 new styles of beer every year."

He brings that same authenticity to Bull City's beers. They are classic examples of English-style ales, whether milds, bitters, porters, stouts, ESBs, or IPAs. He and brewer Luke Studer work meticulously to have the highest-quality beer available to match their food.

Studer, a graduate of Vermont's American Brewing Guild, was working at nearby Triangle Brewing Company when he heard rumors of Gross's plan and approached him about the possibility of working with him. "Triangle was wonderful, but I always wanted to work in a brewpub," he says.

Gross found Studer to be an excellent match. "He has been fantastic, hard-working, and reliable, and we have an understanding that we won't make any bad beer."

That doesn't mean they don't play outside the boundaries of style, though. In addition to the English-style lineup, patrons are likely to find at least one unusual offering, such as the Blonde Stout or the chocolate-inspired HsaWaknow Ale (Wonka Wash backwards).

The compact size of the brewery and the quick brewing schedule mean that something new is always on the horizon at BCBB. Although Gross is looking forward to adding a new fermenter to the brewing space, he has no current plans to distribute outside the local area that gave Bull City Burger and Brewery its name.

FULLSTEAM BREWERY

726 Rigsbee Avenue
Durham, NC 27701
919-682-BEER (2337)
Email: sean@fullsteam.ag
Website: fullsteam.ag
Hours: Monday–Thursday, 4 P.M.–midnight;
    Friday, 2 P.M.–2 A.M.; Saturday, noon–2 A.M.;
    Sunday, noon–midnight
Owner: Sean Lilly Wilson
Brewmaster: Brian Mandeville
Opened: 2010

ꓶULLSTEAM

SEAN LILLY WILSON HAD NO PLANS TO START A BREWERY when he was the Pop the Cap spokesman.

"I don't know the exact date," he says, "but when the law was looking like it was going to change, I thought, *I like this. I like the industry. I like the people.*" And he saw an opportunity.

After the law changed and beer with an alcohol content of over 6 percent was finally allowed in North Carolina, he asked himself, *So the law changed. So what?* He was excited by craft beer and enthused to tell people about it. "You become this evangelist of sorts," he says. "So the mission of Pop the Cap after the law changed became celebrating craft beer in North Carolina." Pop the Cap was never really a job for Wilson. He didn't get paid. He talks about it as a labor of love, but it also turned into a good way for him to grow familiar with the industry. *I can do this*, he thought.

What Wilson felt was missing from the market was a brewery that celebrated local ingredients and Southern agriculture. He had developed his love for Southern seasonal food and drink at age 21 as a waiter at Magnolia Grill, the iconic Durham restaurant that closed in 2012. He learned about Southern food traditions and what would grow in the Southern soil. Thinking back to those days, it

Fullsteam Brewery
Erik Lars Myers

became obvious to Wilson that this niche wasn't being served in the beer world.

So he began to close the doors on Pop the Cap and to start work on his brewery. To develop Fullsteam's initial beer offerings, Wilson teamed with Chris Davis, a talented homebrewer interested in turning professional. Together, they created beers that celebrated traditional Southern ingredients, such as a cream ale with grits and an amber lager with sweet potatoes (named Carver Sweet Potato, after George Washington Carver). Davis has since moved on. Brian Mandeville has now taken the helm, working side by side with Wilson to create new popular beers.

As Fullsteam has grown, so has its array of local ingredients and partnerships. For example, patrons can find Fullsteam beers made with basil, pawpaws, persimmons, and pears sourced from local farms and foragers. Its Cack-a-lacky ginger pale ale is made in collaboration with the local Cackalacky hot sauce company.

Fullsteam's location in the vibrant "DIY District" of Durham is a sight to see. The building is an old Pepsi bottling plant just a couple of blocks from Durham Athletic Park, best known as the former home of the Durham Bulls and for the starring role it played in the movie *Bull Durham*. Wilson feels incredibly lucky for the find. "I consider it a series of fortunate events that the area that we are in was ready for a renaissance, and that we found a space that was ready to be that."

He adds, "The plan was always to have a community gathering spot and to have a manufacturing environment that would allow us to scale, and luckily enough we found it."

That is an understatement. The building has bloomed. Artwork lines the walls as patrons walk in through the giant metal door graced with Fullsteam's distinctive backward *F*. The open space in the brewery's taproom (nicknamed "R&D") is filled with picnic tables, ping-pong tables, and old-school pinball machines. Behind large wooden doors built from fermentation tanks from the old Falstaff Brewery is a neat, sleek taproom with taps sticking directly out of the brick wall. Large chalkboards on each end display each day's taps and North Carolina guest taps. A strip of dry-erase board runs down the center of the bar from one end to the other. Patrons are encouraged to draw on the bar.

The brewery part of Fullsteam is partitioned off from the taproom by a giant glass wall that affords visitors a clear view of the brewing operation, its gleaming fermenters in a long array. Patrons who come early enough in the day can watch brewers at work making new batches of the beers they're enjoying. Over time, Fullsteam has grown its production, adding fermenters and sending 22-ounce bottles and cans of select styles into the marketplace. In addition to Cack-a-lacky, Fullsteam plans to distribute cans of its pilsner and IPA across the South.

Since its opening, Fullsteam has seen great success, winning numerous accolades, including Good Food Awards in 2013 and 2016. To Wilson, this is just the beginning. "We want to be a landmark brewery for the South," he says. "We're just getting started. But this is my life now. It's my career, and I want to build a multigenerational brewery. Something that will last longer than just me."

PONYSAURUS BREWING COMPANY

219 Hood Street
Durham, NC 27701
978-482-7701
Email: ponysaurus@ponysaurusbrewing.com
Website: ponysaurusbrewing.com
Hours: Monday–Thursday, 4 P.M.–11 P.M.;
    Friday, 4 P.M.–midnight;
    Saturday–Sunday, noon–midnight
Founders: Nick Hawthorne-Johnson,
    David Baldwin, Keil Jansen
Head Brewer: Keil Jansen
Brewing Staff: Eric Lebsack
Opened: 2013

WHEN PONYSAURUS STARTED SELLING BEER IN 2013, it caught people's attention, and not just because of its offbeat dinosaur-pony logo. No, Triangle residents were fascinated by Ponysaurus's location inside The Cookery, Durham's commercial kitchen and food incubator space.

Keil Jansen, cofounder and head brewer at Ponysaurus, remembers the splash it made: "Media attention focused on the odd nature of the brewery, and many superlatives were thrown around to describe the brewery: smallest, highest, etc." Jansen has his own opinion of the matter. "I preferred dumbest," he says, referring either to his brewery's tiny size or to its spot on a platform hovering above The Cookery's event space, reachable only by a scissor lift.

The setup may have seemed dumb, but the beer was anything but. Thanks to Ponysaurus's partnership with The Cookery and coordination with its owners (Ponysaurus cofounder Nick Hawthorne-Johnson and his wife, Rochelle), the small brewery was able to reach into the local market. Drinkers loved Jansen's recipes, and he literally could not make enough beer. And so, less than two years after opening, Jansen and his business partners planned their expansion: a separate, larger space with a 15-barrel system that wouldn't be suspended in midair over anything.

Ponysaurus's new space on Hood Street in Durham opened in September 2015. In addition to the upgraded brewing system, the building has a gorgeous,

Great at being delicious, terrible at arm wrestling: the Ponysaurus logo graces each tasting glass.
Erik Lars Myers

funky taproom with a roof deck that promises to be an outstanding place to spend summer evenings. At the bar, patrons can order a guest beer or one of Ponysaurus's offerings. Jansen's beers run the gamut from classic British styles including IPA and Scottish ale to French and Belgian farmhouse and abbey ales. "We brew the beer beer would drink if beer could drink beer," he likes to say.

Like its hybrid dinosaur-pony logo (designed by cofounder David Baldwin), Ponysaurus celebrates playful combinations and collisions of ideas. Following the recent launch of its larger system, it is poised to bring more innovative hybrid beers to the Triangle area.

TRIANGLE BREWING COMPANY

918 Pearl Street
Durham, NC 27713
919-683-BEER (2337)
Website: trianglebrewery.com
Owner: Andy Miller
Opened: 2007

TRIANGLE BREWING COMPANY DEVELOPED FROM THE VISION OF TWO FRIENDS, Rick Tufts and Andy Miller. "Rick and I went to high school together," Andy explains. "I came down here for school, and Rick came down and visited a couple of times and kind of fell in love with the area." Rick ended up moving down in the late 1990s to live near his friend. By that point, he was already an avid homebrewer. He got Andy involved in his hobby and his lofty idea to start a brewery. But it wasn't the right time for either of them.

Andy was employed in the hospitality industry. Rick was a psychologist for the University of North Carolina School of Medicine's TEACCH program, working with kids and adults with autism. For the next seven or eight years, the friends continued to spend time together with beer, especially homebrew. Finally, they got to a point where it just seemed right.

"My wife told me, 'If you're going to start a brewery, it's got to be right now,'" laughs Rick.

So Rick and Andy sat down and started to think about it in earnest. They decided to take a trip to the Craft Brewers Conference, which was in Seattle that year, to check out the industry. "To say that we had a good time is probably an understatement," Andy said. "We learned a lot, we met a lot of people, we got a lot of good contact, and more than anything else, we kind of got comfortable with the industry. I think we started our business plan on the plane ride back."

Soon afterward, Rick enrolled in Vermont's American Brewers Guild to learn the craft. He followed that with an apprenticeship at Flying Fish Brewery in Cherry Hill, New Jersey, where he fell in love with Belgian beers. The two

The canning line at Triangle Brewing Company
Erik Lars Myers

friends then worked on getting a brewery going. Since Andy's background was in hospitality, he took care of sales and distribution. Rick made the beer and focused on the brewery.

Originally, they were going to open with a pale ale and an IPA, but after Rick spent time at Flying Fish, he realized that a whole range of beers—Belgian-style beers—wasn't typically being made in North Carolina. That's what the partners decided to focus on.

"We were told by a few people in the industry that we had lost our minds for having our flagship be Belgian-style Strong Golden Ale, that it would never work in North Carolina," Andy admits. "We're proud to say that a year and a half later, we had 70 accounts and we were looking for a distributor."

When taking one of Triangle Brewing Company's tours or attending its Black Friday Cask Festival, hosted every year the day after Thanksgiving, it's impossible not to notice the small coffin set up somewhere around the brewery. It's not actually a coffin but rather a jockey box—a device used to serve beer at events. But the reason it's coffin-shaped is significant. The building Triangle inhabits was constructed in the 1950s. It has a two-story basement—part built out of cement and part that's just natural clay. When the friends were renovating the building for the brewery, the construction crew found a body partially buried in the clay.

"The bag was obviously tied from the outside," says Rick, "so he didn't put himself there. And the cops weren't able to find anything out about him except that he was a male, just because of his rib structure. There were no dental records back then, no DNA records. So we sat down and we thought, *We've got to name this guy!* We thought that Rufus James sounded like a good Southern name, and now he's the patron saint of Triangle Brewing Company."

"He oversees all aspects of the brewery," Andy adds. "He sees everything. And when he's not happy, things are not good in here—clogged filter, stuck mash, canning line throwing cans at you, whatever. And we pour a little bit of beer down the drain every once in a while to appease him."

In 2015, after eight years of partnership, Rick decided to separate from Triangle to pursue other goals. Triangle continues to brew its now-classic beers, which can be found in cans on shelves and in coolers at local stores. Triangle was one of the earliest breweries in North Carolina to put its beers in cans and was the first packaging brewery to do so. At the time, it got skeptical looks, since craft beer in cans was uncommon in North Carolina. Since then, craft beer canning has taken off, and skeptics have to admit that Triangle was just ahead of the curve.

CAROLINA BREWING COMPANY

140 Thomas Mill Road
Holly Springs, NC 27540
919-557-BEER (2337)
Email: carolinabrewing@aol.com
Website: carolinabrew.com
Retail Hours:
    Monday–Tuesday, 9 A.M.–5 P.M.;
    Wednesday–Thursday, 9 A.M.–10 P.M.;
    Friday, 9 A.M.–11 P.M.;
    Saturday, noon–11 P.M.
Taproom Hours:
    Wednesday–Thursday, 4 P.M.–10 P.M.;
    Friday, 4 P.M.–11 P.M.;
    Saturday, noon–11 P.M.
Owners: Joe Zonin, Greg Shuck, Van Smith,
    Mark Heath
Brewmaster: Mark Heath
Opened: 1995

CAROLINA BREWING COMPANY

outside

WHEN JOE ZONIN AND GREG AND JOHN SHUCK MOVED TO NORTH CARO-
LINA, they did so to start a brewery. The friends had met at Cornell University
in Ithaca, New York, and moved to the Pacific Northwest together. Once there,
they fell in love with brewing culture and small craft breweries and decided they
wanted to start their own. Feeling the Pacific Northwest was too crowded for
another brewery, they looked elsewhere and finally settled on North Carolina.

"When we moved here from Seattle in 1993, there were 12 breweries in
downtown Seattle. There were two in the state of North Carolina," says Joe
Zonin.

The friends didn't want only to found a brewery, though. They wanted to
do it right. They visited over 100 breweries and took ideas from all of them. And
unlike the other breweries in North Carolina at the time, theirs started with all
new equipment, including kegs.

They opened their doors and made their first sale on July 3, 1995, to the
42nd St. Oyster Bar in downtown Raleigh, a spot they return to annually for a

Joe Zonin pours beer at the tasting room at Carolina Brewing Company.
Dave Tollefsen, NC Beer Guys

full beer dinner to celebrate another successful year in business. In 1997, they added their bottling line. "We bought a bottling line that was too big for us, and in a few years when we hit 20 years old and we've increased production, it'll still be too big for us," Zonin says with a laugh. That has meant they've put little wear and tear on their equipment. On a bottling line that is beyond 15 years old, they still see less than a 1 percent loss rate, something most bottling breweries can only dream of.

Despite such a long time in business, Carolina Brewing Company is committed to being a local brewery and a local business. "When we started, we were in three counties," says Zonin, "and today . . . we're in eight." The partners don't have plans for wide growth. "We might try to add on a few areas occasionally," Zonin says, "but we like to sit back and enjoy it. We're not stressed out trying to grow. We're enjoying ourselves."

Owning one of the longest-operating breweries in the state has given the partners the chance to see the brewing industry grow up around them. "It's fun," says Zonin. "We like the competition. We originally felt like we were competing against British imports. Now, we've got all this other small craft. It's great. The consumer is more interested. It's good for everyone. And we've been thrilled to see that we've actually grown over the past five years, even with all of these breweries opening up."

One of the things Carolina Brewing Company is known for around the state is its iconic logo. "We wanted to use an animal, from lions to tigers to bears," says Zonin. "We considered local animals—dogs, cats, turtles, whatever. We even considered Accidental Yak Brewing Company for a while, but we felt like that had too many bad connotations. We settled on a lion because it's regal and aggressive." The company's original logo had a lion emerging from an eggshell resting on a bed of hops and barley, signifying the birth of the brewery.

Carolina Brewing Company's front entrance originally led patrons into a small, informal bar with no taps, a wall full of T-shirts, plaques the brewery earned from its long commitment to the National Multiple Sclerosis Society, and a picture of beer being drunk from the Stanley Cup. "That's Carolina Pale Ale!" notes Zonin, a huge hockey fan. For him, seeing CPA drunk from the Stanley Cup after the Carolina Hurricanes' victory in 2006 was one of the highlights of his career. After 20 years, the entrance got an upgrade to a real operating taproom with a tidy wooden bar and taps pouring CBC's beers for paying customers.

Past the door adjoining the bar, patrons walk into a full-production brewery. The bottling line looms to the left, large 40- and 80-barrel fermenters stand in a row, and every available space is filled with kegs, bottles, packaging, and ingredients. The 20-barrel brewhouse—the same one the partners have brewed in since they opened—is at the far left of the brewery, opposite the cold room and the informal tasting area, a small, three-sided bar that stands in front of the taps sticking out the side of the cold room.

Another thing the brewery is known for is its tour, conducted every Saturday at 1 P.M. for the past 17 years. During the tour, that informal tasting area is filled with eager patrons. "I do about 95 percent of the tours," says Zonin. "We try to walk the line between fun and technical without being too boring." On average, Carolina Brewing Company hosts between 75 and 100 people on the tour. But on busy days, it can see as many as 250 to 300. The tours have helped the brewery build and maintain its fan base in the diverse and growing North Carolina craft beer scene.

BOMBSHELL
BEER COMPANY

120 Quantum Drive
Holly Springs, NC 27540
919-823-1933
Email: events@bombshellbeer.com
Website: bombshellbeer.com
Hours: Wednesday–Thursday, 4 P.M.–10 P.M.;
    Friday, 3 P.M.–11 P.M.;
    Saturday, noon–midnight;
    Sunday, noon–6 P.M.
Founders: Ellen Joyner, Jackie Hudspeth,
    Michelle Miniutti
Head Brewer: Joshua Sattin
Opened: 2014

A RED AND BLACK BOMBSHELL SIGN GREETS VISITORS TO THIS HOLLY SPRINGS BREWERY and taproom. While the outside of the building is utilitarian gray metal, the inside is a cheerful, friendly gathering place filled with high-top tables and a long, shining bar. A large rendition of the Bombshell logo dominates one wall, and windows trimmed in that same cheerful red give bar patrons a view of the brewing equipment. On nice days, a large rolling door provides access to the outdoor beer garden, stocked with picnic tables, umbrellas, and a cornhole game.

Bombshell is the brainchild of three women: Ellen Joyner, Jackie Hudspeth, and Michelle Miniutti. Ellen was a longtime homebrewer who introduced Michelle to the craft in 2011 after the pair had toured numerous breweries together. They started building a business plan for their own craft brewery, bringing Jackie into the process in 2012. With backgrounds in sales, business, and operations, the three partners were ideally suited to work together running a small business.

Although they had homebrewing experience, they decided to bring in a professional to manage the brewing side of things. They opened their doors with the help of Stephen O'Neill, formerly of Church Brew Works in Pittsburgh, Penn-

The bar at Bombshell Beer Company
Dave Tollesfen, NC Beer Guys

sylvania. Now, in the brewhouse behind the bar, Joshua Sattin crafts Bombshell's regular lineup (a pilsner, an IPA, a cream ale, and a black ale) and a rotating slate of seasonal and specialty beers.

As women in the beer industry, Bombshell's owners think a lot about how to encourage women to become craft beer drinkers. Unlike some other brands, Bombshell doesn't focus on female-oriented packaging, colors, or fruity flavors. In an interview with Glenn Cutler and Dave Tollefsen as part of their "NC Beer Buzz" series, Ellen Joyner pointed out that "all three of us [founders] have different tastes." In her opinion, the way to convince women to drink craft beer is to provide them with a consistent and approachable product and let their taste buds do the rest.

Bombshell is currently available only on draft and in growlers, but its equipment is designed for growth. A canning line and wider distribution are part of Bombshell's future plans.

BRÜEPRINT
BREWING COMPANY

1229 Perry Road, Suite 101
Apex, NC 27502
919-387-8075
Email: jessica@brueprint.com
Website: brueprint.com
Hours: Tuesday–Thursday, 4 P.M.–10 P.M.;
    Friday, 4 P.M.–11 P.M.;
    Saturday, noon–11 P.M.; Sunday, noon–8 P.M.
Founder: Eric Wagner
Head Brewer: Brad Fogleman
Sales and Distribution Manager: Reid Huntley
Opened: 2014

BRÜEPRINT BREWING COMPANY, APEX'S FIRST CRAFT BREWERY, can be found in Suite 101 of a nondescript mixed-use office building on Perry Road. Through the doors, patrons will find a taproom filled with high-top tables and a bar serving up Brüeprint's four flagship beers and a rotating list of seasonal recipes. Windows allow visitors a glimpse of Brüeprint's 20-barrel brewing system and shining fermenters. Healthy beer fans will appreciate the brewery's Tuesday Run Club, while hungry drinkers can look forward to the occasional food truck.

Brüeprint's founder, Eric Wagner, describes the brewery as a marriage between his longtime hobby of cooking and his former job as an engineer working in wastewater treatment. Eric views craft beer as a balancing act between science and cooking, with the goal of producing a delicious, unique flavor every time—a viewpoint that's highlighted by the fingerprint in the center of Brüeprint's logo.

After homebrewing for about seven and a half years, Eric decided to take the plunge into the business of craft beer. Together with his brewer, Brad Fogleman, and Reid Huntley, he redesigned and scaled up the homebrew recipes he wanted to bring to the masses.

Brüeprint's regular lineup features a range of styles, from a pale ale to a Scottish ale. All the beer names feature the trademark *brüe* in them somewhere. Seasonals such as the Zambrüeni lager tend to have sports-related names.

A flight of delicious beer at Brüeprint Brewing Company
Dave Tollesfen, NC Beer Guys

AVIATOR BREWING COMPANY

Brewery and bar:
209 Technology Park Lane
Fuquay-Varina, NC 27526
919-567-BEER (2337)
Hours: Wednesday–Friday, 5 P.M.–10 P.M.;
    Saturday, noon–10 P.M.; Sunday, noon–7 P.M.

Aviator Tap House:
600 East Broad Street
Fuquay-Varina, NC 27526
919-552-8826
Hours: Sunday–Thursday, noon–midnight;
    Friday–Saturday, noon–2 A.M.

Aviator SmokeHouse:
525 East Broad Street
Fuquay-Varina, NC 27526
919-557-7675
Hours: Monday–Thursday, 11:30 A.M.–10 P.M.;
    Friday–Saturday, 11:30 A.M.–11 P.M.;
    Sunday, noon–9 P.M.

Website: aviatorbrew.com
Owner: Mark Doble
Opened: 2008

A SHORT DRIVE SOUTHWEST OF RALEIGH, IN A SMALL INDUSTRIAL SUBDIVISION called Technology Park Lane in the burgeoning suburb of Fuquay-Varina, is the original home of Aviator Brewing Company. It's a fitting location, given founder Mark Doble's previous career as a software engineer. Before software, though, there was beer.

Back in the 1980s, Mark and his older brother Jim opened The Brew Shack, a homebrew shop in Tampa, Florida. It did well, and the family wanted to expand to a brewpub.

"My mom is British, and her family had owned pubs all over England and Wales," Mark says, "so she was really focused on getting a pub opened. And my

Assorted decorations at Aviator Brewing Company
Erik Lars Myers

brother really wanted to do the brewing, so we opened a brewpub. I wanted to do a packaging brewery. I wasn't really into the restaurant side of it." The family went on to open Tampa Bay Brewing Company in the city's historic Ybor City neighborhood.

Mark moonlighted at the brewery. But he had just graduated from college and wanted to focus on the career he had prepared himself for, so he got a job at Hewlett-Packard. He ended up working there for over 15 years.

"But time went on, and I kinda got sick of working there," he says. "I always wanted to come back and start a microbrewery." Favorable beer laws brought him to North Carolina.

He moved to Fuquay-Varina and bought a hangar at the Triple W Airport. At that point, he was still doing software design. "I had a small airplane," says Mark, an amateur pilot, "but the hangar was huge. I used to work out of there— just me, my computer, and my airplane." Brewing was still on his mind, though, and he kept his ear to the ground for equipment.

Eventually, he found a brewhouse in Belmont, California, that "needed some work," so he decided to make a cross-country trip to pick up components of his brewhouse, fermenters, and even dairy tanks. It was a tightly orchestrated trip. "I flew on a commercial airline, and an 18-wheeler kind of tracked me across the country. I would rent U-Hauls and drive equipment south to meet him, and then we would off-load stuff. It was crazy. There was literally an inch left in the truck when we packed everything in there."

Finally, he got it all back to his hangar in Fuquay-Varina, and Aviator Brewing Company was born. He rebuilt the equipment he had collected and started making beer.

Eventually, Mark had a small bar in the hangar that he operated a few nights a week and for tours. "People just kept coming," he says. Some nights, he had 500 to 600 patrons hanging out. "They would drink all of the beer that I had!" he laughs. "I had a two-tap kegerator, and I was filling old soda kegs off of the bright tanks. I could never keep up." So he decided to grow.

That growth had two phases. The first was a taproom in downtown Fuquay-Varina in the old Varina train depot. It's a long, warm space with a 38-foot polished wooden bar, wide-plank floors, and tall ceilings. "It's packed all the time," says Mark. The second phase was a larger brewing facility away from the hangar, in a space that could better handle a brewery. That space is on Technology Park Lane.

Now, Mark has so much more. After expanding to a new bottling line, canning came next. And with the new packaging options came new markets, including multiple states and multiple countries: Korea, Taiwan, and Brazil. Aviator has opened a bottle shop in addition to its barbecue restaurant and taproom. And recently, it started plans to expand to a new five-acre site that will include a distillery and yet another restaurant.

FAINTING GOAT
BREWING COMPANY

330 South Main Street
Fuquay-Varina, NC 27526
919-346-7915
Website: facebook.com/FaintingGoatBeer
Hours: Thursday, 4:30 P.M.–11:30 P.M.;
    Friday, 4:30 P.M.–midnight;
    Saturday, noon–midnight
Owners: Tim Potwora, Tim Reichert,
    MaryAnn Durborrow
Brewmaster: Tim Reichert
Opened: 2015

DOWN AT THE END OF THE BUSINESS PART OF SOUTH MAIN STREET, visitors to Fuquay-Varina will find Fainting Goat Brewing Company.

The narrow taproom features a concrete-topped bar down one long side and a series of tables where patrons can sit and enjoy the beers on tap. The back corner of the room, which is cordoned off during taproom hours, showcases the brewing equipment of this nanobrewery. Other business areas including the grain storage and the cooler are accessed through a hall in the back.

Fainting Goat is the brainchild of Tim Potwora and Tim Reichert, who serve together in the North Carolina Army National Guard, and MaryAnn Durborrow. The name Fainting Goat comes from a nickname of Reichert's, a story he'll probably tell if you ask.

According to Reichert, zoning laws demand that at least 70 percent of the building's space be dedicated to retail operations, so Fainting Goat's small-sized system is ideal for the location. He brews three days a week while the taproom is closed and then leaves the brewing equipment, neatly arranged and shining, for taproom visitors to view when they come in for a beer.

Because of the system's small size, Fainting Goat can easily make a variety of recipes. Its four regular beers are a mix of the ordinary (pale ale) and the unusual

The brewhouse at Fainting Goat Brewing Company
Sarah H. Ficke

(tart pomegranate wheat beer), complemented by a rotating dark beer. Reichert says he's well aware that beer fans love seasonal change, so he plans to keep the new recipes coming.

DRAFT LINE
BREWING COMPANY

341 Broad Street, Suite 151
Fuquay-Varina, NC 27526
919-557-7121
Website: draftlinebrewing.com
Hours: Monday–Thursday, 4 P.M.–10 P.M.;
   Friday, 4 P.M.–midnight;
   Saturday, noon–midnight;
   Sunday, 1 P.M.–8 P.M.
Owners: Scott Palmieri, Scott Wood
Opened: 2014

DRAFT LINE BREWING'S HOME IS A CONVERTED WAREHOUSE just down the street from Aviator Brewing's tap house and smokehouse. Set back from the road, the large warehouse is home to a lively taproom and spacious production area. The front is all business. But when visitors drive around the back of the building, they're greeted by a raised and covered patio area packed with picnic tables and a large glass garage-style door that allows the outdoor and indoor spaces to blend into one welcoming area. Inside, a curved wooden bar separates the taproom from the equipment, which towers shining behind it.

The owners, Scott Palmieri and Scott Wood, took a hands-on approach to building their brewery, which seems fitting for an engineer and a general contractor. In fact, the brewery's name is drawn from the term for lines on blueprints—and, of course, the lines that move beer.

Parts of the brewery have been automated using a system they designed, giving them close control over the process. Their 30-barrel system produces enough beer to supply the taproom and draft accounts in a wider area. The regular tap list features classic styles including pilsner, porter, and IPA. But Draft Line also produces a steady stream of limited-release beers with experimental flavors that in the past have included a braggot, a Berliner weisse, and a molasses porter.

Draft Line, Fuquay-Varina's second brewery to open, has become a lively community spot featuring regular events, food trucks, and live music.

Taps line up in front of the brewhouse at Draft Line Brewing Company.
Sarah H. Ficke

The taproom contains a loft overlooking the space that can be rented for special groups. In the currently unused part of the warehouse, patrons play friendly games of foosball, ping-pong, and cornhole.

With all that space and a distribution contract, Draft Line is poised to grow.

LINCOLN BREWING COMPANY

2912 North Main Street
Fuquay-Varina, NC 27526
919-285-2318
Website: lincolnbrewery.com
Hours: Sunday–Thursday, noon–10 P.M.;
    Friday–Saturday, noon–midnight
Owner: Richard Camos
Opened: 2015

RICHARD CAMOS, THE OWNER OF LINCOLN BREWING COMPANY, didn't start out in the brewing business. He's the proprietor of the successful Camos Brothers Pizza restaurants in the Triangle area. But when he thought about his next business, his mind turned to beer.

His first venture into the beer world was Lincoln Bottle Shop and Taproom on Six Forks Road in Raleigh, which stocks a variety of craft beers from around the world in bottles and on draft. Camos didn't stop with a bottle shop, though. Brewing his own beer was his goal, so he began work on Lincoln Brewing Company.

Lincoln Brewing is located in a shopping center on North Main Street in Fuquay-Varina, around the corner from a location of Camos Brothers Pizza. It's a good-sized space with a granite bar dominating one side of the room, tables on the other end, and a separate room with pool tables and other games. Bold posters featuring Abraham Lincoln decorate the walls. The production side of the space contains the elements expected in a small startup brewery. But there is considerable room to grow. As time goes on, more of the items listed on the electronic signs above the bar will be Lincoln-made brews. For the time, Lincoln's beers share space with a selection of other high-quality craft beers.

Life, liberty, and pursuit of good beer: the mantra at Lincoln Brewing Company
Sarah H. Ficke

FORTNIGHT BREWING COMPANY

1006 Southwest Maynard Road
Cary, NC 27511
919-342-6604
Email: info@fortnightbrewing.com
Website: fortnightbrewing.com
Hours: Monday–Thursday, 4 P.M.–10 P.M.;
    Friday, 2 P.M.–11 P.M.;
    Saturday, noon–11 P.M.;
    Sunday, noon–7 P.M.
Founders: David Gardner,
    Will and Bob Greczyn
President: Stuart Arnold
Head Brewer: Derek Garman
Opened: 2014

BEER DRINKERS SEARCHING FOR UK-STYLE BEERS AND CASK ALE will be happy to find Fortnight Brewing Company, Cary's first craft brewery. *Fortnight* is a traditionally British term used to describe a period of two weeks. It struck the owners as appropriate because that is also approximately the time it takes to ferment a craft beer.

Not all of Fortnight's team members are British (some are local North Carolinians), but all are committed to the flavors of traditional English beers. Fortnight's regular lineup includes several session beers including English Ale (designed like an ordinary bitter) and ESB (English ale kicked up a notch or two). It also occasionally plays around with other styles or alternate ingredients—such as new hop varieties—that bring a twist to its classic recipes. Fortnight's cask ales are entirely traditional—no crazy fruits, no elaborate spices, just straightforward beer carbonated naturally in the metal cask. While many breweries tap casks for special occasions, Fortnight's casks are a regular feature, pouring smoothly carbonated beer that should please Anglophile drinkers.

Visitors to Fortnight's rectangular white brick building on Southwest Maynard Road will find a friendly, modern taproom—no faux pub-style paneling or mirrored bar. The mixture of wooden tables and soft leather armchairs gives the

Gorgeous and comfortable seating in Fortnight Brewing Company's taproom
Dave Tollefsen, NC Beer Guys

room a comfortable feel and encourages patrons to hang out. A wall of windows opens onto the brewing floor, where bourbon barrels for aging share space with kegs, casks, and the large kettle and fermenters. Live music, trivia, bingo, and a variety of other events make the taproom an entertaining place to sit down to enjoy a craft beer.

LONERIDER BREWING COMPANY

8816 Gulf Court, Suite 100
Raleigh, NC 27617
919-442-8004
Website: loneriderbeer.com
Hours: Monday–Thursday, 2 P.M.–10 P.M.;
    Friday–Saturday, 2 P.M.–11 P.M.;
    Sunday, 2 P.M.–7 P.M.
Owners: Steve Kramling (VP of brewery
    operations), Mihir Patel (CFO), and Sumit
    Vohra (CEO)
Head Brewer: Galen Smith
Opened: 2008

LONERIDER BREWING COMPANY IS THE BRAINCHILD OF THREE COLLEAGUES— Sumit Vohra, Mihir Patel, and Steve Kramling—who worked as software quality-assurance engineers at Cisco Systems in Research Triangle Park. For a while, they were all on the same floor within a five-second walk of each other. They've even been on each other's teams at different points in time. To say they had experience working together would be an understatement.

Kramling and Patel had been homebrewing together when Vohra started working on Kramling's team. "He was just getting into beer at the time," Kramling remembers, "and he was very excited about the homebrew." Together, the three talked about the possibility of opening a brewery, but nothing came of it until a friend let them know that Mad Boar Brewery in Myrtle Beach, South Carolina, was ending operations and putting its equipment up for sale. They were offered a good deal and decided this was their chance.

They bought the equipment and found a space in North Raleigh that would accommodate it. Unable to afford a general contractor, they did most of the work themselves on nights and weekends. By November 2008, they were ready to open their doors.

The trio decided that the best strategy for their bottom line was a staged exit from Cisco. They needed only one thing: a full-time brewer.

Enter Ian VanGundy, a homebrewer and student of the craft. In fact, VanGundy had worked for years at a local homebrew supply store, American

Lonerider's distinctive logo peers over the brewing equipment.
Sarah H. Ficke

Brewmaster, quietly honing his craft until he saved enough money to head to brewing school. He enrolled at the Siebel Institute and spent the better part of a year in Chicago and Munich learning the best practices in brewing. He returned from his training just in time for Lonerider.

VanGundy joined the staff and immediately started building what were already fantastic recipes into brilliant beers that not only showcased their ingredients but were also excellent examples of their styles. In fact, within just three years of opening, Lonerider brought home two medals from the Great American Beer Festival, the largest and most prestigious beer competition in the country: a gold for Sweet Josie Brown in 2010 and a silver for Deadeye Jack in 2011. VanGundy left Lonerider in 2013 to become director of brewery operations for White Street Brewing, but Lonerider's recipes have continued to develop in the capable hands of new head brewer Galen Smith.

It might seem odd that a brewery owned by two Indians and their Southern white friend ("I'm the token white guy," Kramling jokes) should be called Lonerider Brewing Company, something that celebrates the Wild West. But there's more to the name. In their original concept, Lonerider was going to be called Outlaw Brewing Company.

"We're the guys who said, 'We don't want to do what we do. We want to do what we like,'" says Vohra. "It's always something that resonates with everybody. If I asked you, 'Have you ever done something in your life that somebody else thought you shouldn't have done?' the answer is usually yes. There are very few people who say no. In some sort of fashion, every one of us tries to do something different and is some sort of an outlaw."

Their outlaw nature is on full display at the brewery, where their logo—a Clint Eastwood–esque cowboy—graces the side of the building. When the business opened, a small taproom shared space inside with the brewing equipment, but Lonerider's growth has pushed the taproom out to a glassed-in patio against the exterior wall of the brewery. No-frills picnic tables and a wooden bar complement the Old West aesthetic. The bartender might well be wearing a cowboy hat. Inside the building, Lonerider has seen exponential growth, installing a bigger brewing system and more fermenters and replacing its bottling line with canning equipment, something Galen Smith is proud to show off.

The rapid growth of the craft beer market has allowed Lonerider to expand its distribution as far north as Maryland and as far west as Tennessee. The appeal of this outlaw-themed beer is undeniable, which suggests bright things for Lonerider's future.

GIZMO BREW WORKS

5907 Triangle Drive
Raleigh, NC 27617
919-782-2099
Email: info@gizmobrewworks.com
Website: gizmobrewworks.com
Hours: Wednesday–Thursday, 4 P.M.–10 P.M.;
    Friday, 3 P.M.–10 P.M.;
    Saturday, 1 P.M.–10 P.M.;
    Sunday, 1 P.M.–7 P.M.
Founders: Bryan Williams, Matt Santelli,
    Bryan Shaw, Elizabeth Morgan, Jeff Sgroi
Head Brewer: Joe Walton
Brewing Staff: Eric Hill
Opened: 2013

THE ROAD TO GIZMO BREW WORKS IS A REMINDER THAT BREWING IS AN INDUSTRY as well as a craft.

Winding through Umstead Industrial Park, beer drinkers pass a variety of warehouses before arriving at the mixed-use brewing and taproom space that houses Gizmo. Although the building is an ordinary warehouse, Gizmo's owners have added welcoming touches that make it a place where people gather to hang out and enjoy a good beer (or several). An outdoor area with picnic tables and sun shades expands Gizmo's seating in nice weather. Cornhole and darts are available for patrons who want to engage in some friendly competition. Visitors will almost always find a local food truck parked outside, and live music or some other special event is often scheduled for weekend nights. The interior of the taproom is dominated by the wooden bar and a row of shining taps pouring Gizmo's current beers, which include three year-round styles and a variety of rotating seasonal and experimental recipes, many available only at the taproom.

Gizmo Brew Works is first and foremost a testament to the passion craft beer fans bring to their local breweries. According to cofounder Bryan Williams, Gizmo was born when patrons learned that Roth Brewing Company (2010–12) was getting ready to close its doors and "a group of regulars joined forces to purchase it." After the purchase, the new owners "set forth on a slow journey to

Taps and fermenters at Gizmo Brew Works
Sarah H. Ficke

rebuild the brewery from the ground up." Part of this rebuilding effort was an expansion that exponentially enlarged the brewery's production from 120 barrels per year to roughly 1,000.

The screws, clamps, and gears that make up Gizmo's logo are more than just decorative. Williams explains that Gizmo is "a DIY brewery. Anytime we can do something ourselves to save money, we do."

The results of the hard work are visible to patrons from the taproom bar to the gleaming steel brewhouse that takes up the bulk of the small space. Gizmo's founders see their name and their approach as a nod to "the thinkers, tinkerers, and inventors who make up RTP and Umstead Industrial Park," Williams says.

Gizmo's inventive work isn't done yet. The owners hope to expand the facility further to make over 2,000 barrels of beer per year, being careful to ensure that Gizmo remains the kind of vibrant local brewery that inspired them to join the craft beer world.

RALEIGH BREWING COMPANY

3709 Neil Street
Raleigh, NC 27607
919-400-9086
Email: kristie@raleighbrewingcompany.com
Website: raleighbrewingcompany.com
Hours: Monday–Thursday, noon–10 P.M.;
   Friday–Saturday, noon–midnight;
   Sunday, noon–6 P.M.
Founders: Kristie and Patrik Nystedt
Head Brewer: Alex Smith
Brewing Staff: Scott Craddock, Seth Berry
Opened: 2013

THERE ARE MANY BREWERIES IN RALEIGH, BUT RALEIGH BREWING COMPANY is the only one that invites patrons to "Tap the Capital." From its logo—a large *R*—to its flight trays shaped like the state of North Carolina, Raleigh Brewing embraces its location. Its goal is to be Raleigh's one-stop shop for all things craft beer, and it makes a good case for it. In addition to running a successful packaging brewery and taproom, Raleigh Brewing is partnered with Atlantic Brew Supply, a homebrew store that sells ingredients and equipment for aspiring and expert homebrewers, and with ABS Commercial, a supplier of professional brewing equipment. Brewers and drinkers alike will find what they're looking for at Raleigh Brewing Company.

The business model makes sense, given the background of owners Kristie and Patrik Nystedt. They got interested in craft beer as drinkers and homebrewers, then improved their knowledge and skill for 10 years before seeing an opportunity to found a professional brewery. Homebrewing is also how they met their original head brewer, John Federal, who was working at a local homebrew store at the time. After several discussions about beer, brewing, and business plans, the trio developed a two-pronged approach. Atlantic Brew Supply, the homebrew side, opened in January 2013 and Raleigh Brewing Company a short time later.

An impressive tap lineup at Raleigh Brewing Company
Sarah H. Ficke

In addition to sharing ownership, Atlantic Brew Supply and Raleigh Brewing share a space just off Hillsborough Street between the campuses of North Carolina State and Meredith College. Visitors who venture down the side street to find it will see a building painted with Raleigh Brewing's signature bright red. The taproom is painted that same red, with large murals of the Raleigh landscape splashed across the walls. High-top tables and padded seats along the wooden bar give patrons somewhere to sit and sip their pints.

The bar serves up Raleigh Brewing's year-round offerings as well as seasonal and guest beers. In addition to the beer, visitors can enjoy darts, sports playing on the TVs on the wall, and a variety of activities including a weekly social running club. Raleigh Brewing also sponsors special events such as the Carolina Quarterly Brew Off homebrew competition, which leads up to an annual Best of Show tasting that is open to the public.

The year 2015 was big for Raleigh Brewing. That April, John Federal left to become head brewer at River Dog Brewing, a regional brewery in South Carolina. Alex Smith, Federal's co-brewer, stepped into the head brewer role at Raleigh Brewing. Also that spring, the brewery switched from packaging its regular lineup in 22-ounce bottles to canning its beers, using a mobile canning company until it can get its own line up and running. It distributes its cans and kegs in Raleigh and the Triangle area.

TROPHY BREWING COMPANY

Trophy Brewing & Pizza:
827 West Morgan Street
Raleigh, NC 27603
919-803-4849
Hours: Monday–Wednesday, 5 P.M.–midnight;
  Thursday–Friday, 3 P.M.–2 A.M.;
  Saturday, noon–2 A.M.;
  Sunday, noon–midnight

Trophy on Maywood:
656 Maywood Avenue
Raleigh, NC 27603
919-803-1333
Hours: Monday–Thursday, 3 P.M.–midnight;
  Friday, 3 P.M.–2 A.M.; Saturday, noon–2 A.M.;
  Sunday, noon–midnight

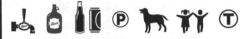

Website: trophybrewing.com
Founders: David "Woody" Lockwood, Chris
  Powers, David Meeker, Les Stewart
Head Brewer: Les Stewart
Opened: 2013

CHRIS POWERS AND DAVID "WOODY" LOCKWOOD MET IN 2001. They were both working in bars and restaurants in Raleigh, and both seeing a lot of success. They quickly became friends, bonding over the bar and restaurant businesses in Glenwood South and over their mutual love of good beer. Over time, they even contemplated opening a place of their own.

Enter David Meeker, son of former mayor Charles Meeker, who is largely credited with revitalizing downtown Raleigh. David met Chris and Woody while bartending at a local beer hotspot, The Raleigh Times. David was bartending to learn about business in downtown, but he was also a budding real-estate

The crowded bar at Trophy's original location
Erik Lars Myers

developer. It was the perfect team. Soon, the three returned an old Raleigh establishment, The Busy Bee, to Wilmington Street.

The original Busy Bee was a lunch counter and restaurant in the 1950s. The new incarnation became a temple to great beer. When Chris, Woody, and David opened The Busy Bee in 2009, it was part coffee shop, part restaurant, and part beer bar, but it soon found its place as a brilliant gastropub serving creative food next to outstanding beer in a warm, inviting atmosphere. Upstairs, The Hive had the atmosphere of a dance club, bringing people out to enjoy a roof deck and a laid-back atmosphere.

The Busy Bee thrived. Only a few years after opening, it was named by *Draft* magazine as one of the Best 100 Beer Bars in America. But the ownership team was just getting started.

Together, they worked at expanding the types of beer available at The Busy Bee, asking breweries to produce styles that weren't always available and making long trips out of state to pick up barrels to give to breweries for barrel aging. After a time, it became apparent that what they really needed to do was open their own brewery. Enter Trophy Brewing.

Trophy started small—really small. The building is the old Burger Hut. From the outside, it feels like a 1950s restaurant, its white metal awning jutting out from a brick façade. When the partners opened their doors in 2013, just a dozen or so seats were available at the bar. The place was so small that the stalls in the bathrooms made up a large percentage of the seating capacity.

Luckily, it didn't take long to tear down a wall, build a patio and a grain silo, and get the pizza kitchen operating at full strength. Inside, the space is still packed. The exterior window is just a few feet behind the seats at the bar, and it seems like every available space is used for seating.

It's still difficult to find a seat at Trophy, but chalk that up to popularity. The pizza is fantastic. And the beer that head brewer Les Stewart creates on Trophy's tiny three-barrel system is nothing short of outstanding. In Trophy's brewery, every nook and cranny is filled with equipment to churn out as much beer as possible.

Fortunately, the ownership team has been working on that problem as well. After launching a successful pair of businesses—Runologie (a running store) and State of Beer (a bottle shop)—in Glenwood South, the partners have been working on Trophy on Maywood, nicknamed, "Big Trophy," this time with Stewart as a part of the team.

At Big Trophy, which opened at the end of 2015, the group finally has a chance to stretch its wings. The 20,000-square-foot space houses a beautiful 20-barrel system. In the new space—which has a taproom, a barrel aging room, and a cooler that might be larger than the original brewery—the partners have the capacity to brew up to 4,000 barrels per year, a huge step up from the backbreaking work of 650 barrels on a three-barrel system.

Trophy finally has plenty of room to grow.

BOYLAN BRIDGE BREWPUB

201 South Boylan Avenue
Raleigh, NC 27603
919-803-8927
Email: rob@boylanbridge.com
Website: boylanbridge.com
Hours: Sunday–Thursday, noon–10 P.M.;
　　Friday–Saturday, noon–11 P.M.
Owner: Andrew Leager
Brewmaster: Laren Avery
Opened: 2009

THE CORNER OF HARGETT STREET AND BOYLAN AVENUE features one of the most spectacular views of downtown Raleigh—a view best seen from the patio of Boylan Bridge Brewpub.

Boylan Bridge is the brainchild of architect and cabinetmaker Andrew Leager, owner of Special Projects, a custom woodworking and design firm in Raleigh. Leager was a homebrewer for just shy of a decade before opening the brewpub. Drawing a parallel between his beer and his cabinetry, he says he likes to take raw materials and have his way with them.

Appropriately, the brewpub is an architectural masterpiece. It resides in an old metal fabrication and welding shop but no longer bears any resemblance to it whatsoever. The pub is wrapped in floor-to-ceiling windows that allow natural light to flow into and illuminate the space. All the woodwork inside and outside was done by Leager and Special Projects. The brewpub's notable features include a beautiful, sweeping bar, a friendly dining area, and an expansive patio crowned by a gorgeous post-and-beam structure.

The brewery, visible behind tall double doors in the bar area, is a small seven-barrel brewpub system that Leager bought used from Peckerhead Brewing Company in Douglasville, Georgia.

The bar at Boylan Bridge Brewpub
Erik Lars Myers

When Boylan Bridge opened in 2009, it sold out of beer in two weeks, forcing it to double its capacity almost instantly. Since then, it has been a local stop for the Boylan Heights crowd and many others who look to enjoy their beer in the beautiful setting Leager has designed.

CRANK ARM BREWING

319 West Davie Street
Raleigh, NC 27601
919-324-3529
Website: crankarmbrewing.com
Hours: Monday–Thursday, 4 P.M.–midnight;
    Friday, 4 P.M.–2 A.M.;
    Saturday, noon–2 a.m.;
    Sunday, noon–10 P.M.
Founders: Adam Eckhardt, Michael Morris,
    Craig Gee, Dylan Selinger
Head Brewer: Michael Morris
Opened: 2013

BIKES AND BEER ARE THE TWIN PASSIONS THAT DRIVE CRANK ARM BREWING, Raleigh's cycling-themed brewery.

Two years before the brewery opened, sharp-eyed Raleigh residents may have noticed Crank Arm's distinctive logo popping up on the side of new yellow rickshaws around the city. Crank Arm Rickshaw was Adam Eckhardt's first business, moving people around downtown Raleigh neighborhoods. However, Eckhardt was also a homebrewer whose love of beer wouldn't be denied. Crank Arm Brewing, opened in 2013, fuses his passions into one business that promotes an active lifestyle and a refreshing beer at the end of every long ride.

Eckhardt discovered a kindred spirit in his cofounder and head brewer, Michael Morris. Morris had a track record of brewing great beer both in the Washington D.C., area and at North Carolina mainstays Big Boss and Natty Greene's. At Crank Arm, he maintains three year-round beers, including Rickshaw Rye IPA, which won Best in Show in the 2014 NC Brewers Cup competition. Where Crank Arm shines, though, is in its seasonal beers, which range from classic styles to inventive experiments with ingredients including beets, mint, and peanut butter. Much like his regular beers, Morris's experiments have been rewarded. In 2015, Crank Arm won first place in the Sour Ale category at the NC Brewers Cup for its Brett Saison, aged with tart cherries in a white wine barrel.

Thanks to Morris's hard work, drinkers both adventurous and not will find something to enjoy at Crank Arm's taproom. Visitors unable to make up their

Functional art built from bicycles graces the wall at Crank Arm Brewing.
Erik Lars Myers

minds can try a sampler flight of beers, delivered on a gear-shaped tray that nods at Crank Arm's bicycle theme. More striking than the flight trays are the large artworks on the walls made from reassembled bicycle parts, the spokes and gears moving gently while patrons congregate at the tables below. The bicycle theme continues outside on the patio, where bright yellow racks invite drinkers to park their bikes and stay for a beer or two—an invitation anyone should be glad to accept.

NICKELPOINT BREWING COMPANY

506 Pershing Road
Raleigh, NC 27608
919-916-5961
Email: info@nickelpointbrewing.com
Website: nickelpointbrewing.com
Hours: Monday–Thursday, 4 P.M.–10 P.M.;
    Friday–Saturday, noon–midnight;
    Sunday, noon–10 P.M.
Founders: Bruce and Matt Corregan, Mark
    Kanczak, Shaluka Perera, Greg
    Weerasinghe
Head Brewer: Bruce Corregan
Opened: 2014

outside

NICKELPOINT IS IN RALEIGH'S FIVE POINTS AREA, which is fast becoming one of the Triangle's brewery hotspots. It's a good location—an industrial zone just minutes from a large residential area. Nickelpoint is often crowded with locals sitting at the picnic tables in the concrete courtyard outside the brewery or inside at the bar chatting with the bartender or watching a game on the television. The brewery is clearly enthusiastic about its community. Local art for sale decorates the walls. And a picture board celebrates the Nickelpoint dog of the month—although the dogs themselves have to stay outside at the picnic tables, due to regulations.

Matt Corregan and his brother, Bruce, got into the beer business through homebrewing, a hobby they picked up together after a motorcycle accident landed Matt in a wheelchair in 2004. As the brothers gained a reputation among their friends for tasty beer, they started to think about going pro. Ten years later, they and their partners successfully opened Nickelpoint's doors.

The beers served at the small wooden taproom bar—among them Belgian Golden Ale, Vienna Lager, and IPA—are mainly examples of classic recipes. Nickelpoint's owners have nothing against more unusual styles of beer, but their

Tanks line the wall at Nickelpoint.
Erik Lars Myers

main focus is on high-quality beer that will appeal to a variety of customers. In fact, one notable thing about Nickelpoint is its lab setup, which was developed under Matt's direction using his background in biochemistry. Thanks to his scientific know-how, Nickelpoint can ensure that every 20-barrel batch meets its high standards and pleases the palates of the drinkers who come through the door.

NEUSE RIVER BREWING COMPANY

NEUSE ⚑ RIVER
BREWING COMPANY

518 Pershing Road
Raleigh, NC 27608
404-386-7522
Email: info@neuseriverbrewing.com
Website: neuseriverbrewing.com
Hours: Thursday, 5 P.M.–10 P.M.;
    Friday, 5 P.M.–11 P.M.;
    Saturday, noon–11 P.M.;
    Sunday, noon–10 P.M.
Founders and Partners: Ryan and
    Jennifer Kolarov, David Powell,
    Ethan and Caroline Barbee
Head Brewers: Ryan Kolarov, David
    Powell
Opened: 2015

MANY CRAFT BREWERIES ARE BUILT ON FRIENDSHIPS. Raleigh's Neuse River Brewing Company is a great example. Cofounders Ryan Kolarov and David Powell grew up together, playing on the banks of the Neuse. A move separated their families while the boys were in their teens. When they reconnected years later, they discovered a mutual interest in homebrewing and set their sights on opening a brewery in Raleigh.

Neuse River Brewing is located in the kind of large industrial spot that seems ideal for a brewery. It was originally designed for a company that built and repaired fire engines in the 1940s, so space isn't an issue. However, as cofounder Jennifer Kolarov explains, starting up wasn't simple. "The building the taproom and brewhouse are located in had only previously been for commercial use. There was no plumbing and minimal electrical. Adding all of this for a brewhouse and taproom and gaining approval from the city was quite an undertaking, two years in the making."

The finished brewery is a testament to the Neuse River team's hard work and vision for the space. An herb garden flourishes along one side of the open

The spacious taproom at Neuse River Brewing Company
Erik Lars Myers

concrete seating area in front of the brewery, providing a nice splash of color in that commercial area. The outdoor and indoor spaces are separated by big garage doors that are open on nice days. Inside, scattered wooden tables provide seating, and the beer is served from a long concrete bar that stretches across the back of the space. Off to the side, another door opens into the part of the building that houses the brewing equipment.

The atmosphere at Neuse River is relaxed. "We pride ourselves on providing a place where people feel comfortable bringing their families," Jennifer says. "Many of our guests have expressed an appreciation for the time taken to create an inviting space and the little details like fresh flower arrangements and a children's area."

The founders are serious about their beer, though. Their focus is on Belgian styles and IPAs, and it isn't unusual for them to offer high-octane beers such as Affluent, their Belgian tripel, and Caleb's High Noon, their imperial IPA. In addition to their regular lineup, they're starting a barrel aging program with both wine and whiskey barrels.

Looking forward, Jennifer identifies bottling or canning and distribution as "major priorities." Until then, the taproom is the best place to sample Neuse River's offerings and find out what's coming next.

SUB NOIR
BREWING COMPANY

2039 Progress Court
Raleigh, NC 27608
919-480-2337
Email: imbibe@subnoir.net
Website: subnoir.net
Hours: Friday, 6 P.M.–midnight;
  Saturday, noon–8 P.M.
Owners: Michael Stagner, Brennan Watson
Head Brewer: Michael Stagner
Opened: 2013

VISITORS LOOKING FOR A NANOBREWERY EXPERIENCE will find it at Sub Noir, Raleigh's smallest brewery. The location, a compact suite in an office park, was renovated to have taproom space in the front and a production area in back. The taproom features a small counter typically pouring four beers, along with a local cider. The drafts, a mix of Sub Noir and guest taps, always showcase a mix of funky and interesting flavors. For entertainment, a TV shows sports, while several retro gaming systems with racks of games delight players. Patrons with children will appreciate the shelf of board games and the entire wall covered in chalkboard paint. Buckets of chalk wait for young artists to add to the décor.

Sub Noir's owners, Michael Stagner and Brennan Watson, developed their recipes as homebrewers. They were interested in taking their recipes in a professional direction but decided to buck the trend and start small. With Sub Noir's tiny system, Stagner and Watson can brew on weekends and still work full-time at their non-beer jobs. Although this schedule keeps the taproom hours limited, the brewery's small size and brewing schedule allow Stagner and Watson to explore a range of interesting recipes. They both love sour beers and creative flavors, so patrons of Sub Noir can always expect something fun on draft, such as a stout brewed with Count Chocula cereal or a witbier made with lavender. The closest they have to a flagship beer is their saison, brewed with Brettanomyces and New Zealand hops, a twist on the classic European style.

Sub Noir in a nutshell: barrel aging next to a tiny brewhouse
Erik Lars Myers

Although Stagner and Watson haven't ruled out expansion, they're committed to slow growth and building community around their brand. Visitors who enjoy a homey taproom and funky beers will find the trip to Sub Noir well worth it.

LYNNWOOD BREWING CONCERN

Lynnwood Grill & Brewing Concern:
4821 Grove Barton Road
Raleigh, NC 27613
919-785-0043
Hours: Daily, 11 A.M.–2 A.M.

Taproom and production facility:
1053 East Whitaker Mill Road
Raleigh, NC 27604
919-424-7533
Hours: Monday–Thursday, 4 P.M.–11 P.M.;
    Friday, 3 P.M.–1 A.M.; Saturday, noon–
    1 A.M.; Sunday, noon–10 P.M.

Email: info@lynnwoodgrill.com
Website: lynnwoodgrill.com
Owner: Ted Dwyer
Head Brewer: Bill Gerds
Opened: 2013

LYNNWOOD GRILL ON GROVE BARTON ROAD IN RALEIGH IS A CLASSIC SPORTS BAR and grill, with one notable difference: it serves excellent house-brewed beer. In 2013, Lynnwood, already a popular restaurant, added a brewhouse and quickly gained a reputation for high-quality ales and lagers. The credit largely belongs to head brewer Bill Gerds, who came to Raleigh from Michigan, where he was a lead brewer at Crankers Brewing Company and Arbor Brewing. With a wealth of experience behind him, Gerds was poised to make Lynnwood into one of the best breweries in the state. How successful was he? Just one year after opening, Lynnwood won a silver medal at the World Beer Cup for its American-style black ale, named Once You Go.

High-top tables lead to the bar in the tasting room at Lynnwood Brewing Concern.
Erik Lars Myers

American-style ales are what Gerds is best known for. His mix of bold hop flavors and balanced malt notes is a big hit with local drinkers as well as international judges. His beers have medaled in numerous local competitions as well.

In fact, Lynnwood's beers proved so popular that just two years after opening, it expanded in a big way. In the fall of 2015, Lynnwood purchased the facility previously occupied by Blackjack Brewing in Raleigh's Five Points area. The new, much larger brewery will allow Lynnwood to start packaging and distributing on a larger scale. The new spot is an industrial building with high ceilings and an open feel. Floor-to-ceiling windows separate the production floor from the taproom, so visitors sitting at the sturdy wooden tables can see the source of the delicious beverages listed on the two giant chalkboard signs above the bar. Patrons can also enjoy foosball and skee-ball or venture to the parking lot, where a food truck is likely to be parked.

In the near future, the owners plan to open a small outdoor patio for additional seating in good weather.

BIG BOSS
BREWING COMPANY

1249-A Wicker Drive
Raleigh, NC 27604
919-834-0045
Email: info@bigbossbrewing.com
Website: bigbossbrewing.com
Hours: Monday, 3 P.M.–midnight;
   Tuesday–Thursday, 3 P.M.–2 A.M.;
   Friday–Saturday, 2 P.M.–2 A.M.;
   Sunday, 1 P.M.–7 P.M.
Owner: Geoff Lamb
Brewmaster: Brad Wynn
Opened: 2007

THE BUILDING BIG BOSS BREWING COMPANY OCCUPIES has been a brewery for much longer than Big Boss has been around. In 1996, Tomcat Brewing opened its doors at 1247 Wicker Drive in Raleigh. A year later, Tomcat closed and was replaced by Pale Ale Brewery, which lasted just two years before being taken over by a brewery out of Pennsylvania, Rock Creek Brewing. With Rock Creek came brewer Brad Wynn. Rock Creek lasted only a couple of years before being bought by Chesapeake Bay Brewing.

When Chesapeake Bay closed in 2003, Wynn was ready with business partner Brian Baker. They bought the old brewery and turned it into Edenton Brewery. Edenton stuck around longer than its predecessors before Geoff Lamb, a UNC–Chapel Hill grad with a background in corporate law, bought a majority stake in the business in 2007. Lamb and Wynn renamed the brewery once more to reduce the confusion of having it honor a city it didn't reside in. The new name was Big Boss, after one of Edenton Brewery's most popular beers. The brewery was also rebranded, using a design aesthetic reflecting Lamb's affinity for World War II aircraft.

Wynn started brewing new beers, as well as old favorites under new names, and Big Boss Brewing Company took off. Within the next few years, it expanded its distribution. Its bottles are now available almost statewide, from Asheville and the mountains through Charlotte and, of course, the Triangle.

The bottling line at Big Boss Brewing Company
Big Boss Brewing Company

The brewery is definitely a large manufacturing environment. On Big Boss's monthly tours, patrons enter through the loading dock. The warehouse spills open in front of them, the brewhouse stands tall on the right-hand side, and the fermentation and bottling operations are nestled into rooms along the back wall. One of the highlights of the space is the attached taproom, which resides upstairs from the brewery and is reachable via an interior staircase or an exterior entrance. The taproom is dark and homey. Its wooden booths bear the patina of years of use. Across from the small seating area stands a short bar featuring Big Boss's regular beers and some experimental brews that don't see regular distribution. Other small rooms hold a pool table, a ping-pong table, and darts. The place is a popular hangout for many locals.

Big Boss has become synonymous with fun outdoor events in Raleigh. Among its regular events are a weekly run club, food-truck rodeos, during which a vast array of food trucks arrive while Big Boss pours beer, and Casktoberfest, an English-style celebration of a German festival.

COMPASS ROSE BREWERY

3201 Northside Drive, Suite 101
Raleigh, NC 27615
919-875-5683
Email: Sharon@compassrosebrewery.com
Website: compassrosebrewery.com
Hours: Daily, noon–midnight
Founders: John Coulter, Jose Martinez,
    Gary Kohake
Head Brewer: Thomas Vincent
Opened: 2015

IF YOU WANT TO FIND COMPASS ROSE BREWERY, SET YOUR SIGHTS NORTH—
that is, to the North Raleigh area. The brewery is in an industrial complex that
sits shoulder-to-shoulder with residential neighborhoods. And it is those neighborhoods that help drive Compass Rose's business. Head brewer Thomas Vincent points out that the area had no brewery before Compass Rose opened.

The brewery's large building is divided into a brewing side and a spacious
taproom, with a wall of glass windows between them. Dartboards off to one
side give patrons with a competitive streak something to do. The bar stretching
across the back of the room is decorated with iron tap handles and a beer list that
mixes Compass Rose brews with offerings from other local and national craft
beer brands.

Through the wall of windows, visitors can see Compass Rose's 10-barrel
brewing system and assortment of fermentation vessels. The brewhouse is the
domain of Vincent, a brewer with a long history in North Carolina craft beer.
Before joining Compass Rose, Vincent brewed for the popular Natty Greene's.
He is also an instructor for the craft beer brewing program at Wake Technical
Community College, which is designed to give students practical hands-on experience in a variety of brewery jobs.

Brewing is Vincent's passion, though, and it shows in his beer. Every recipe
is crafted to showcase the best qualities of its ingredients, and Vincent won't let

The taps at Compass Rose, ready to pour a beer to thirsty patrons
Sarah H. Ficke

any beer hit the taps unless it meets his high quality standards. As an example, he describes brewing an early batch of his Agave Cream Ale that didn't quite meet the mark. Even though he dearly wanted to serve it, he didn't put it out until he was certain the beer was everything it ought to be.

Agave beer? Although Compass Rose isn't consumed by exotic styles and flavors, its recipes have a definite creative bent. As Vincent explains, the brewery's ownership has "connections with the food industry" that give him easy access to unusual ingredients such as agaves. From the outset, the brewery was designed to have an international flair. In fact, the owners were searching for a name evocative of travel and adventure when they happened across an image of a compass rose, the icon that displays cardinal direction points on a map. While the compass rose suggests adventure, Vincent sees it another way. For him, the four directions represent the four main ingredients of beer—hops, water, malt, and yeast—which combine to take drinkers on a journey with every pint.

Although Compass Rose is relatively new, the founders planned the brewery with eventual expansion in mind. Currently empty space will someday be filled with more fermenters and the wooden barrels Vincent will use to create a line of aged and sour ales.

WHITE RABBIT BREWING COMPANY

219 Fish Drive
Angier, NC 27501
919-527-2739
Email: info@WhiteRabbitBrewery.com
Website: whiterabbitbrewery.com
Hours: Thursday, 6 P.M.–10 P.M.;
    Friday, 6 P.M.–11 P.M.;
    Saturday, 3 P.M.–11 P.M.;
    Sunday, 4 P.M.–9 P.M.
Owner: Ken Ostraco
Brewmaster: Matt Ehlers
Opened: 2012

WHITE RABBIT BREWING COMPANY, ANGIER'S FIRST BREWERY, is located in an unassuming brick building shared with several other businesses. Inside the small taproom, visitors will find two long wooden tables, dartboards, a Jenga set, and a popcorn machine that makes the whole space smell like warm butter. Behind the corner bar, a row of taps carved like rabbit ears pour the beers crafted in the brewhouse visible through the window at the back of the bar.

So far, owner Ken Ostraco and brewer Matt Ehlers have used their three-barrel system to produce 15 different styles of beer, which are rotated in the taproom. Twenty-two-ounce bottles sporting the eye-catching White Rabbit artwork (taken from John Tenniel's original *Alice in Wonderland* illustrations) can be found in shops throughout the Triangle area.

White Rabbit's beers draw inspiration from many brewing traditions. For example, a Belgian-style tripel rubs elbows with a German-style Oktoberfest and a California common. However, Ostraco is on the record as stating that big hop bombs like the IPAs produced by so many breweries are not in the cards for White Rabbit.

White Rabbit's local, homegrown, balanced approach to beer has been a hit with drinkers in Angier and the surrounding area. A wall of photos in the

White rabbit ear tap handles complete the *Alice in Wonderland*–themed White Rabbit Brewing Company.
Sarah H. Ficke

taproom of people posing with the White Rabbit logo is a testament to the brewery's community appeal. And with two new fermenters and other equipment upgrades in the works, growth is in the future.

WHITE STREET BREWING COMPANY

218 South White Street
Wake Forest, NC 27587
919-647-9439
Email: brewery@whitestreetbrewing.com
Website: whitestreetbrewing.com
Hours: Monday–Thursday, 4 P.M.–10 P.M.;
 Friday, 4 P.M.–midnight; Saturday, noon–
 midnight; Sunday, noon–10 P.M.
Founders: Dino and Tina Radosta
Director of Brewery Operations:
 Ian VanGundy
Head Brewer: Chris Bivins
Opened: 2012

WHITE STREET BREWING MAKES ITS HOME ON THE STREET OF THE SAME NAME in the small, bustling downtown area of Wake Forest. The street holds a mixture of small businesses, restaurants, and coffee shops. White Street Brewing fits in as the go-to local taproom.

Inside the old building, visitors will find wooden ceilings and gracefully aged brick walls. The space is divided by a low wooden wall that keeps patrons from wandering into the brewing operation while allowing them an unfettered view of the shining 10-barrel brewhouse. The taproom side of the wall is filled with high-top tables and chairs, a shuffleboard table, and darts. The bar thrusts out from one wall, offering patrons beer, merchandise, growlers, and a place to lean to chat with the bartender or watch the televisions above. A colorful chalkboard lists the current beers on tap.

White Street's beer list is built around a core lineup of standard styles, including an IPA, a Scottish ale, and a Kölsch-style ale. In 2014, just two years after the opening, the Kölsch-style ale won a gold medal at the prestigious World Beer Cup, which cemented White Street's reputation for high-quality, well-crafted beer. In addition to its mainstream styles, it occasionally branches out into more

The brewhouse at White Street Brewing Company
Sarah H. Ficke

elaborate seasonals, such as its Koschei the Deathless Russian imperial stout, which made a splash during its release in the spring of 2014.

Even before the brewery won a gold medal, local enthusiasm for its beer had encouraged the owners to start thinking of expansion. They brought in Ian Van-Gundy, formerly of Lonerider Brewing, as director of brewery operations and launched a larger production facility in Youngsville, which opened at the end of 2014. The 56,000-foot Youngsville location is home to a 30-barrel brewing system, rows of large fermenters, and a bottling line that churns out 12-ounce bottles of White Street's core beers. The expansion is fueling increased distribution outside the immediate Raleigh area. Growth within the North Carolina market continues to be White Street's goal.

DEEP RIVER
BREWING COMPANY

700 West Main Street
Clayton, NC 27520
919-585-2296
Website: deepriverbrewing.com
Hours: Thursday–Friday, 4 P.M.–9 P.M.;
    Saturday, 1 P.M.–9 P.M.;
    Sunday, 1 P.M.–6 P.M.
Founders: Paul and Lynn Auclair
Head Brewer: Paul Auclair
Opened: 2013

DEEP RIVER BREWING, BILLED AS "JOHNSTON COUNTY'S FIRST LEGAL BREW-ERY," opened its doors in 2013 in a brick warehouse in downtown Clayton. The large Deep River logo on the exterior wall, framed by climbing hop vines in the growing season, lets visitors know they've reached their destination. A broad concrete patio covered in picnic tables provides outside seating. Inside, the brick is relieved by weathered wood paneling on the wall behind the bar, which faces the door. Tall, narrow tables offer more seating. A chalkboard sign announces the beers that are pouring that day, while a cooler behind the bar carries Deep River beer in cans to go.

The big, open taproom space is only the front of the brewery. Behind the wall lies the production floor, which boasts a 15-barrel brewhouse and a canning line.

Deep River's signature beers are a mix of styles. In cans are a witbier, a rye, a black IPA, and Watermelon Lager, one of the brewery's most recognizable brands. The draft beers offer even more variety, with seasonal recipes rotating in and out. Owner and head brewer Paul Auclair's background is in civil engineering, but he

Rows of tanks lead to the brewhouse at Deep River Brewing Company.
Erik Lars Myers

and his wife, Lynn, were longtime homebrewers before they started Deep River. Experimenting with recipes comes naturally to them.

Deep River has been steadily expanding. Its canning line was installed just one year after the opening, and more fermentation space followed on its heels. At this point, Deep River distributes its beer around the Triangle and many parts of the state, taking it beyond a truly local experience.

DOUBLE BARLEY BREWING

3174 US 70W
Smithfield, NC 27577
919-934-3433
Email: cheryl@DoubleBarleybrewing.com
Website: doublebarleybrewing.com
Hours: Wednesday–Thursday, 4 P.M.–10 P.M.;
 Friday, 3 P.M.–11 P.M.;
 Saturday, noon–11 P.M.;
 Sunday, noon–6 P.M.
Founders: Cheryl and Larry Lane
Brewmaster: Mark Kirby
Assistant Brewer: Ritchie Marraccini
Opened: 2013

FROM THE OUTSIDE, SMITHFIELD'S DOUBLE BARLEY BREWING LOOKS LIKE a generic business building, only the recognizable logo sign letting beer lovers know they've arrived at the right place. Inside the doors, though, the building is full of personality. The lobby features work from a local artist and a display of historic moonshine bottles. An open door invites patrons into the taproom side of the business, where a curved concrete bar dominates the space. High-top wooden tables and low upholstered chairs make up the rest of the furniture. The walls are lined with old wood and tin panels that used to be part of a local barn. A side door leads to an outside beer garden shielded by wooden walls from the traffic on the nearby highway. Inside or out, the atmosphere is relaxed and invites drinkers to settle in to enjoy the beers on tap, the bar menu, and the occasional live band.

As the name suggests, Double Barley Brewing is not afraid to go big when it comes to its beer. The lineup features an array of styles, every one weighing in at a minimum 6 percent ABV and most hovering in the 8- to 11-percent range.

The big styles and bold flavors reflect the personalities of founders Cheryl and Larry Lane, who threw themselves into brewing with a passion after Cheryl

A view into the taproom at Double Barley Brewing reveals the man himself: Larry Lane behind the bar, chatting with customers.
Erik Lars Myers

gave Larry his first homebrew kit for his 40th birthday. According to Cheryl, that kit turned into "a fast-track obsession with brewing." Double Barley followed just a few years later. Although the brewery started with a limited distribution area, its 20-barrel system is now cranking out beer that can be found statewide.

Many of Double Barley's beers draw on Cheryl, Larry, and their family and friends for inspiration. The Sexy Rexy Red Rye ale is named after Cheryl's father, Abby's Amber is named for the daughter of a friend, and Richard's Black EyePA commemorates a ping-pong match gone wrong (the complete story is on the Double Barley website). One of the beers, Thrilla in Vanilla—a porter brewed with vanilla extract—made an appearance in the background of a scene in the season 27 premiere of *The Simpsons*.

At the moment, the beers are sold in 22-ounce bottles with vividly illustrated labels, but the Lanes are planning to transition to cans in the near future as they continue to expand their market within North Carolina.

SANDHILLS AND COAST BREWERIES

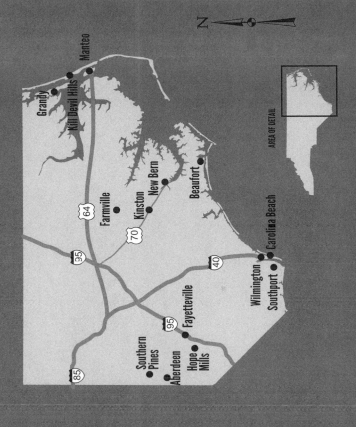

Aberdeen
Railhouse Brewery

Southern Pines
Southern Pines Brewing Company

Fayetteville
The Mash House Brewery
Huske Hardware House Restaurant & Brewing Company

Hope Mills
Dirtbag Ales

Wilmington
Front Street Brewery
Ironclad Brewery
Flytrap Brewing
Wilmington Brewing Company
Broomtail Craft Brewery

Southport
Check Six Brewing Company

Carolina Beach
Good Hops Brewing

Farmville
The Duck-Rabbit Craft Brewery

Kinston
Mother Earth Brewing

New Bern
Brewery 99

Beaufort
Mill Whistle Brewing

Manteo
Full Moon Cafe & Brewery

Kill Devil Hills
Outer Banks Brewing Station

Grandy
Weeping Radish Farm Brewery

RAILHOUSE BREWERY

105 East South Street
Aberdeen, NC 28315
910-783-5280
Website: railhousebrewery.com
Hours: Monday–Wednesday, 4 P.M.–11 P.M.;
    Thursday, noon–midnight;
    Friday–Saturday, noon–2 A.M.;
    Sunday, noon–10 P.M.
Founders: Mike Ratkowski, Brian Evitts
Head Brewer: Brian Evitts
Assistant Brewer: Michael Bacon
Opened: 2010

MIKE RATKOWSKI AND BRIAN EVITTS MET WHILE WORKING AT FERRELLGAS, a propane company. They found they had similar backgrounds. They're both ex-military guys—Ratkowski was in the army and Evitts in the navy—and had complementary skills. "We've always had a real good working relationship," says Ratkowski. "Brian's a real numbers guy—in fact, he just got his MBA from N.C. State—and I'm more of a people person, marketing person, operations person."

They discussed going into business together. "We had talked about maybe getting into real estate," Ratkowski says, "and of course the housing market crashed, and that became a poor option."

The epiphany came when they were in Alexandria, Virginia, on a sales call. On their way back, they stopped at an Uno Pizzeria for lunch. "It was raining," says Ratkowski, "so there were all these contractors at the bar drinking and eating lunch, and we noticed that they were all drinking all these craft beers. And I thought, *That's kinda weird, because they seem like blue-collar Bud Light, Miller Lite kinda guys.* I just didn't realize how widespread the craft beer phenomenon had gotten. I actually wrote it on a napkin: 'We should start a brewery.' "

They still have that napkin.

Following the sales trip, Ratkowski and Evitts started looking for equipment. They found a good deal on a system in Kentucky from Bowling Green Brewing Company, which was going out of business. Soon, they were looking for a space to install that equipment. They decided on the name Railhouse Brewery

Fermenters stand over low-top tables in Railhouse's taproom.
Sarah H. Ficke

several months before locating a space. Through a stroke of luck, they found a spot next to the train depot in Aberdeen, right on the tracks.

"It was a little overwhelming," says Ratkowski of their first few months. "We got all the equipment put in here on Easter Sunday—just pallets of hoses and pumps and motors and everything. It took us about three months to get everything up and working."

One of the highlights of their first year in business, says Ratkowski, was seeing the void they filled in the area. They had contemplated the North Raleigh/ Zebulon area. What drew them south to Aberdeen were the golf and military communities, both of which, they felt, would provide a good customer base for a new brewery.

Ratkowski says, "We didn't realize it at the time, but there are a huge amount of homebrewers in the area. We actually have a homebrew club that we started even before we were open. We have 65 to 70 guys in the homebrew club that get together one Saturday a month, order pizzas, bring samples in, and try beers. The guys in the club are a great volunteer work force." In fact, the partners called on that volunteer work force a few times in the first year to help get their brewery up and running.

Railhouse has enjoyed considerable success in a short time. Ratkowski and Evitts saw about twice as much growth in their first year as they anticipated and experienced 216 percent sales growth from 2012 to the end of 2013. They've already expanded their fermentation space, added six-packs of bottles to their packaging options, and started distributing to neighboring states.

S**OUTHERN**
P**INES**
BREWING CO.

565 Air Tool Drive, Suite E
Southern Pines, NC 28387
910-365-9925
Email: info@southernpinesbrewing.com
Website: southernpinesbrewing.com
Hours: Monday–Saturday, noon–10 P.M.
Founders: Micah Niebauer, John Brumer,
   Jason Ginos
Brewers: Micah Niebauer, John Brumer,
   Jason Ginos
Opened: 2014

NORTH CAROLINA HAS A SIGNIFICANT NUMBER OF VETERAN-OWNED BREW-
ERIES. Southern Pines Brewing Company, located in the town of the same name,
is one of them. Cofounders Micah Niebauer, John Brumer, and Jason Ginos
served together as Green Berets in the United States Army. They were stationed
at Fort Bragg when they all faced turning points in their careers. Homebrewing
had been a casual hobby, but they started to think about brewing as a career
when they learned more about the booming craft beer industry in North Carolina. A business plan was born, and the three men left the army to join the world
of beer.

   In order to take their brewing to the next level, Niebauer and Brumer took
the Siebel Institute's concise course in brewing and also attended the essential
quality control course at White Labs in San Diego, California. While at White
Labs, they learned about yeast management and quality control, but the thriving
local brewing industry was also an inspiration.

   Armed with scientific knowledge and information gathered from brewery
visits, Niebauer and Brumer returned to Southern Pines, where Ginos had been
handling other aspects of the startup. The three then finished converting their
business plan into a reality.

   Southern Pines Brewing is located in a large industrial space. Taking up
most of the back is the brewery production floor. Southern Pines has two sys-

Windows peek in from the brewery to a well-designed bar at Southern Pines Brewing Company
Sarah H. Ficke

tems: a 15-barrel production system and a 2.5-barrel pilot system. The pilot system allows the brewer-owners to test recipe ideas and create small batches to release in their taproom, while the larger system enables full-scale production of their regular recipes designated for distribution. Currently, they employ a mobile canning line to package their flagship beers for market, but at some point a canning line will probably join the equipment on the production floor.

The front of the space is a taproom, where visitors can enjoy the offerings from Southern Pines. Design touches give it personality and a welcoming feeling. The bar is covered with a tall wooden arbor canopy that dominates the room. The arbor, together with the wooden facing on the bar and the wooden tables, makes the room feel rustic, almost outdoorsy. Low leather chairs grouped around the room encourage visitors to relax and chat over their beers. Large windows on either side of the bar allow patrons to see into the brewing facility, while an additional window provides a view of a room stacked with wooden barrels.

Southern Pines Brewing makes some straightforward recipes, such as its Duck Hook cream ale, designed to appeal to people who like light, crisp beers or who are new to craft beer flavors. However, the brewer-owners aren't afraid to dip into more elaborate styles. One of their flagships is a saison, and their limited releases have included beers made with peaches, beers fermented with Brettanomyces yeast, and historical styles such as a Scottish fraoch (heather ale).

As the taste for craft beer grows in the Sandhills region, Southern Pines Brewing is poised to grow with it, both in complexity and distribution.

THE MASH HOUSE BREWERY

4150 Sycamore Dairy Road
Fayetteville, NC 28303
910-867-9223
Email: gm@themashhouse.com
Website: themashhouse.com
Hours: Monday–Thursday, 4 P.M.–11 P.M.;
    Friday, 4 P.M.–midnight;
    Saturday, noon–2 A.M.;
    Sunday, noon–midnight
General Manager: Steve Groveunder
Brewmaster: Richard Young
Opened: 2000

THE MASH HOUSE IS A MEMBER OF THE ROCKY TOP HOSPITALITY GROUP, a small North Carolina–based chain owned by Dean Ogan, who was named the 2011 Restaurateur of the Year by the North Carolina Restaurant and Lodging Association. Back in 2000, Ogan created The Mash House in Fayetteville as a cross between fine and casual dining. The menu ranges from gourmet fusion to burgers and sandwiches. The Mash House uses as many North Carolina–grown products as possible and is consistently ranked among the best restaurants in Fayetteville.

The Mash House's original brewer, Zach Hart, was a native of Texas. He began brewing in his backyard and soon found himself volunteering at Big Horn Brewery in Arlington and wondering if making beer was what he wanted to do with his life. After getting his feet under him, he attended the University of California–Davis. He subsequently graduated with a degree in brewing science and engineering and received an offer to brew at a large-scale brewery in Chicago. He turned it down in favor of a job in Fayetteville at a startup called Cross Creek Brewing Company—now The Mash House—where he was given the exciting opportunity of beginning with a blank slate, making his own recipes from scratch. Soon afterward, he was rewarded for his decision when he received a silver medal at the Great American Beer Festival in one of the most highly populated, and thus most difficult, categories: IPA.

The Mash House Brewery
Erik Lars Myers

Hart has moved on from The Mash House, but his replacement, Richard Young, brings the same attention to detail to the beers. Young, who joined The Mash House in 2014, is also an award-winning brewer with a long history in the industry. He caught the brewing bug while serving in the United States Army, where he was introduced to homebrewing. When Young left active service, he moved into a position with Seabright Brewery in California and then traveled to New England to brew with companies in Massachusetts and New Hampshire. In 1995, he was the driving force that reinstated the New England chapter of the Master Brewers Association of the Americas after a 17-year lapse. After a stint in Toledo, Ohio, at Maumee Bay Brewing Company, Young finally made his way to The Mash House, drawn by Fayetteville's strong connection to the military.

Young uses The Mash House's 15-barrel brewing system to supply beer to the on-site restaurant and its sister restaurants, Tribeca Tavern locations in Raleigh and Cary. Visitors to The Mash House and the Tribeca Taverns will find a slate of classic styles including porter, IPA, and hefeweizen, as well as some rotating specialty and fruit beers to match the seasons.

HUSKE HARDWARE HOUSE RESTAURANT & BREWING COMPANY

405 Hay Street
Fayetteville, NC 28301
910-437-9905
Website: huskehardware.com
Hours: Monday–Thursday, 11 A.M.–10 P.M.;
   Friday–Saturday, 11 A.M.–2 A.M.;
   Sunday, noon–9 P.M.
Owner: Josh Collins
Head Brewer: Matthew Bisceglia
Opened: 1996

IN 1903, WHEN BENJAMIN HUSKE CONSTRUCTED THE BUILDING that would become his landmark department/hardware store—"the Home Depot of its day," says current owner Josh Collins—in the middle of nowhere in North Carolina's coastal plain, people thought he was crazy. During the years that followed, it became a center of commerce and eventually the center of what is now downtown Fayetteville. After the store closed in the 1970s, the building hosted a variety of tenants ranging from a furniture store to a jewelry store. In 1996, part of the structure was renovated, and a brewery/restaurant was installed by Dr. William Baggett.

In 2006, Josh Collins and his wife, Tonia, the owners of Blue Moon Café in downtown Fayetteville, saw that the brewery/restaurant was in its waning days and decided to take a shot at it. Josh assembled some friends—his "Band of Brothers," he calls them, all active-duty Special Ops soldiers—who pooled their savings to buy Huske Hardware House around the end of 2007.

What followed was a long renovation. "It used to look more industrial, with this hard concrete-and-metal look to it," Josh says. "Now, it's all custom woodwork, all maples and red oaks. All the woodwork is handmade. The brewery was a mess. It had 13 years of low maintenance."

Remnants of the hardware store linger, especially in the brickwork. In some areas, the parapets that were the original exterior walls are still visible.

Huske Hardware House Restaurant & Brewing Company
Erik Lars Myers

After a year of work, Josh and Tonia reopened Huske Hardware House. The brewpub is beautiful. It is an enormous open space with warm wooden accents throughout. The main room of the brewery is two stories tall. A mezzanine that seats well over 100 encircles the room. A sheltered brick patio with abundant outdoor seating stands to the left of the restaurant. In the rear of the seating area behind tall glass walls lies the brewhouse and fermentation space. All in all, this is one of the largest brewpubs in the state.

To get their brewing operation going, Josh and Tonia hired Julie Baggett, formerly of Abita Brewing Company and at that time the only female brewmaster in North Carolina. "Julie was awesome," Josh says. "I had a huge stack of résumés, and I interviewed about a dozen brewers. They were all these gold medal winners, people with huge amounts of experience. But one of my key questions was, 'Are you willing to compete side by side with guest beers?' " Unlike many brewpubs, Huske offers a wide variety of competitors' beers alongside its own. "She was the only one that said yes," Josh recalls. "She was just the right person to bring in to restore the brewery to its pristine state. She invented the flagship beers that we've stuck with to this day."

Huske's current brewmaster is Matthew Bisceglia, who started homebrewing during his time in college at the University of Connecticut, drawn by the combination of creativity and science it demanded. He joined the team at Huske in 2014 as assistant brewer and took over the head position in the summer of 2015.

One of the noteworthy things about Huske Hardware House is its commitment to the military. Fayetteville has a large military community, being the major city nearest Fort Bragg and Pope Army Airfield. The commitment makes even more sense because of the involvement of Huske's six active-duty partners. "These guys are guys that I've been in combat with," Josh says with reverence. "They're good friends that I trust with my life."

Craft beer at its source

WHAT IS CRAFT BEER?

The Brewers Association, the professional association of brewers and breweries, defines a craft brewer as small, independent, and traditional.

SMALL: Based on taxation laws, a small brewery is one that makes under 6 million barrels of beer per year. Very few small breweries come anywhere near that mark. The 10 largest craft brewers in the country averaged a million barrels in 2014, but the median size of breweries is 500 barrels per year.

INDEPENDENT: A brewery must not be owned or controlled by another alcoholic industry member that is itself not a craft brewer.

TRADITIONAL: The majority of a brewery's total volume must be in beers whose flavor derives from traditional or innovative brewing ingredients and their fermentation. Flavored malt beverages (alcopops) are not considered beers.

The following market segments are defined within the category of craft beer:

MICROBREWERY: A brewery that makes fewer than 15,000 barrels of beer each year. Most small breweries in the country are microbreweries.

REGIONAL BREWERY: A brewery that makes between 15,000 and 6 million barrels of beer each year.

What defines a craft beer, however, is ultimately in the mind of the beer drinker. For many people, craft is about having a full-flavored beer. For others, it's about artisan craftsmanship, or about breweries that use the best possible ingredients. As more of the large beer companies produce craft-style beers, an increasingly common discussion point centers around what exactly makes a beer a craft beer. In the end, it's up to you.

DIRTBAG ALES

MADE IN NORTH CAROLINA

DIRTBAG ALES

3623 Legion Road
Hope Mills, NC 28348
904-434-1606
Website: dirtbagales.com
Hours: Thursday–Friday, 5 P.M.–9 P.M.;
 Saturday, 2 P.M.–6 P.M.;
 Sunday, noon–5 P.M.
Founders: Vernardo Simmons-Valenzuela,
 Eric Whealton, Jerry Hall
Head Brewer: Vernardo Simmons-Valenzuela
Brewing Staff: Claire Simmons-Valenzuela,
 Jackie Hall, Richard Batchelor, Kylie and
 Brandon Ferraz
Opened: 2013

DIRTBAG ALES' WEBSITE PROCLAIMS THAT IT BREWS BEER "FOR THE REFINED TASTE OF THE COMMON MAN." A glance at its beer list verifies that statement. The styles on the list are straightforward—Kölsch, IPA, pale ale—but each beer has a creative twist, such as the blood orange in the Kölsch or the passion fruit concentrate in the pale ale. According to the owners, their goal "is to make beers that are innovative while continuing to be both accessible and well put together." With that approach to beer, Dirtbag has something to appeal to both new and experienced craft beer drinkers.

The man behind Dirtbag's beer recipes is Vernardo Simmons-Valenzuela. He started as a homebrewer while in the military, serving up beers to an increasingly appreciative group of friends. The name Dirtbag comes from Vernardo's homebrew days. He explains, "A coworker overheard a conversation about a 30-pound ale—we were discussing a recipe—and she asked what a Dirtbag Ale was, and I replied, 'It's a damn good name for a company.' "

While working at Womack Army Medical Center at Fort Bragg, Vernardo met Eric Whealton and got him interested in beer. Fast-forward to August 2013. "I was on my way out of the military," Vernardo explains, "and had an opportunity to turn my love of beer into a profession, and I took it." Because starting a brewery is so expensive, the owners of Dirtbag decided to begin by contracting

The shining brewhouse at Dirtbag Ales
Dirtbag Ales

out their recipes at Railhouse, an established craft brewery in Aberdeen. This allowed them to spread the word about their beers.

The community was so responsive that it was only a short year later when Dirtbag invested in a 17-barrel system and moved into its own space. Vernardo describes the move, especially getting the equipment into the space, as "the ultimate DIY story" because of the strong group effort it took.

Dirtbag has been brewing in its new space since September 2014. In November 2015, it successfully cleared its last permit hurdle and opened a taproom at the brewery. Thanks to a deal with a local distributor, Dirtbag now has beer on draft in accounts around the southeastern part of the state, and some bottles as well, filled on a new bottling line it installed in the summer of 2015. Dirtbag's owners have "a lot of great big ideas" for the future, Vernardo says, and are looking forward to expanding their distribution while keeping strong ties to their community.

FRONT STREET BREWERY

9 North Front Street
Wilmington, NC 28401
910-251-1935
Email: frontstreetbrewery@gmail.com
Website: frontstreetbrewery.com
Hours: Daily, 11:30 A.M.–midnight
Owner: Tom Harris
Director of Brewing Operations: Kevin Kozak
Head Brewer: Kelsie Cole
Opened: 1995

THOSE WALKING FRONT STREET IN HISTORIC DOWNTOWN WILMINGTON find it impossible to miss Front Street Brewery. Although the brewery's tall neon sign has been lighting up the street since 1995, the building has been there for 130 years. The brewery occupies Front Street's only freestanding building (alleys are on both sides of it). Prior to housing the brewery, it served as a clothing shop and a candy store. "I like to tell people it was a brothel," says Kevin Kozak, Front Street's director of brewing operations, "but I have no evidence of that whatsoever."

Kozak took the helm at Front Street after an extended remodeling closure in 2006. When the brewery reopened, he faced the daunting task of creating new recipes from scratch for a drinking public that had a decade of expectations. "Basically, they told me to make whatever I wanted, but to include the four flagship beers: Lumina Lager, Port City IPA, River City Raspberry Wheat, and Dram Tree Scottish Ale. It was a little intimidating, but it worked out all right." At the start, the Scottish ale wasn't popular, but then "it just took off." Today, it's one of Front Street's best sellers. Kozak has been so successful that he's been able to move up into a management position in the brewery and bring on another brewer full-time in Kelsie Cole.

Front Street is a gorgeous brewpub full of warm lighting and dark-stained

The bar at Front Street Brewery
Erik Lars Myers

wood. Upon entering, patrons are greeted by the brewery—first the fermenters, then the small Bohemian copper kettle system. Seating radiates from the brewhouse toward the long, dark bar. Toward the back of the space, stairs climb to additional seating. The tall restaurant space is crowned by an ornate skylight that looks onto the building's top floor, a space used for parties, events, and even the occasional mystery dinner theater.

A piece of lore is connected to Front Street. "The brewery is haunted," says Kozak. "People see things. Weird things happen at night." It seems fitting that the brewery is a stop on the city's Haunted Pub Crawl. According to Kozak, the building is inhabited by the ghost of Henry Wenzel, a German immigrant who fell to his death while painting the ceiling in the early 1900s. Wenzel's obituary said he had previously worked as a driver for Palmetto Brewing Company in South Carolina. To Kozak, it all makes sense: "A German immigrant and an old brewery worker? No wonder he sticks around the brewery."

While Front Street Brewery is a model of a successful brewpub, it is nonetheless looking toward further expansion. "We've been talking about the possibility of a production brewery to bottle the flagship brands," says Kozak.

IRONCLAD BREWERY

115 North Second Street
Wilmington, NC 28401
910-769-0290
Website: ironcladbrewery.com
Hours: Monday–Saturday, noon–midnight;
   Sunday, 1 P.M.–10 P.M.
CEO: Ted Coughlin
Brewmaster: Ethan Hall
Assistant Brewers: Lydia Berzonsky,
   Nash Fralick
Opened: 2015

DOWNTOWN WILMINGTON LIVES AND BREATHES HISTORY. Ironclad Brewery, one of the newest additions to the city's beer scene, proudly connects itself to that history. The brewery's name comes from the ironclad ships manufactured at the aptly named Beery's Shipyard during the Civil War. And it is located in a 1925 building that over the years housed an undertaker, a millinery shop, a confectioner's shop, a general store, a car dealership, and an auto repair shop. In its current incarnation, the building is a polished and attractive two-story brewery, bar, and event space.

CEO Ted Coughlin teamed up with beer veteran Ethan Hall to open Ironclad in 2015. Hall is a Wilmington native who started his career in beer when he opened a homebrew store. In 2004, he was a founding member of Wilmington's Azalea Coast Brewery, which closed in 2008. Hall then did stints with Millennium Beverage, a distributor based in Charlotte, and Thomas Creek Brewery in South Carolina. When he got the call to join Ironclad, Hall pulled the Azalea Coast brewing equipment out of storage and got it in working shape to bring beer to a new set of Wilmington drinkers.

At Ironclad, Hall and his assistant brewers produce beer in a variety of styles ranging from an IPA to a chocolate stout, all appropriately named after local icons such as the "Old Baldy" lighthouse and famous pirate Edward Teach, better known

The original brewhouse from Wilmington's now-defunct Azalea Coast Brewery makes its home at Ironclad.
Erik Lars Myers

as Blackbeard. Ironclad Brewery isn't just tapped into local history, though. It is adding to it with a beer known as Gib's Pumpkin Ale—Gib being an acronym for Ghost of Ironclad Brewery, a spirit that manifested itself as the old building was being renovated. According to Coughlin, workers restoring the building reported "doors opening, footsteps upstairs when no one was upstairs, all the bathroom urinals and toilets flushing at once," and other unexplained occurrences. Coughlin jokes that the spirit "must be related to Casper" because of the friendly—or at least nonthreatening—nature of the haunting.

Visitors to Ironclad may note a ghostly presence, but it's unlikely to distract them from the glowingly restored wood, the weathered brick of the historic building, and the worn copper of Hall's original brewhouse from Azalea Coast. Live music on Saturdays adds to the attraction at this downtown watering hole. Coughlin is proud of the way his business has transformed the historic building but is looking forward to bigger things, including canning Ironclad's beer and perhaps opening a small distillery to add to North Carolina's burgeoning craft distilling movement.

FLYTRAP BREWING

319 Walnut Street
Wilmington, NC 28401
910-769-2881
Email: barfly@flytrapbrewing.com
Website: flytrapbrewing.com
Hours: Monday–Wednesday, 3 P.M.–10 P.M.;
    Thursday, 3 P.M.–midnight;
    Friday–Saturday, noon–midnight;
    Sunday, noon–10 P.M.
Founders: Mike and Emily Barlas
Head Brewer: Mike Barlas
Brewing Staff: Kristian Marioni
Opened: 2014

FLYTRAP BREWING, A SMALL NEIGHBORHOOD BREWERY, is located in a white-brick building at the corner of Walnut and North Fourth Streets in downtown Wilmington. Just a few blocks from the waterfront in the Brooklyn Arts District, the combination brewery and taproom is an easy stop for Wilmington beer lovers and visitors from out of town. Inside, patrons are greeted by a sweeping L-shaped bar with a bright lineup of beer faucets and a constantly rotating tap list featuring Flytrap's own Belgian and American-style ales and an array of guest beers. A window behind the bar provides a glimpse into the cold-storage room containing serving tanks of Flytrap beer.

The brewery is the brainchild of husband-and-wife team Mike and Emily Barlas. Mike moved to Wilmington in 2004 to pursue an MBA from the university but in the process discovered a love of homebrewing and the local craft beer scene. Like many other homebrewers, he decided to turn his passion into a profession, opening Flytrap Brewing 10 years after his arrival in the city. Coincidentally, Emily's brother, John Savard, was working on expanding his homebrewing store into Wilmington Brewing Company at the same time, creating a small beer renaissance in the Wilmington area.

And why name the brewery after a carnivorous plant? As Mike points out, the beautiful bright green species is native to the coastal area surrounding

This tiny brewhouse makes an enormous amount of delicious beer.
Erik Lars Myers

Wilmington. Like many other native species, it is in danger of dying out due to loss of habitat. Naming the brewery after this unique plant roots the brewery in its local ecosystem and allows Mike and Emily to raise awareness about the plant's important and precarious place in the environment.

Flytrap is a small operation. Its system generates only a handful of kegs. Fermenters are primarily stored inside normal kitchen refrigerators lining the walls of the brewery space. While it's small, the brewery is neat and trim, and its cleanliness is evident in the beer it produces.

The Flytrap team sees the future in terms of "small, organic growth" for the brewery. In addition to upgrades to the brewing equipment, it plans to help foster the local artistic community through rotating displays of art on the walls and live music on weekends.

With such a small operation, Mike and Emily often find themselves working overtime. But if you ask Mike, he'll tell you their pride in building this business from the ground up makes up for the work: "We love the hell out of what we do."

WILMINGTON BREWING COMPANY

824 South Kerr Avenue
Wilmington, NC 28403
919-392-3315
Website: wilmingtonbeer.com
Hours: Tuesday–Thursday, 10 A.M.–9 P.M.;
    Friday–Saturday, 10 A.M.–10 P.M.;
    Sunday, noon–6 P.M.
Founders: John and Michelle Savard
Head Brewer: John Savard
Brewing Staff: Blair Ferguson, Lee Murray
Opened: 2014

WHEN VISITORS PULL UP TO 824 SOUTH KERR AVENUE IN WILMINGTON, they're faced with two signs. The one on the left reads, "Wilmington Homebrew Supply," while the one on the right announces, "Wilmington Brewing Company." Although the two signs look distinct, those entering will find one interconnected space that celebrates both the brewing and drinking of craft beer.

Owners John and Michelle Savard are natives of Wilmington who discovered the joys of homebrewing during their college years in Asheville. Their first business venture was Wilmington Homebrew Supply, which opened in 2012. The company's original home was an 800-square-foot space on Wrightsville Avenue. Business was good, leading John and Michelle to expand the homebrew shop and add a professional brewery of their very own. They were in excellent company. It was around the same time that John's sister, Emily, and her husband, Mike Barlas, were working on putting together their brewery, Flytrap.

The transition from homebrew shop to a joint homebrewing and professional space was daunting. John jokes that "our old whole homebrew shop could have easily fit in our taproom, twice." It took the couple 11 months to complete the move and the new brewery. But the community makes it all worthwhile. "The people that come through our doors every day are incredible," John says.

People visiting Wilmington Brewing Company will find up to 15 original

A family sits and enjoys a Wilmington Brewing Company beer inside the adjoining homebrew store.
Erik Lars Myers

beers on tap, ranging from mainline styles such as IPA and Kölsch to more unusual offerings including Lemon Ginger Saison and a weekly cask beer. Customers have the option of hanging out in the small taproom bar or wandering over to the homebrew shop, where soft seating awaits them near recipe kits for some of those same beers. Drinkers interested in the beer-making process can come to one of the free brewing classes on Saturdays, while families with children will enjoy the child-friendly zone inside and the outdoor beer garden.

Big changes are on the horizon for Wilmington Brewing Company. John and Michelle are in the process of moving from their three-barrel brewing system to a 25-barrel system that will allow them to distribute kegs to individuals and retail accounts in the surrounding area. It's a significant step, but one John and Michelle are excited to make as they continue to spread the joy of beer and brewing to craft beer fans.

BROOMTAIL CRAFT BREWERY

BroomTail Craft Brewery
Wilmington, NC

6404 Amsterdam Way #100
Wilmington, NC 28405
910-264-1369
Email: info@broomtailcraftbrewery.com
Website: broomtailcraftbrewery.com
Hours: Wednesday–Thursday, 4 P.M.–9 P.M.;
   Friday, 4 P.M.–10 P.M.;
   Saturday, 2 P.M.–10 P.M.;
   Sunday, 2 P.M.–8 P.M.
Founders: Lisa and Barry Owings, Kim and
   Randy Shelton
Head Brewer: Barry Owings
Assistant Brewer: Randy Shelton
Opened: 2014

TO REACH BROOMTAIL CRAFT BREWERY, CRAFT BEER DRINKERS FIND THEIR WAY to Dutch Square Industrial Park, an industrial zone sandwiched between residential areas on the northeast side of Wilmington. Though the area isn't designed for retail visitors, outdoor seating and the friendly Broomtail logo welcome people to the brewery's taproom. Inside, the bright blue walls and multicolored chalkboard draft list give the small space a lively feel that is enhanced by a close look at the beer list.

Broomtail focuses on inventive beers distributed to the local area. While some of its beer styles are familiar, others such as its smoked IPA play with style and expectations. The owners have had plenty of experience experimenting with their recipes. Barry Owings says he and his wife, Lisa, started homebrewing with Kim and Randy Shelton 24 years before Broomtail was created. Over those years, the couples perfected their recipes and processes until Lisa suggested it was time to start a business.

Lisa is the driving mind behind Broomtail, managing sales, distribution, and the business side of things with Kim Shelton's help. Meanwhile, Barry and Randy brew the beer on the weekends around their full-time jobs. Among the ingredients that make Broomtail stand out is the one you'd least expect: the

Broomtail Craft Brewery's comfortable taproom
Erik Lars Myers

water. Barry Owings has a background in water chemistry, so adjusting the mineral content and water profile for each beer is a big part of his brewing process. He says it can take up to six hours to create water that matches the profile he wants for a specific style.

That detail-oriented approach is working out big time for Broomtail. It makes six barrels at a time, distributing most of it in the Wilmington area. In addition to its regular lineup, it makes special brews for several restaurants around town that are available only at those restaurants and at Broomtail's taproom. The brewery has been successful enough in its first year that the owners are already planning an expansion and shopping around for a larger location.

Although Broomtail is named after the term for a wild, undesirable horse, Broomtail the brewery is clearly a smoothly working business creating some highly desirable brews.

CHECK SIX
BREWING COMPANY

5130 Southport-Supply Road
Southport, NC 28461
910-477-9280
Website: checksixbeer.com
Hours: Monday–Wednesday, noon–10:30 P.M.;
    Thursday–Saturday, noon–midnight
Founders: Tim Hassel, Noah and
    Michael Goldman, Norm Weiss
Head Brewer: Noah Goldman
Brewing Staff: Justin Maggard, Jared Hassel,
    Nick Coren
Opened: 2015

12-ounce   outside

LOCATED IN A SMALL STRIP OF BUSINESSES IN SOUTHPORT, Check Six Brewing Company has a bright, modern feel. The colorful Check Six logo welcomes patrons into the company's narrow taproom, which features a gleaming wooden bar, a long, thin standing rail, and a few high-top tables. A window behind the bar shows off bright silver fermenters labeled with nicknames of investors and gives patrons a glimpse into the brewing area, which takes up a large portion of the space. The other walls in the taproom are decorated with images of classic airplanes and airplane memorabilia.

The airplane theme comes naturally to Check Six. Cofounder Tim Hassel is a lieutenant colonel and fighter pilot in the United States Air Force. Cofounder Noah Goldman explains that Check Six is "a military term used a lot by the air force. It means look behind you, at your six o'clock position. It's the weak spot." He adds that " 'I've got your six' means someone is looking behind you and has your back. When it comes to craft beer, we have your six." The airplane theme continues with the beer names, which are mostly inspired by aviation lore from World War I.

Goldman and Hassel became acquainted at a meeting of Cub Scout leaders and discovered a joint passion for beer and a shared curiosity about the brewing process. The pair's early experiments were a hit, "and all of our friends urged us

The gleaming wooden bar overlooks the brewery and showcases shiny fermenters.
Erik Lars Myers

to take the next step," Goldman says. Check Six is the result of that step. Now, the brewery serves a wide variety of beer styles, from IPA and cream ale to imperial porter and Irish stout.

The founders are already planning to expand their market beyond the local area and hope to start canning some of their brands for wider distribution. Goldman adds, "We are already looking into a larger brewhouse" to meet increased demand.

GOOD HOPS BREWING

811 Harper Avenue
Carolina Beach, NC 28428
706-713-1594
Website: goodhopsbrewing.com
Hours: Monday–Thursday, 1 P.M.–8 P.M.;
    Friday–Saturday, 1 P.M.–9 P.M.;
    Sunday, 1 P.M.–7 P.M.
Founders: Richard and Patricia Jones, John
    Garcia, William and Sharon Gorczynski
Head Brewer: Richard Jones
Opened: 2014

GOOD HOPS BREWING, LOCATED IN CAROLINA BEACH JUST SOUTH OF WILMINGTON, has the type of casual vibe you'd expect in a beach-town brewery. Housed in a low, glass-fronted building with a curved white roof, Good Hops focuses on providing tasty, accessible beer in a comfortable and friendly atmosphere. Bright blue padded chairs line the bar, which stretches across the small tasting room. A window behind the bar highlights the brewing equipment in the room beyond. In good weather, patrons can enjoy the outside picnic tables, cornhole games, and occasional live music by local musicians.

The founders of Good Hops have truly adopted beer as a family business. After helping their son, John Garcia, start Lookout Brewing in Black Mountain, Richard and Patricia Jones took a divide-and-conquer approach to the North Carolina beer scene, coming east to start a companion brewery in the popular area around Wilmington. Richard explains that their business model is driven by the local market: "Locating in a tourist-driven economy, we concentrated our effort on distribution in the Wilmington and beaches-area bars and restaurants." Recognizing his customers' constant thirst for new beers, Richard, the brewmaster, does his best "to stay ahead of customer demand by innovating new beer almost monthly." While Good Hops has a slate of regular beers, its tap menu changes frequently, though the recipes tend to remain rooted in classic English styles.

The inviting bar at Good Hops Brewing looks into the brewhouse.
Erik Lars Myers

The owners of Good Hops did so well that just one year after opening they ran a successful Kickstarter campaign to expand their fermentation space. However, according to Richard, the plan is not to stop there. "Our goal is to purchase a 10-barrel system in the next few years to better serve our local community," he says. Until then, visitors to Good Hops can continue to enjoy small-batch beers in the taproom or take home a "grumbler" (a 32-ounce Mason jar growler) to share later.

THE DUCK-RABBIT CRAFT BREWERY

4519 West Pine Street
Farmville, NC 27828
252-753-7745
Email: info@duckrabbitbrewery.com
Website: duckrabbitbrewery.com
Hours: Thursday–Saturday, 3 P.M.–10 P.M.
Owner: Paul Philippon
Brewmaster: Paul Philippon
Opened: 2004

12-ounce   outside

TUCKED AWAY IN AN INDUSTRIAL WAREHOUSE IN RURAL FARMVILLE lies The Duck-Rabbit Craft Brewery, "the Dark Beer Specialist." Farmville, a quaint little town representative of North Carolina's coastal plain, is surrounded by tobacco fields and other farmland just a few miles outside Greenville, the home of East Carolina University.

"Where else would you want to start a brewery but Farmville?" asks Duck-Rabbit founder and brewmaster Paul Philippon, a jovial man with a quick smile and a big laugh. "I didn't want to rent, I wanted to own. And I wanted to own enough real estate so that I never had to move." Philippon's four-acre lot allows him a good deal of room to grow. "It's a very friendly town," he continues, "and they've been very welcoming to us. It means a lot to me."

Duck-Rabbit's emblem, a classic optical illusion made famous by 20th-century philosopher Ludwig Wittgenstein, is a reference to Philippon's former life as a philosophy professor. After graduate school at the University of Michigan, he took a few teaching jobs. His longest stint was at Eastern Michigan University. But academia was not the life for him. "I love beer, I love brewing beer—and I love philosophy, too! But I could see colleagues of mine who I thought were more talented than me in philosophy struggling to get tenure-track jobs. I saw a lot of people unhappy, and it looked like something that I didn't want to go through." It was time for him to look for an alternate career.

The brewhouse at The Duck-Rabbit Craft Brewery
Erik Lars Myers

Philippon enrolled at the Siebel Institute in Chicago to learn brewing and never looked back. After Siebel, his career took him on a slow but steady path south: from Brewmasters in Cincinnati, Ohio (now closed), to Pipkin Brewing Co. in Louisville, Kentucky (now Bluegrass Brewing Co.), to Williamsville Brewery in Wilmington, North Carolina (now closed). Finally, in 2004, he achieved his dream. "The goal was always to open my own brewery," he says, "but I wanted to make sure I was familiar with the industry first. I think that's very important."

Philippon's experience has served him well. Though Duck-Rabbit brews on a modestly sized system, it's a strong and successful business with a wide distribution network. Duck-Rabbit beer can be found on tap and in bottles across North Carolina and in many other states, including Georgia, Tennessee, Virginia, and Pennsylvania.

The facility looks like many craft breweries that make the most efficient use of their space. The equipment is squashed together on one side of the warehouse, while storage—empty cases, kegs, and bottles—fills the rest. The bottling line—the piece of equipment that allows this relatively small brewery to distribute up and down the Atlantic coast—sits with its back against the fermenters. The brewhouse backs up to the loading dock.

The Duck-Rabbit Craft Brewery specializes in dark beers. "I brew what I like," says Philippon of his specialty. It's clear that many others like it, too. Duck-Rabbit's Milk Stout and Baltic Porter have both won medals at the prestigious Great American Beer Festival, and the Milk Stout won a gold medal at the 2010 World Beer Cup, the largest professional brewing competition in the world.

"I'm proud to have made something that people enjoy," says Philippon. "When I go out to festivals and events, people are coming up to me, telling me that they enjoy the beer, and it's been very rewarding."

But he saves his kindest words for employees who have moved on from Duck-Rabbit. "It's bittersweet," he says, "because you feel like you've nurtured them. I feel like Duck-Rabbit has made the brewers who have left here what they are. But to see them move on, to become successful elsewhere, and even start their own breweries—it's what I'm most proud of, that I've been able to make a positive difference in their lives. They will always be a part of Duck-Rabbit."

In 2011, Duck-Rabbit opened its tasting room, a small affair attached to the front of the brewery. A couple of tall, round tables occupy space next to the short, sleek wooden bar, which sports four Duck-Rabbit taps. Tall windows and a glass door look into the brewery and offer a close-up view of fermentation vessels. Outside, a picnic table waits to greet patrons on warm Farmville afternoons.

MOTHER EARTH BREWING

311 North Heritage Street
Kinston, NC 28501
252-208-BIER (2437)
Email: info@motherearthbrewing.com
Website: motherearthbrewing.com
Hours: Tuesday–Thursday, 4 P.M.–10 P.M.;
    Friday–Saturday, 1 P.M.–10 P.M.
Owners: Stephen Hill, Trent Mooring
Head Brewer: Josh Brewer
Opened: 2009

MOTHER EARTH BREWING MIGHT BE ONE OF THE MOST BEAUTIFUL packaging breweries patrons will ever see. It is located in downtown Kinston, a city that was once a center of textile production and is now seeing a revitalization, thanks in no small part to Mother Earth.

Mother Earth was started by Trent Mooring and his father-in-law, Stephen Hill, both of whom were born and raised in Kinston. Hill had been a home-brewer and a lover of beer in the past but hadn't touched it in years. Mooring had been interested in beer since the first craft beer renaissance of the 1990s, when he clerked in a grocery store that had a good selection of beer. But it wasn't until Hill introduced his new son-in-law to an old family recipe—a "Red Eye," a mixture of beer and spiced tomato juice—that Mooring caught the bug. "I was hooked," says Mooring, who began to try his own hand at homebrewing.

They batted around the idea of starting a business that would combine the passions they held in common: beer, agriculture, and, most importantly, Kinston. They both saw a new business as a wonderful way to give back to their hometown. Soon, they had a plan and went in search of a brewer.

After posting an ad on ProBrewer.com, they located Josh Brewer, who likes to joke about the way he found the brewery. "That's our shtick at beer dinners or events when people ask us how we met. We say we met on Match.com."

Fresh beer at Mother Earth Brewing
Erik Lars Myers

Brewer had a long history with beer. Back in 1997, a friend of his received a homebrew kit for Christmas, and they brewed their first batch of beer together. "That first batch had a whole bunch of muck turning around in the fermenter, and we looked at that and thought that it probably wasn't supposed to be like that, so we dumped that batch in the backyard. But I figured I still wanted to do something with it, so I took the kit from him, and it started from there. He never made another batch of beer in his life, and I kept going."

Brewer worked a few odds-and-ends jobs in the late 1990s. At first, his brewing experience came in dribs and drabs. He used to pass a brewpub on his way home from a job at Sears and kept bringing homebrew to the brewer there. After a while, that brewer got to a point where he needed help cleaning kegs, taplines, and even the occasional tank. "I never got to brew there," Brewer remembers, "but I got to put in three or four hours three days a week."

Finally, he got a job in Georgia as head brewer at Hilton Head Brewing

Company, an all-extract seven-barrel brewpub, where he ended up having to do extra work to make beer of the quality he wanted. "It was a good step into brewing," he says, "but it was the most hodgepodge system ever."

While at Hilton Head Brewing, he started working part-time at Moon River Brewing Company in nearby Savannah. He calls his time there his "big foot in the door" in the brewing industry. After a couple of years, he moved on. "I got a wild hair to move to Hawaii at that point." He and his fiancée packed up everything, sold their cars, and headed to Hawaii. There, Brewer worked as a cellarman for Kona Brewing Company before buying a defunct bicycle tour business, building it back up, and running it for a few years. Eventually, though, he and his fiancée found themselves back in Georgia, where he picked up exactly where he had left off at Moon River.

A couple years later, Brewer and his now-wife took another step toward every brewer's dream and started their own brewpub, Brewer's, in Beaufort, South Carolina. The concept was a good one—a small brewery with an 80-seat restaurant serving organic food—but they just didn't have enough money, and the restaurant went out of business. Once things settled down, Brewer found the listing on ProBrewer.com. Soon, he was part of the Mother Earth team and, what's more, in charge of building the brewery from scratch.

"The cool thing was, I came here before they even bought the building," he says. "Trent and Stephen have the business background and no real brewing background, so everything was up to me. 'What kind of equipment do you want? Where's it going to go? Where's the bottling line going to go? Where does the walk-in go?' I got to do the full design. I was here for the full build-out and the construction and everything. We have the equipment and the backing to do things the way they're supposed to be done."

The Mother Earth building was actually a suite of businesses—an old drive-through pharmacy, a stable, and a barbecue restaurant. The new owners gutted it and gave it a completely new life. Today, most of a city block is connected via the building's interior, even though many of the storefronts have been retained. The owners installed large, open windows and cut away portions of the floor not only to accommodate large brewery tanks but to flood the interior with bright, natural light. The bottling operation is in what used to be the barbecue restaurant. The canning line is in a gallery "next door," even though they are feet from each other inside. A small, dark barrel room connects the brewery warehouse to the taproom, located in yet another former storefront, this one repainted and redecorated with modern lights, chairs, and a high, white, square bar in the middle of the space. Mother Earth also has a beer garden and a roof deck. A spiral slide taken from an old playground Hill used to visit as a child leads from the upstairs offices to the canning room downstairs. All of the design and renovation was handled by Hill, Mooring, and Brewer. The result is a testament to how well they work together.

Recently, Mother Earth put the finishing perfect touch on Stephen Hill's old Red Eye recipe, releasing a brew called Homegrown. "We've brewed more pilot batches of this beer than any other to make sure [we got it right,]" says Brewer on the company's website, calling the beer, "a beautiful blend of tomato, spice, salt, and corn beer."

In addition, Mother Earth has spawned a successful distillery, Mother Earth Spirits. Just off the end of the canning line is the still where Mother Earth produces whiskey, rum, and a gin that won a silver medal at the 2015 Distilling Institute Craft Spirits Competition.

Mooring predicts a bright future for Mother Earth, but all in due time. "We want to grow to be a regional brewery. We just have to make sure we grow at a controlled pace so that our quality doesn't dip."

BREWERY 99

BREWERY 99

417F Broad Street
New Bern, NC 28560
252-259-6393
Website: brewery99.com
Hours: Friday–Saturday, 2 P.M.–10 P.M.
Founder: Peter Frey
Head Brewer: Peter Frey
Brewing Staff: Dan Frey
Opened: 2015

NINETY-NINE IS A LUCKY NUMBER. At least that's what Pete Frey, the owner of Brewery 99, believes. Frey's birthday is September 9 (9/9), and 1999 is the year he moved to New Bern. Now, 99 is the name of Frey's startup business, an accomplishment he is very proud of.

Brewery 99 is a nanobrewery operating out of a small white building off Broad Street in downtown New Bern. The bulk of the space is taken up with the brewing equipment and a cooler, but a slender bar that is open Friday and Saturday afternoons and evenings gives patrons a place to sip and sample Frey's beers. He uses his one-barrel system to create a series of beers. Some are familiar styles such as a normal India pale ale, while others use innovative ingredients such as bay leaf. Because of the small size of Frey's system, drinkers visiting Brewery 99 can expect to see new beers popping up regularly.

Frey's first trips to a homebrew store weren't for ingredients. He was buying bottles of craft beer to drink at home. But after some serious encouragement from the store's owner, Frey decided to see what homebrewing was all about. His experiments were so successful that he decided to make beer his profession. However, he didn't jump straight into brewery ownership. Instead, he spent two years working at Mother Earth Brewing in Kinston, learning the ropes. He also picked up business education from Craven Community College's program for entrepreneurs before he decided to take the plunge into brewery ownership.

Brewery 99's one-barrel system creates a series of beers.
Brewery 99

When asked about his path to brewery ownership, Frey says that "translating my education and experience into my own business has been both challenging and rewarding." While his early challenge was getting the permits lined up to start the business, his current one is making enough beer to supply his eager customers. Although he's been open only since February 2015, Frey is already considering an expansion that would double the brewery's capacity. He explains that the goal of the expansion will be to "increase our product offering, quality, and profitability."

His plans spell good news for New Bern craft beer drinkers and visitors squeezing in a trip to this small local brewery.

MILL WHISTLE BREWING

1354 Lennoxville Road
Beaufort, NC 28516
252-247-6929
Email: millwhistlebrewing@gmail.com
Website: facebook.com/MillWhistleBrewing
Founders: Tom and Barb Backman, Brian
    Riso, Joe Roomsburg, Bob Safrit,
    Dean Ochsner
Head Brewer: Tom Backman
Brewing Staff: Brian Riso, Barb Backman
Opened: 2015

MILL WHISTLE IS A NEWCOMER TO THE NORTH CAROLINA BEER SCENE, but its name connects it to a long history of manufacturing in the state. Its location (not open to the public as of this writing) is the old Scarboro-Safrit lumber mill on Lennoxville Road in Beaufort. The steam-driven mill was a significant employer in the early part of the 20th century. In the latter part of the century, the Safrit family closed the mill to focus on other aspects of its business.

The building got new life when Bob Safrit convinced his business partners that the old mill was the ideal location for their startup brewery. According to owner Barb Backman, the brewery's name comes from the lumber mill's tradition of blowing a 4:45 P.M. whistle every day, a tradition Barb says the brewery is keeping alive: "We have the original whistle, and it now signals beer at 4:45 daily."

The brewery's approach to beer and business is hands-on and local. Until Mill Whistle opens its taproom in 2016, its brightly colored 22-ounce bottles can be found in craft beer–friendly accounts in the immediate Beaufort–Morehead City area. Mill Whistle's owners have contracted with several artists to design their labels, providing a funky variety of styles. That funkiness is matched by the creative beers inside the bottles. The offerings include a sour wheat ale, a tart blueberry ale, an ale aged in wine barrels, and the more traditional IPA and amber.

The brewhouse at Mill Whistle Brewing
Mill Whistle Brewing

Mill Whistle's next goal is to open a tasting room at its facility, allowing it to start welcoming guests for pints and growler fills. Until then, visitors to Beaufort can listen for the old mill whistle announcing another successful day of tasty beer in this North Carolina coastal town.

FULL MOON CAFÉ & BREWERY

208 Queen Elizabeth Street
Manteo, NC 27954
252-473-MOON (6666)
Email: fullmoonmanteo@msn.com
Website: thefullmooncafe.com
Hours: 11 A.M.–9 P.M. (varies by season)
Owners: Paul Charron and Sharon Enoch
Brewmaster: Paul Charron
Opened: 2011

FULL MOON, NESTLED IN THE MIDDLE OF HISTORIC MANTEO, has been around since Paul Charron and Sharon Enoch started their café in 1995. At the time, it was a small sandwich shop serving tourists during Manteo's busy season. Soon, though, the café started expanding into the shops around it, creating a larger and larger presence. Enoch even opened a small pottery gallery next door.

Through that time, Charron—a former airline pilot and a longtime disciple of great beer—was homebrewing. "The batches just kept getting bigger and bigger," he says. That's when he considered making beer for the café.

"I thought we could just make one beer and put it on tap, and we could probably make it in the kitchen," says Charron. "We don't really get year-round business, so I figured we could carry all North Carolina beer, and ours would be a complement. But we were quickly overwhelmed."

They decided to open a small brewery in the space that was once Enoch's pottery gallery. And so their brewery was born. It uses a "Brutus 10" system that Charron built with plans from *Brew Your Own* magazine and small Blichmann fermenters. He currently has the ability to make about one barrel of beer at a time. "I'm overjoyed to say that it is way too small," he says. "We haven't even advertised. We just put a sign up outside, and we can't keep up."

Charron came to the industry with no professional credentials. "It's all homebrew experience," he says. "People come in all the time and ask if I'm the

Full Moon Café & Brewery in Manteo
Erik Lars Myers

brewmaster, and I tell them, 'No, I'm the guy who brews the beer, but I'm not the brewmaster.' I have an enormous amount of respect for guys with loads of schooling." He notes that the brewers from the other area breweries—Weeping Radish and Outer Banks Brewing Station—were "beyond helpful" while he was getting his brewery up and running. In fact, they are even planning to come over to brew with him in the winter—"the slow season."

Charron currently brews and ferments in the same room that serves as his tasting room and pub. It's a small taproom with a bright, polished copper bar gleaming in front of the brew kettles and fermenters. Full Moon doesn't have temperature control like most large breweries. "We've got central air and some other air-conditioning units," Charron says. In the summer, it gets hot. "Sometimes, to try to control temperature, we have to brew at three and four o'clock in the morning, when it's cool outside and easier to keep the room cool."

Down the road, Charron hopes for continued success. But his plans are really only to supply his own café. "If it keeps going this way," he says, "I'd like to move to a bigger site and move up to a seven-barrel system and just brew for the restaurant."

AMERICA'S FIRST WIND POWERED BREW PUB

OUTER BANKS BREWING STATION
MP 8½ • KILL DEVIL HILLS, NORTH CAROLINA • WWW.OBBREWING.COM

600 South Croatan Highway
Kill Devil Hills, NC 27948
252-449-BREW (2739)
Website: obbrewing.com
Hours: Monday–Thursday, opens at 3 P.M.;
　　　Friday–Sunday, opens at 11:30 A.M.
Owners: Eric Reece, Aubrey Davis
Brewmaster: Bart Kramlik
Opened: 2001

ON AN ISLAND IN THE ATLANTIC OCEAN JUST A FEW HUNDRED YARDS from where the Wright brothers' home-built flying machine made the first controlled, powered, sustained human flights is Outer Banks Brewing Station. It's hard to miss. The large red-and-white building stands out among the businesses surrounding it on the main strip of the island, and a wind turbine—taking advantage of the blustery winds on the northern Outer Banks—looms overhead.

The origins of the Outer Banks Brewing Station's beers trace back to California. The first head brewer at Outer Banks, Scott Meyer, had been involved in fermentation for a long time. He was working as a vintner in the wine industry in Northern California when he started seeing tap handles in bars from new breweries—microbreweries. Intrigued, he sought out a local microbrewery—Bison Brewing—and started volunteering and learning how it all worked. He was hooked.

Soon afterward, the head brewer and assistant brewer both left the company, and Meyer was promoted to head brewer. He hired Eric Reece—a lab tech at nearby Bear Technologies—as an assistant brewer. Or, as Reece puts it, "I tasted Scott's beers, and I quit my job."

As luck would have it, Bison Brewing (now Bison Organic) was bought out, and the new owners were brewers. Meyer and Reece found themselves out of

Outer Banks Brewing Station
Erik Lars Myers

jobs. Meyer went back to the wine industry, and Reece went with him, working at Rosenblum Cellars.

Meanwhile, Aubrey Davis, an old friend of Reece's, got tired of his job. He convinced Reece to return to an idea they had come up with while they were in Thailand in the Peace Corps together: starting a brewpub.

Davis had grown up visiting his grandparents' house on the Outer Banks. He felt it would be the perfect location—and it was, except for actually getting everything built.

"It's hard to find contractors out here," says Meyer when asked about the construction, echoing Reece's early frustrations. "Plumbers and electricians don't move out here to work. They move out here to surf or to fish. They'll get work done, but they're doing it on beach time, and nobody's really prepared for any sort of industrial setting. These are residential guys that are here for the life-style. It's hard to fault them, though. When you live in paradise, it kind of infects you."

Eventually, they got their brewery built—all except for the windmill, which was in the original business plan. It took five and a half years of fighting with the city's mayor and zoning board before they finally got it through. Now, as the state of North Carolina considers a wind farm offshore, the turbine already offsets about 8 percent of Outer Banks Brewing Station's power needs. "It would be a lot more if we didn't have a brewery," says Reece, "but then we wouldn't have the great beer."

When Reece and Davis opened the brewery, they called Meyer to see if he was interested in helping them. He eagerly accepted and was head brewer at Outer Banks for almost 15 years, though he has moved on to help start another brewery. Bart Kramlik replaced him as the chief creator of Outer Banks Brewing Station's beers.

The brewing system is an amalgam of used equipment. Reece and Davis found a brewery in foreclosure and got a trailer full of equipment. In fact, they ended up selling equipment they didn't need in order to finance the rest of what they required. The result is a quirky brewery tucked into an impossibly small space away from the restaurant. Patrons can see it from the dining room. It is situated half a story below floor level and stands two stories tall. A catwalk runs across the brewery at restaurant level. The only entrances to the brewhouse are outside around the back of the restaurant and a secret-wall-type access through the back of the cold room.

Brewing on the Outer Banks poses some interesting challenges. "The water is horrible out here." Meyer jokingly refers to it as "the three threads of the Outer Banks," in reference to traditional beer in England, which was a blend of three different types of ale. "What we have is basically a mix of desalinated ocean water, water from a coastal aquifer, and good ol' swamp water. The blend changes constantly. . . . So we just strip it down entirely and rebuild it using brewing salts." The salt air also poses a problem, corroding motors and any metal that has to spend time outside.

The final challenge is the seasonality. For Reece, the issue is making sure to capitalize on the four months of tourism to keep the restaurant and brewery open the rest of the year. Fortunately, the popularity of the restaurant has allowed Outer Banks year-round success. It has recently added an outdoor beer garden and features live music seven days a week throughout the year.

The restaurant is magnificent, boasting vaulted ceilings and a long, beautiful bar running the length of its back half. "What really sets us apart," Reece says, "is that we care about the food." In fact, Reece's wife, Tina McKenzie, a graduate of the California Culinary Institute, works in the restaurant. "You've got to try her carrot cake," says Reece. "It'll make you cry."

Outer Banks Brewing Station has been in operation over a decade now. Its continued success is a testament to the determination and skill of old friends. "We have to continually try to reinvent ourselves to keep things fresh," Reece says. "We're very involved in the community, and we like to try to keep the community involved with us. It's very important to us."

WEEPING RADISH
FARM BREWERY

6810 Caratoke Highway
Grandy, NC 27947
252-491-5205
Website: weepingradish.com
Hours: Wednesday, 11 A.M.–4 P.M.;
   Thursday–Saturday, 11 A.M.–8 P.M.;
   Sunday, noon–5 P.M.
Owner: Uli Bennewitz
Brewmaster: Uli Bennewitz
Opened: 1986

16-ounce

"I'VE BEEN HERE SINCE 1980. I'M A GERMAN IMMIGRANT," says Uli Bennewitz, founder of Weeping Radish. "I came here to farm, and I still farm. Farming is my life." When Uli moved to North Carolina and Hyde County, he worked as a farm manager, becoming the only resident on a 30,000-acre farm. "We had 60 miles of roads that I was in charge of patrolling," he remembers. "It was what you expect pioneering to be."

The trouble was that he never really thought farm management would be sufficient for paying the bills and raising a family. In 1985, Uli's brother—who lived in Munich—called him with an idea. He had a friend with a brewery that was up for sale and asked if Uli was interested in buying it.

"I was not very enthralled with American beers at the time," says Uli. "Your choices were either Bud or Coors, which was no choice at all." He immediately agreed to his brother's plan, subject to Uli's finding the capital to enable him to buy the brewery.

He remembers talking to the owner of The Christmas Shop in Manteo, a popular tourist destination. The owner told Uli that the question he was most often asked in his shop was, "Is there someplace to eat?" So the two got together, pooled their resources, and decided to open a sandwich stand and brewery.

Goats greet visitors at Weeping Radish Farm Brewery.
Erik Lars Myers

At that point, after he had committed to the brewery, Uli faced his first stumbling block. "I didn't know what the ABC was. I thought it was some sort of learning center. Coming from Germany, I never thought that in the land of the free there would ever be such a thing as an alcohol control board," he says, referring to the state's Alcoholic Beverage Control commission. He met with the ABC and told it of his plan to open a brewery/restaurant. The board broke the news to him that it was illegal. However, the ABC thought it was a great idea and proposed to help him get the law changed.

Soon afterward, Uli began meeting regularly with the chief legal counsel of the ABC, who was drafting the new law. It flew through the legislature in the hands of then–freshman senator Marc Basnight, becoming law just six months after Uli first approached the ABC with his question. Weeping Radish opened on July 4, 1986.

Interestingly, Uli doesn't take full credit for the law change. "It was really Biltmore that did the share of the work," he says. In 1980, Biltmore Estate Winery in Asheville wanted the ability to serve its own wine on the premises, which was illegal at the time. Using its considerable resources, Biltmore had pursued a change in the law for wine. "When I came along, we just used the exact same argument, but we just changed the word *wine* to *beer*," Uli says. "I've always wondered if Biltmore knows that it is essentially responsible for the microbrewery boom in North Carolina."

Weeping Radish, now legal, did not see instant success. "You do not open a brewpub in a dry town," says Uli. At the time, liquor was outlawed in Manteo. Although beer and wine were technically legal, they were frowned upon. "They were not amused to have a brewery in town." Furthermore, the idea behind Weeping Radish was not immediately popular with the local clientele. "Don't open a Bavarian-themed restaurant in the South. There aren't any Bavarian-themed restaurants in the South, and there's a reason—nobody wants one. We did great in the summer when tourists from Midwestern states—Ohio, Wisconsin, Minnesota, Iowa—were in town, but the rest of the year it was dead."

Still, Uli continued to pursue his idea. In 1988, he opened a Weeping Radish in downtown Durham near the Brightleaf Square area. "It was gorgeous. It was a beautiful building with great architecture, and it was a beautiful brewery, but it was about 25 years ahead of schedule." Uli notes that if he opened the Durham location today, it would likely be immensely popular. As it was, it lasted about a year and a half and then shut down. The city was just not ready.

Back in Manteo, Weeping Radish ran into a new problem. In 2000, the brewhouse fell through the floor of the brewery. "We had an all-wooden structure," says Uli, "a heavy, water-intensive operation on a wood floor."

At that point, he decided to take the brewery to the next level. He had long been interested in the local food movement and was beginning to realize the connection between natural beer and natural food. "They're both crafts," he says. "Beer is a craft, meat is a craft, vegetables are a craft. They're all the same."

After looking at the market, he realized there were no craft butchers in North Carolina. He then put out an ad in a German journal for a master butcher and began his plans for a full farmhouse brewery in Currituck County. "Literally, all I had was a field," he says. He constructed a 20,000-square-foot building, which he calls "a celebration of craft brewing, butchering, and organic farming—all of these wrapped into one concept."

The building is immense and impressive. Visitors enter a large room with a restaurant at the far end. A rough wooden outdoor façade stands over a short bar decorated with newspaper articles about the Outer Banks in the early 20th century. Although the brewing operation is out of sight from patrons, they can take a tour that allows them to see the brewpub-sized brewhouse tucked into an enormous cavern of a brewery. Outside, visitors can see fields stretching in back of the brewery. Those are the fields Uli farms. He fertilizes them with waste from the brewery, including spilled beer. In fact, he calls the fields "the first true beer garden in America, without a table, without a chair, without a patron."

In 2011, Weeping Radish's Doppelbock was the first beer in the state to feature 100 percent North Carolina–grown and –malted ingredients. Uli is a supporter of Asheville's Riverbend Malt House, a new craft maltster using North Carolina–grown barley. "We want to end up growing our own barley and have Riverbend malt it for us," Uli says, "so that we can have a complete closed loop, even more integrated into the farming operation." He notes that he has many more ideas about how to combine beer and food. "There's a lot going on in both worlds that we want to explore."

GLOSSARY

Adjunct: A source of fermentable sugar that is not malted barley.

Ale: A beer that is brewed using an ale yeast (*Saccharomyces cerevisiae*).

Barrel: A unit of measurement used in beer, also written "bbl." One barrel equals 31 gallons.

Brewhouse: A set of equipment used on the "hot side" of brewing, comprised of the mash tun/lauter tun, kettle, and whirlpool.

Brewpub: A combination brewery and restaurant.

Bright tank: A tank used specifically for carbonating beer.

CAMRA: The Campaign for Real Ales, a movement in Britain dating to the 1970s. Its aim is to return tradition to the way beer is served, focusing primarily on cask-conditioned and bottle-conditioned beers. For more information, visit camra.org.uk.

Cask-conditioned: Refers to beer that has gone through an additional fermentation step within the vessel it will be served from. Cask-conditioned beer is generally served at cellar temperature by gravity via hand pump.

CIP: Clean in place. This generally refers to brewery tanks equipped with spray balls designed to be used with high-pressure pumps and industrial cleaning solutions to wash or sanitize a tank with little manual labor.

Cold room: A large walk-in (or sometimes drive-in) refrigerator.

Ester: A chemical compound formed by yeast during fermentation. Esters generally taste fruity.

Fermenter: A vessel in which beer is fermented, where yeasts eat sugars to create ethanol and CO_2.

GABF: The Great American Beer Festival, a yearly beer festival sponsored by the Brewers Association in Denver, Colorado. It includes the largest professional beer competition in the country.

Growler: A refillable hard-sided container for beer, often a glass jug with a screw top, or sometimes with a ceramic swing top. In North Carolina, growlers must be 64 ounces (four pints) or less in volume.

Hops: The flowering and fruiting body of the plant *Humulus lupulus,* used to impart both bitterness and flavor to beer.

Keezer: A kegerator built from a freezer.

Kegerator: A refrigerator built to hold kegs and serve beer.

Lager: Literally, "to store." Lager beers are those made with lager yeast (*Saccharomyces pastorianus*).

Lautering: The step in brewing in which sugar is rinsed from grain in order to create wort.

Lauter tun: The vessel in the brewhouse in which lautering takes place, often combined with the mash tun.

Malt: Grain, most often barley, that has been forced through a false germination process and then kilned, creating a reserve of starches and enzymes. Malted barley is the main source of sugar in beer.

Maltster: A company that malts barley for use in brewing.

Mash tun: The vessel in the brewhouse in which mashing takes place, often combined with the lauter tun.

Mashing: The step in the brewing process when hot water is added to malted barley in order to activate enzymes that break down starches into sugars.

Microbrewery: A brewery that brews fewer than 15,000 barrels of beer per year.

Nanobrewery: A brewery that brews small batches of beer. While there is no official definition, a nanobrewery is generally considered to be a brewery that makes four barrels or less per batch.

Reinheitsgebot: The German Purity Law of 1516, which stated that beer could be made of three ingredients only: water, barley, and hops. Yeast wasn't discovered for another 340 years and therefore was not included. The Reinheitsgebot also included a rigorous pricing schedule for beer that is no longer observed.

Sparging: The act of rinsing hot water over grain during lautering, which assists in removing sugar from the grain.

Taproom: A small beer bar attached to, or associated with, a brewery.

World Beer Cup: The world's largest professional beer competition. It is held in even-numbered years in conjunction with the Brewers Association's Craft Brewers Conference.

Wort: Unfermented beer.

Yeast: A unicellular fungus that metabolizes sugar and secretes ethanol, CO_2, and hundreds of other compounds that affect the mouth-feel, flavor, and body of beer.

INDEX